NEW
TABERNACLE
SERMONS

BY

T. DE WITT TALMAGE, D.D.

DELIVERED IN THE
BROOKLYN TABERNACLE

NEW YORK
GEORGE H. DORAN COMPANY

Fac-Similie of

DR. TALMAGE'S

LETTER OF AUTHORITY

FOR ISSUING THIS SERIES OF SERMONS.

E. B. Treat Esqr has
authority for publishing
a book called "New
Tabernacle Sermons."

T. De Witt Talmage

Brooklyn April 16th 1886.

CONTENTS.

BRAWN AND MUSCLE.

" And Samson went down to Timnath."—JUDGES xiv: 1.

THERE are two sides to the character of Samson. The one phase of his life, if followed into the particulars, would administer to the grotesque and the mirthful; but there is a phase of his character fraught with lessons of solemn and eternal import. To these graver lessons we devote our morning sermon.

This giant no doubt in early life gave evidences of what he was to be. It is almost always so. There were two Napoleons—the boy Napoleon and the man Napoleon—but both alike; two Howards—the boy Howard and the man Howard — but both alike; two Samsons — the boy Samson and the man Samson—but both alike. This giant was no doubt the hero of the playground, and nothing could stand before his exhibitions of youthful prowess. At eighteen years of age he was betrothed to the daughter of a Philistine. Going down toward Timnath, a lion came out upon him, and, although this young giant was weaponless, he seized the monster by the long mane and shook him as a hungry hound shakes a March hare, and made his bones crack, and left him by the wayside bleeding under the smiting of his fist and the grinding heft of his heel.

There he stands, looming up above other men, a mountain of flesh, his arms bunched with muscle that can lift the gate of a city, taking an attitude defiant of everything. His hair had never been cut, and it rolled down in seven great plaits over his shoulders, adding to his bulk, fierceness, and terror. The Philistines want to conquer him, and therefore they must find out where the secret of his strength lies.

There is a dissolute woman living in the valley of Sorek by the name of Delilah. They appoint her the agent in the case. The Philistines are secreted in the same building, and then Delilah goes to work and coaxes Samson to tell what is the secret of his strength. " Well," he says, " if you should take seven green withes such as they fasten wild beasts with and put them around me I should be perfectly powerless." So she binds him with the seven green withes. Then she claps her hands and says: " They come—the Philistines!" and he walks out as though they were no impediment. She coaxes him again, and says: " Now tell me the secret of this great strength?" and he replies: " If you should take some ropes that have never been used and tie me with them I should be just like other men." She ties him with the ropes, claps her hands, and shouts: " They come—the Philistines!" He walks out as easily as he did before—not a single obstruction. She coaxes him again, and he says: " Now, if you should take these seven long plaits of hair, and by this house-loom weave them into a web, I could not get away." So the house-loom is rolled up, and the shuttle flies backward and forward and the long plaits of hair are woven into a web. Then she claps her hands, and says: " They come—the Philistines!" He walks out as easily as he did before, dragging a part of the loom with him.

But after awhile she persuades him to tell the truth. He says: " If you should take a razor or shears and cut off this long hair, I should be powerless and in the hands of my enemies." Samson sleeps, and that she may not wake him up during the process of shearing, help is called in. You know that the barbers of the East have such a skill-ful way of manipulating the head to this very day that, in-stead of waking up a sleeping man, they will put a man wide awake sound asleep. I hear the blades of the shears grinding against each other, and I see the long locks fall-ing off. The shears or razor accomplishes what green withes and new ropes and house-loom could not do. Sud-denly she claps her hands, and says: " The Philistines be upon thee, Samson!" He rouses up with a struggle, but his strength is all gone. He is in the hands of his enemies.

I hear the groan of the giant as they take his eyes out, and then I see him staggering on in his blindness, feeling his way as he goes on toward Gaza. The prison door is open, and the giant is thrust in. He sits down and puts his hands on the mill-crank, which, with exhausting hori-zontal motion, goes day after day, week after week, month after month—work, work, work! The consternation of the world in captivity, his locks shorn, his eyes punctured, grinding corn in Gaza!

I. First of all, behold in this giant of the text that physical power is not always an index of moral power. He was a huge man—the lion found it out, and the three thousand men whom he slew found it out; yet he was the subject of petty revenges and out-gianted by low passion. I am far from throwing any discredit upon physical stamina. There are those who seem to have great admiration for delicacy and sickliness of constitution. I never could see any glory in weak nerves or sick headache. Whatever effort in our day is made to make the men and women more robust should have the favor of every good citizen as well as of every Christian. Gymnastics may be positively religious.

Good people sometimes ascribe to a wicked heart what they ought to ascribe to a slow liver. The body and the soul are such near neighbors that they often catch each other's diseases. Those who never saw a sick day, and who, like Hercules, show the giant in the cradle, have more to answer for than those who are the subjects of life-long infirmities. He who can lift twice as much as you can, and walk twice as far, and work twice as long, will have a double account to meet in the judgment.

How often it is that you do not find physical energy indicative of spiritual power! If a clear head is worth more than one dizzy with perpetual vertigo—if muscles with the play of health in them are worth more than those drawn up in chronic " rheumatics "—if an eye quick to catch passing objects is better than one with vision dim and uncertain—then God will require of us efficiency just in proportion to what he has given us. Physical energy ought to be a type of moral power. We ought to have as good digestion of truth as we have capacity to assimilate food. Our spiritual hearing ought to be as good as our physical hearing. Our spiritual taste ought to be as clear as our tongue. Samsons in body, we ought to be giants in moral power.

But while you find a great many men who realize that they ought to use their money aright, and use their intelligence aright, how few men you find aware of the fact that they ought to use their physical organism aright! With every thump of the heart there is something saying, "Work! work!" and, lest we should complain that we have no tools to work with, God gives us our hands and feet, with every knuckle, and with every joint, and with every muscle saying to us, "Lay hold and do something."

But how often it is that men with physical strength do not serve Christ! They are like a ship full manned and full rigged, capable of vast tonnage, able to endure all stress of weather, yet swinging idly at the docks, when these men ought to be crossing and recrossing the great ocean of human suffering and sin with God's supplies of mercy. How often it is that physical strength is used in doing positive damage, or in luxurious ease, when, with sleeves rolled up and bronzed bosom, fearless of the shafts of opposition, it ought to be laying hold with all its might, and tugging away to lift up this sunken wreck of a world.

It is a most shameful fact that much of the business of the Church and of the world must be done by those comparatively invalid. Richard Baxter, by reason of his diseases, all his days sitting in the door of the tomb, yet writing more than a hundred volumes, and sending out an influence for God that will endure as long as the " Saints' Everlasting Rest." Edward Payson, never knowing a well day, yet how he preached, and how he wrote, helping thousands of dying souls like himself to swim in a sea of glory! And Robert M'Cheyne, a walking skeleton, yet you know what he did in Dundee, and how he shook Scotland with zeal for God. Philip Doddridge, advised by his friends, because of his illness, not to enter the ministry, yet you know what he did for the " rise and progress of religion " in the Church and in the world.

Wilberforce was told by his doctors that he could not live a fortnight, yet at that very time entering upon philanthropic enterprises that demanded the greatest endurance and persistence. Robert Hall, suffering excruciations, so that often in his pulpit while preaching he would stop and lie down on a sofa, then getting up again to preach about heaven until the glories of the celestial city dropped on the multitude, doing more work, perhaps, than almost any well man in his day.

Oh, how often it is that men with great physical endurance are not as great in moral and spiritual stature! While there are achievements for those who are bent all their days with sickness — achievements of patience, achievements of Christian endurance—I call upon men of health to-day, men of muscle, men of nerve, men of physical power, to devote themselves to the Lord. Giants in body, you ought to be giants in soul.

II. Behold also, in the story of my text, illustration of the fact of the damage that strength can do if it be misguided. It seems to me that this man spent a great deal of his time in doing evil—this Samson of my text. To pay a bet which he had lost by guessing of his riddle he robs and kills thirty people. He was not only gigantic in strength, but gigantic in mischief, and a type of those men in all ages of the world who, powerful in body or mind, or any faculty of social position or wealth, have used their strength for iniquitous purposes.

It is not the small, weak men of the day who do the damage. These small men who go swearing and loafing about your stores and shops and banking-houses, assailing Christ and the Bible and the Church—they do not do the damage. They have no influence. They are vermin that you crush with your foot. But it is the giants of the day, the misguided giants, giants in physical power, or giants in mental acumen, or giants in social position, or giants in wealth, who do the damage.

The men with sharp pens that stab religion and throw their poison all through our literature; the men who use the power of wealth to sanction iniquity, and bribe justice, and make truth and honor bow to their golden scepter.

Misguided giants—look out for them! In the middle and the latter part of the last century no doubt there were thousands of men in Paris and Edinburgh and London who hated God and blasphemed the name of the Almighty; but they did but little mischief—they were small men, insignificant men. Yet there were giants in those days.

Who can calculate the soul-havoc of a Rousseau, going on with a very enthusiasm of iniquity, with fiery imagination seizing upon all the impulsive natures of his day? or David Hume, who employed his life as a spider employs its summer, in spinning out silken webs to trap the unwary? or Voltaire, the most learned man of his day, marshaling a great host of skeptics, and leading them out in the dark land of infidelity? or Gibbon, who showed an uncontrollable grudge against religion in his history of one of the most fascinating periods of the world's existence—the Decline and Fall of the Roman Empire—a book in which, with all the splendors of his genius, he magnified the errors of Christian disciples, while, with a sparseness of notice that never can be forgiven, he treated of the Christian heroes of whom the world was not worthy?

Oh, men of stout physical health, men of great mental stature, men of high social position, men of great power of any sort, I want you to understand your power, and I want you to know that that power devoted to God will be a crown on earth, to you typical of a crown in heaven; but misguided, bedraggled in sin, administrative of evil, God will thunder against you with His condemnation in the day when millionaire and pauper, master and slave, king and subject, shall stand side by side in the judgment, and money-bags, and judicial ermine, and royal robe shall be riven with the lightnings.

Behold also, how a giant may be slain of a woman. Delilah started the train of circumstances that pulled down the temple of Dagon about Samson's ears. And tens of thousands of giants have gone down to death and hell through the same impure fascinations. It seems to me that it is high time that pulpit and platform and printing-press speak out against the impurities of modern society. Fastidiousness and Prudery say: " Better not speak—you will rouse up adverse criticism; you will make worse what you want to make better; better deal in glittering generalities; the subject is too delicate for polite ears." But there comes a voice from heaven overpowering the mincing sentimentalities of the day, saying: "Cry aloud, spare not, lift up thy voice like a trumpet, and show my people their transgressions and the house of Jacob their sins."

The trouble is that when people write or speak upon this theme they are apt to cover it up with the graces of belles-lettres, so that the crime is made attractive instead of repulsive. Lord Byron in "Don Juan" adorns this crime until it smiles like a May queen. Michelet, the great French writer, covers it up with bewitching rhetoric until it glows like the rising sun, when it ought to be made loathsome as a small-pox hospital. There are to-day influences abroad which, if unresisted by the pulpit and the printing-press, will turn New York and Brooklyn into Sodom and Gomorrah, fit only for the storm of fire and brimstone that whelmed the cities of the plain.

You who are seated in your Christian homes, compassed by moral and religious restraints, do not realize the gulf of iniquity that bounds you on the north and the south and the east and the west. While I speak there are tens of thousands of men and women going over the awful plunge of an impure life; and while I cry to God for mercy upon their souls, I call upon you to marshal in the defense of your homes, your Church and your nation. There is a banqueting hall that you have never heard described. You know all about the feast of Ahasuerus, where a thousand lords sat. You know all about Belshazzar's carousal, where the blood of the murdered king spurted into the faces of the banqueters. You may know of the scene of riot and wassail, when there was set before Esopus one dish of food that cost $400,000. But I speak now of a different banqueting hall. Its roof is fretted with fire. Its floor is tesselated with fire. Its chalices are chased with fire. Its song is a song of fire. Its walls are buttresses of fire. Solomon refers to it when he says: " Her guests are in the depths of hell."

Our American communities are suffering from the gospel of Free Loveism, which, fifteen or twenty years ago, was preached on the platform and in some of the churches of this country. I charge upon Free Loveism that it has blighted innumerable homes, and that it has sent innumerable souls to ruin. Free Loveism is bestial; it is worse — it is infernal! It has furnished this land with about one thousand divorces annually. In one county in the State of Indiana it furnished eleven divorces in one day before dinner. It has roused up elopements, North, South, East, and West. You can hardly take up a paper but you read of an elopement. As far as I can understand the doctrine of Free Loveism it is this: That every man ought to have somebody else's wife, and every wife somebody else's husband. They do not like our Christian organization of society, and I wish they would all elope, the wretches of one sex taking the wretches of the other, and start to-morrow morning for the great Sahara Desert, until the simoom shall sweep seven feet of sand all over them, and not one passing caravan for the next five hundred years bring back one miserable bone of their carcasses! Free Loveism! It is the double-distilled extract of nux vomica, ratsbane, and adder's tongue. Never until society goes back to the old Bible, and hears its eulogy of purity and its anathema of uncleanness—never until then will this evil be extirpated.

IV. Behold also in this giant of the text and in the giant of our own century that great physical power must crumble and expire. The Samson of the text long ago went away. He fought the lion. He fought the Philistines. He could fight anything, but death was too much for him. He may have required a longer grave and a broader grave; but the tomb nevertheless was his terminus.

If, then, we are to be compelled to go out of this world, where are we to go to? This body and soul must soon part. What shall be the destiny of the former I know— dust to dust. But what shall be the destiny of the latter? Shall it rise into the companionship of the white-robed, whose sins Christ has slain? or will it go down among the unbelieving, who tried to gain the world and save their souls, but were swindled out of both? Blessed be God, we have a Champion! He is so styled in the Bible: A Champion who has conquered death and hell, and he is ready to fight all our battles from the first to the last. "Who is this that cometh from Edom, with dyed garments from Bozrah, mighty to save?" If we follow in the wake of that Champion death has no power and the grave no victory. The worst man trusting in Him shall have his dying pangs alleviated and his future illumined.

V. In the light of this subject I want to call your attention to a fact which may not have been rightly considered oy five men in this house, and that is the fact that we must be brought into judgment for the employment of our physical organism. Shoulder, brain, hand, foot—we must answer in judgment for the use we have made of them. Have they been used for the elevation of society or for its depression? In proportion as our arm is strong and our step elastic will our account at last be intensified. Thousands of sermons are preached to invalids. I preach this sermon this morning to stout men and healthful women. We must give to God an account for the right use of this physical organism.

These invalids have comparatively little to account for, perhaps. They could not lift twenty pounds. They could not walk half a mile without sitting down to rest. In the preparation of this subject I have said to myself, how shall I account to God in judgment for the use of a body which never knew one moment of real sickness? Rising up in judgment, standing beside the men and women who had only little physical energy, and yet consumed that energy in a conflagration of religious enthusiasm, how will we feel abashed!

Oh, men of the strong arm and the stout heart, what use are you making of your physical forces? Will you be able to stand the test of that day when we must answer for the use of every talent, whether it were a physical energy, or a mental acumen, or a spiritual power?

The day approaches, and I see one who in this world was an invalid, and as she stands before the throne of God to answer she says, " I was sick all my days. I had but very little strength, but I did as well as I could in being

kind to those who were more sick and more suffering."
And Christ will say, " Well done, faithful servant."

And then a little child will stand before the throne, and
she will say, " On earth I had a curvature of the spine,
and I was very weak, and I was very sick; but I used to
gather flowers out of the wild-wood and bring them to my
sick mother, and she was comforted when she saw the
sweet flowers out of the wild-wood. I didn't do much, but
I did something." And Christ shall say, as He takes her
up in His arm and kisses her, " Well done, well done,
faithful servant; enter thou into the joy of thy Lord."

What, then, will be said to us—we to whom the Lord
gave physical strength and continuous health? Hark! it
thunders again. The judgment! the judgment!

I said to an old Scotch minister, who was one of the best
friends I ever had, " Doctor, did you ever know Robert
Pollock, the Scotch poet, who wrote ' The Course of
Time'?" " Oh, yes," he replied, " I knew him well; I
was his classmate." And then the doctor went on to tell
me how that the writing of " The Course of Time " exhausted the health of Robert Pollock, and he expired. It
seems as if no man could have such a glimpse of the day
for which all other days were made as Robert Pollock had,
and long survive that glimpse. In the description of that
day he says, among other things:

"Begin the woe, ye woods, and tell it to the doleful winds
    And doleful winds wail to the howling hills,
    And howling hills mourn to the dismal vales,
    And dismal vales sigh to the sorrowing brooks,
    And sorrowing brooks weep to the weeping stream,

And weeping stream awake the groaning deep;
Ye heavens, great archway of the universe, put sack-cloth on;
And ocean, robe thyself in garb of widowhood,
And gather all thy waves into a groan, and utter it.
Long, loud, deep, piercing, dolorous, immense.
The occasion asks it, Nature dies, and angels come to lay
    her in her grave."

What Robert Pollock saw in poetic dream, you and I
will see in positive reality—the judgment! the judgment!

THE PLEIADES AND ORION.

———

"Seek Him that maketh the Seven Stars and Orion."—AMOS. **v**: 8

A COUNTRY farmer wrote this text—Amos of Tekoa. He plowed the earth and threshed the grain by a new threshing-machine just invented, as formerly the cattle trod out the grain. He gathered the fruit of the sycamore-tree, and scarified it with an iron comb just before it was getting ripe, as it was necessary and customary in that way to take from it the bitterness. He was the son of a poor shepherd, and stuttered; but before the stammering rustic the Philistines, and Syrians, and Phœnicians, and Moabites, and Ammonites, and Edomites, and Israelites trembled.

Moses was a law-giver, Daniel was a prince, Isaiah a courtier, and David a king; but Amos, the author of my text, was a peasant, and, as might be supposed, nearly all his parallelisms are pastoral, his prophecy full of the odor of new-mown hay, and the rattle of locusts, and the rumble of carts with sheaves, and the roar of wild beasts devouring the flock while the shepherd came out in their defense. He watched the herds by day, and by night inhabited a booth made out of bushes, so that through these branches he could see the stars all night long, and was more familiar with them than we who have tight roofs to our houses, and hardly ever see the stars except among the tall brick chimneys of the great towns. But at seasons of the year when the herds were in special danger, he would stay out in the open field all through the darkness, his only shelter the curtain of the night, heaven, with the stellar embroideries and silvered tassels of lunar light.

What a life of solitude, all alone with his herds! Poor Amos! And at twelve o'clock at night, hark to the wolf's bark, and the lion's roar, and the bear's growl, and the owl's te-whit-te-whos, and the serpent's hiss, as he unwittingly steps too near while moving through the thickets! So Amos, like other herdsmen, got the habit of studying the map of the heavens, because it was so much of the time spread out before him. He noticed some stars advancing and others receding. He associated their dawn and setting with certain seasons of the year. He had a poetic nature, and he read night by night, and month by month, and year by year, the poem of the constellations, divinely rhythmic. But two rosettes of stars especially attracted his attention while seated on the ground, or lying on his back under the open scroll of the midnight heavens—the Pleiades, or Seven Stars, and Orion. The former group this rustic prophet associated with the spring, as it rises about the first of May. The latter he associated with the winter, as it comes to the meridian in January. The Pleiades, or Seven Stars, connected with all sweetness and joy; Orion, the herald of the tempest. The ancients were the more apt to study the physiognomy and juxtaposition of the heavenly bodies, because they thought they had a special influence upon the earth; and perhaps they were right. If the moon every few hours lifts and lets down the tides of the Atlantic Ocean, and the electric storms of last year in the sun, by all scientific admission, affected the earth, why not the stars have proportionate effect?

And there are some things which make me think that it may not have been all superstition which connected the movements and appearance of the heavenly bodies with great moral events on earth. Did not a meteor run on evangelistic errand on the first Christmas night, and designate the rough cradle of our Lord? Did not the stars in their courses fight against Sisera? Was it merely coincidental that before the destruction of Jerusalem the moon was eclipsed for twelve consecutive nights? Did it merely happen so that a new star appeared in constellation Cassiopeia, and then disappeared just before King Charles IX. of France, who was responsible for St. Bartholomew massacre, died? Was it without significance that in the days of the Roman Emperor Justinian war and famine were preceded by the dimness of the sun, which for nearly a year gave no more light than the moon, although there were no clouds to obscure it?

Astrology, after all, may have been something more than a brilliant heathenism. No wonder that Amos of the text, having heard these two anthems of the stars, put down the stout rough staff of the herdsman and took into his brown hand and cut and knotted fingers the pen of a prophet, and advised the recreant people of his time to return to God, saying: "Seek Him that maketh the Seven Stars and Orion." This command, which Amos gave 785 years B.C., is just as appropriate for us, 1885 A.D.

In the first place, Amos saw, as we must see, that the God who made the Pleiades and Orion must be the God of order. It was not so much a star here and a star there that impressed the inspired herdsman, but seven in one group, and seven in the other group. He saw that night after night and season after season and decade after decade they had kept step of light, each one in its own place, a sisterhood never clashing and never contesting precedence. From the time Hesiod called the Pleiades the "seven daughters of Atlas" and Virgil wrote in his Æneid of "Stormy Orion" until now, they have observed the order established for their coming and going; order written not in manuscript that may be pigeon-holed, but with the hand of the Almighty on the dome of the sky, so that all nations may read it. Order. Persistent order. Sublime order. Omnipotent order.

What a sedative to you and me, to whom communities and nations sometimes seem going pell-mell, and world ruled by some fiend at hap-hazard, and in all directions maladministration! The God who keeps seven worlds in right circuit for six thousand years can certainly keep all the affairs of individuals and nations and continents in adjustment. We had not better fret much, for the peasant's argument of the text was right. If God can take care of the seven worlds of the Pleiades and the four chief worlds of Orion, He can probably take care of the one world we inhabit.

So I feel very much as my father felt one day when we were going to the country mill to get a grist ground, and I, a boy of seven years, sat in the back part of the wagon, and our yoke of oxen ran away with us and along a laby-rinthine road through the woods, so that I thought every moment we would be dashed to pieces, and I made a terrible outcry of fright, and my father turned to me with a face perfectly calm, and said: "De Witt, what are you crying about? I guess we can ride as fast as the oxen can run." And, my hearers, why should we be affrighted and lose our equilibrium in the swift movement of worldly events, especially when we are assured that it is not a yoke of unbroken steers that are drawing us on, but that order and wise government are in the yoke?

In your occupation, your mission, your sphere, do the best you can, and then trust to God; and if things are all mixed and disquieting, and your brain is hot and your heart sick, get some one to go out with you into the starlight and point out to you the Pleiades, or, better than that, get into some observatory, and through the telescope see further than Amos with the naked eye could—namely, two hundred stars in the Pleiades, and that in what is called the sword of Orion there is a nebula computed to be two trillion two hundred thousand billions of times larger than the sun. Oh, be at peace with the God who made all that and controls all that—the wheel of the constellations turning in the wheel of galaxies for thousands of years without the breaking of a cog or the slipping of a band or the snap of an axle. For your placidity and comfort through the Lord Jesus Christ I charge you, "Seek Him that maketh the Seven Stars and Orion."

Again, Amos saw, as we must see, that the God who made these two groups of the text was the God of light.

Amos saw that God was not satisfied with making one star, or two or three stars, but He makes seven; and having finished that group of worlds, makes another group— group after group. To the Pleiades He adds Orion. It seems that God likes light so well that He keeps making it. Only one being in the universe knows the statistics of solar, lunar, stellar, meteoric creations, and that is the Creator Himself. And they have all been lovingly christened, each one a name as distinct as the names of your children. " He telleth the number of the stars; He calleth them all by their names." The seven Pleiades had names given to them, and they are Alcyone, Merope, Celæno, Electra, Sterope, Taygete, and Maia.

But think of the billions and trillions of daughters of starry light that God calls by name as they sweep by Him with beaming brow and lustrous robe! So fond is God of light—natural light, moral light, spiritual light. Again and again is light harnessed for symbolization—Christ, the bright and morning star; evangelization, the daybreak; the redemption of nations, Sun of Righteousness rising with healing in His wings. Oh, men and women, with so many sorrows and sins and perplexities, if you want light of comfort, light of pardon, light of goodness, in earnest, pray through Christ, " Seek Him that maketh the Seven Stars and Orion."

Again, Amos saw, as we must see, that the God who made these two archipelagoes of stars must be an unchanging God. There had been no change in the stellar appearance in this herdsman's life-time, and his father, a shepherd, reported to him that there had been no change in his life-time. And these two clusters hang over the celestial arbor now just as they were the first night that they shone on the Edenic bowers, the same as when the Egyptians built the Pyramids from the top of which to watch them, the same as when the Chaldeans calculated the eclipses, the same as when Elihu, according to the Book of Job, went out to study the aurora borealis, the same under Ptolemaic system and Copernican system, the same from Calisthenes to Pythagoras, and from Pythagoras to Herschel. Surely, a changeless God must have fashioned the Pleiades and Orion! Oh, what an anodyne amid the ups and downs of life, and the flux and reflux of the tides of prosperity, to know that we have a changeless God, the same yesterday, to-day, and forever."

Xerxes garlanded and knighted the steersman of his boat in the morning, and hanged him in the evening of the same day. Fifty thousand people stood around the columns of the national capitol, shouting themselves hoarse at the presidential inaugural, and in four months so great were the antipathies that a ruffian's pistol in Washington depot expressed the sentiment of a great multitude. The world sits in its chariot and drives tandem, and the horse ahead is Huzza, and the horse behind is Anathema. Lord Cobham, in King James' time, was applauded, and had thirty-five thousand dollars a year, but was afterward execrated, and lived on scraps stolen from the royal kitchen. Alexander the Great after death remained unburied for thirty days, because no one would do the honor of shoveling him under. The Duke of Wellington refused to have his iron fence mended, because it had been broken by an infuriated populace in some hour of political excitement, and he left it in ruins that men might learn what a fickle thing is human favor. "But the mercy of the Lord is from everlasting to everlasting to them that fear Him, and His righteousness unto the children's children of such as keep His covenant, and to those who remember His commandments to do them." This moment " seek Him that maketh the Seven Stars and Orion."

Again, Amos saw, as we must see, that the God who made these two beacons of the Oriental night sky must be a God of love and kindly warning. The Pleiades rising in mid-sky said to all the herdsmen and shepherds and husbandmen: " Come out and enjoy the mild weather, and cultivate your gardens and fields." Orion, coming in winter, warned them to prepare for tempest. All navigation was regulated by these two constellations. The one said to shipmaster and crew: " Hoist sail for the sea, and gather merchandise from other lands." But Orion was the storm-signal, and said: " Reef sail, make things snug, or put into harbor, for the hurricanes are getting their wings out." As the Pleiades were the sweet evangels of the spring, Orion was the warning prophet of the winter.

Oh, now I get the best view of God I ever had! There are two kinds of sermons I never want to preach—the one that presents God so kind, so indulgent, so lenient, so imbecile that men may do what they will against Him, and fracture His every law, and put the cry of their impertinence and rebellion under His throne, and while they are spitting in His face and stabbing at His heart, He takes them up in His arms and kisses their infuriated brow and cheek, saying, " Of such is the kingdom of heaven." The other kind of sermon I never want to preach is the one that represents God as all fire and torture and thunder-cloud, and with red-hot pitch-fork tossing the human race into paroxysms of infinite agony. The sermon that I am now preaching believes in a God of loving, kindly warn-ing, the God of spring and winter, the God of the Pleiades and Orion.

You must remember that the winter is just as impor-tant as the spring. Let one winter pass without frost to kill vegetation and ice to bind the rivers and snow to enrich our fields, and then you will have to enlarge your hospitals and your cemeteries. "A green Christmas makes a fat grave-yard," was the old proverb. Storms to purify the air. Thermometer at ten degrees above zero to tone up the system. December and January just as im-portant as May and June. I tell you we need the storms of life as much as we do the sunshine. There are more men ruined by prosperity than by adversity. If we had our own way in life, before this we would have been imper-sonations of selfishness and worldliness and disgusting sin, and puffed up until we would have been like Julius Cæsar, who was made by sycophants to believe that he was divine, and the freckles on his face were as the stars of the firma-ment.

One of the swiftest transatlantic voyages made last sum-mer by the "Etruria" was because she had a stormy wind abaft, chasing her from New York to Liverpool. But to those going in the opposite direction the storm was a buffeting and a hinderance. It is a bad thing to have a storm ahead, pushing us back; but if we be God's children and aiming toward heaven, the storms of life will only chase us the sooner into the harbor. I am so glad to believe that the monsoons, and typhoons, and mistrals, and siroccos of the land and sea are not unchained maniacs let loose upon the earth, but are under divine supervision! I am so glad that the God of the Seven Stars is also the God of Orion! It was out of Dante's suffering came the sublime "Divina Commedia," and out of John Milton's blindness came "Paradise Lost," and out of miserable infidel attack came the "Bridgewater Treatise" in favor of Christianity, and out of David's exile came the songs of consolation, and out of the sufferings of Christ came the possibility of the world's redemption, and out of your bereavement, your persecution, your poverties, your misfortunes, may yet come an eternal heaven.

Oh, what a mercy it is that in the text and all up and down the Bible God induces us to look out toward other worlds! Bible astronomy in Genesis, in Joshua, in Job, in the Psalms, in the prophets, major and minor, in St. John's Apocalypse, practically saying, "Worlds! worlds! worlds! Get ready for them!" We have a nice little world here that we stick to, as though losing that we lose all. We are afraid of falling off this little raft of a world. We are afraid that some meteoric iconoclast will some night smash it, and we want everything to revolve around it, and are disappointed when we find that it revolves around the sun instead of the sun revolving around it. What a fuss we make about this little bit of a world, its existence only a short time between two spasms, the paroxysm by which it was hurled from chaos into order, and the paroxysm of its demolition.

And I am glad that so many texts call us to look off to other worlds, many of them larger and grander and more resplendent. "Look there," says Job, "at Mazaroth and Arcturus and his sons!" "Look there," says St. John, "at the moon under Christ's feet!" "Look there," says Joshua, "at the sun standing still above Gibeon!" "Look there," says Moses, "at the sparkling firmament!" "Look there," says Amos, the herdsman, "at the Seven Stars and Orion!" Don't let us be so sad about those who shove off from this world under Christly pilotage. Don't let us be so agitated about our own going off this little barge or sloop or canal-boat of a world to get on some "Great Eastern" of the heavens. Don't let us persist in wanting to stay in this barn, this shed, this outhouse of a world, when all the King's palaces already occupied by many of our best friends are swinging wide open their gates to let us in.

When I read, "In my Father's house are many mansions," I do not know but that each world is a room, and as many rooms as there are worlds, stellar stairs, stellar galleries, stellar hallways, stellar windows, stellar domes. How our departed friends must pity us shut up in these cramped apartments, tired if we walk fifteen miles, when they some morning, by one stroke of wing, can make circuit of the whole stellar system and be back in time for matins! Perhaps yonder twinkling constellation is the residence of the martyrs; that group of twelve luminaries is the celestial home of the Apostles. Perhaps that steep of light is the dwelling-place of angels cherubic, seraphic, archangelic. A mansion with as many rooms as worlds, and all their windows illuminated for festivity.

Oh, how this widens and lifts and stimulates our expectation! How little it makes the present, and how stupendous it makes the future! How it consoles us about our pious dead, that instead of being boxed up and under the ground have the range of as many rooms as there are worlds, and welcome everywhere, for it is the Father's house, in which there are many mansions! Oh, Lord God of the Seven Stars and Orion, how can I endure the transport, the ecstasy, of such a vision! I must obey my text and seek Him. I will seek Him. I seek Him now, for I call to mind that it is not the material universe that is most valuable, but the spiritual, and that each of us has a soul worth more than all the worlds which the inspired herdsman saw from his booth on the hills of Tekoa.

I had studied it before, but the Cathedral of Cologne, Germany, never impressed me as it did this summer. It is admittedly the grandest Gothic structure in the world, its foundation laid in 1248, only two or three years ago completed. More than six hundred years in building. All Europe taxed for its construction. Its chapel of the Magi with precious stones enough to purchase a kingdom. Its chapel of St. Agnes with masterpieces of painting. Its spire springing five hundred and eleven feet into the heavens. Its stained glass the chorus of all rich colors. Statues encircling the pillars and encircling all. Statues above statues, until sculpture can do no more, but faints and falls back against carved stalls and down on pavements over which the kings and queens of the earth have walked to confession. Nave and aisles and transept and portals combining the splendors of sunrise. Interlaced, interfoliated, intercolumned grandeur. As I stood outside, looking at the double range of flying buttresses and the forest of pinnacles, higher and higher and higher, until I almost reeled from dizziness, I exclaimed; "Great doxology in stone! Frozen prayer of many nations!"

But while standing there I saw a poor man enter and put down his pack and kneel beside his burden on the hard floor of that cathedral. And tears of deep emotion came into my eyes, as I said to myself: "There is a soul worth more than all the material surroundings. That man will live after the last pinnacle has fallen, and not one stone of all that cathedral glory shall remain uncrumbled. He is now a Lazarus in rags and poverty and weariness, but immortal, and a son of the Lord God Almighty; and the prayer he now offers, though amid many superstitions, I believe God will hear; and among the Apostles whose sculptured forms stand in the surrounding niches he will at last be lifted, and into the presence of that Christ whose sufferings are represented by the crucifix before which he bows; and be raised in due time out of all his poverties into the glorious home built for him and built for us by 'Him who maketh the Seven Stars and Orion.'"

THE QUEEN'S VISIT.

"Behold, the half was not told me."—I KINGS x: 7.

SOLOMON had resolved that Jerusalem should be the center of all sacred, regal, and commercial magnificence. He set himself to work, and monopolized the surrounding desert as a highway for his caravans. He built the city of Palmyra around one of the principal wells of the East, so that all the long trains of merchandise from the East were obliged to stop there, pay toll, and leave part of their wealth in the hands of Solomon's merchants. He manned the fortress Thapsacus at the chief ford of the Euphrates, and put under guard everything that passed there. The three great products of Palestine—wine pressed from the richest clusters and celebrated all the world over; oil which in that hot country is the entire substitute for butter and lard, and was pressed from the olive branches until every tree in the country became an oil well; and honey which was the entire substitute for sugar — these three great products of the country Solomon exported, and received in return fruits and precious woods and the animals of every clime.

He went down to Ezion-geber and ordered a fleet of ships to be constructed, oversaw the workmen, and watched the launching of the flotilla which was to go out on more than a year's voyage, to bring home the wealth of the then known world. He heard that the Egyptian horses were large and swift, and long-maned and round-limbed, and he resolved to purchase them, giving eighty-five dollars apiece for them, putting the best of these horses in his own stall, and selling the surplus to foreign potentates at great profit.

He heard that there was the best of timber on Mount Lebanon, and he sent out one hundred and eighty thousand men to hew down the forest and drag the timber through the mountain gorges, to construct it into rafts to be floated to Joppa, and from thence to be drawn by ox-teams twenty-five miles across the land to Jerusalem. He heard that there were beautiful flowers in other lands. He sent for them, planted them in his own gardens, and to this very day there are flowers found in the ruins of that city such as are to be found in no other part of Palestine, the lineal descendants of the very flowers that Solomon planted. He heard that in foreign groves there were birds of richest voice and most luxuriant wing. He sent out people to catch them and bring them there, and he put them into his cages.

Stand back now and see this long train of camels coming up to the king's gate, and the ox-trains from Egypt, gold and silver and precious stones, and beasts of every hoof, and birds of every wing, and fish of every scale! See the peacocks strut under the cedars, and the horsemen run, and the chariots wheel! Hark to the orchestra! Gaze upon the dance! Not stopping to look into the

wonders of the temple, step right on to the causeway, and
pass up to Solomon's palace!

Here we find ourselves amid a collection of buildings on
which the king had lavished the wealth of many empires.
The genius of Hiram, the architect, and of the other
artists is here seen in the long line of corridors and the
suspended gallery and the approach to the throne.
Traceried window opposite traceried window.   Bronzed
ornaments bursting into lotus and lily and pomegranate.
Chapiters surrounded by network of leaves in which imitation fruit seemed suspended as in hanging baskets.   Three
branches—so Josephus tells us—three branches sculptured
on the marble, so thin and subtle that even the leaves
seemed to quiver.   A laver capable of holding five hundred barrels of water on six hundred brazen ox-heads,
which gushed with water and filled the whole place with
coolness and crystalline brightness and musical plash.
Ten tables chased with chariot wheel and lion and cherubim.   Solomon sat on a throne of ivory.   At the seating
place of the throne, on each end of the steps, a brazen lion.
Why, my friends, in that place they trimmed their candles
with snuffers of gold, and they cut their fruits with knives
of gold, and they washed their faces in basins of gold, and
they scooped out the ashes with shovels of gold, and they
stirred the altar fires with tongs of gold.   Gold reflected
in the water!   Gold flashing from the apparel!   Gold blazing in the crown!   Gold, gold, gold!

Of course the news of the affluence of that place went
out everywhere by every caravan and by wing of every ship,
until soon the streets of Jerusalem are crowded with cu-

riosity seekers.   What is that long procession approaching
Jerusalem?   I think from the pomp of it there must be
royalty in the train.   I smell the breath of the spices
which are brought as presents, and I hear the shout of the
drivers, and I see the dust-covered caravan showing that
they come from far away.   Cry the news up to the palace.
The Queen of Sheba advances.   Let all the people come
out to see.   Let the mighty men of the land come out on
the palace corridors.   Let Solomon come down the stairs
of the palace before the queen has alighted.   Shake out
the cinnamon, and the saffron, and the calamus, and the
frankincense, and pass it into the treasure house.   Take
up the diamonds until they glitter in the sun.

The Queen of Sheba alights.   She enters the palace.
She washes at the bath.   She sits down at the banquet.
The cup-bearers bow.   The meat smokes.   The music
trembles in the dash of the waters from the molten sea.
Then she rises from the banquet, and walks through the
conservatories, and gazes on the architecture, and she asks
Solomon many strange questions, and she learns about the
religion of the Hebrews, and she then and there becomes a
servant of the Lord God.

She is overwhelmed.   She begins to think that all the
spices she brought, and all the precious woods which are
intended to be turned into harps and psalteries and into
railings for the causeway between the temple and the
palace, and the one hundred and eighty thousand dollars
in money—she begins to think that all these presents
amount to nothing in such a place, and she is almost
ashamed that she has brought them, and she says within

herself: " I heard a great deal about this place, and about
this wonderful religion of the Hebrews, but I find it far
beyond my highest anticipations. I must add more than
fifty per cent. to what has been related. It exceeds everything that I could have expected. The half—the half was
not told me."

Learn from this subject what a beautiful thing it is
when social position and wealth surrender themselves to
God. When religion comes to a neighborhood, the first to
receive it are the women. Some men say it is because
they are weak-minded. I say it is because they have
quicker perception of what is right, more ardent affection
and capacity for sublimer emotion. After the women
have received the Gospel then all the distressed and the
poor of both sexes, those who have no friends, accept
Jesus. Last of all come the people of affluence and high
social position. Alas, that it is so!

If there are those here to-day who have been favored of
fortune, or, as I might better put it, favored of God, surrender all you have and all you expect to be to the Lord
who blessed this Queen of Sheba. Certainly you are not
ashamed to be found in this queen's company. I am glad
that Christ has had His imperial friends in all ages—Elizabeth Christina, Queen of Prussia; Maria Feodorovna,
Queen of Russia; Marie, Empress of France; Helena, the
imperial mother of Constantine; Arcadia, from her great
fortunes building public baths in Constantinople and toiling for the alleviation of the masses; Queen Clotilda, leading her husband and three thousand of his armed warriors
to Christian baptism; Elizabeth of Burgundy, giving her

jeweled glove to a beggar, and scattering great fortunes among the distressed; Prince Albert, singing " Rock of Ages " in Windsor Castle, and Queen Victoria, incognita, reading the Scriptures to a dying pauper.

I bless God that the day is coming when royalty will bring all its thrones, and music all its harmonies, and painting all its pictures, and sculpture all its statuary, and architecture all its pillars, and conquest all its scepters; and the queens of the earth, in long line of advance, frankincense filling the air and the camels laden with gold, shall approach Jerusalem, and the gates shall be hoisted, and the great burden of splendor shall be lifted into the palace of this greater than Solomon.

Again, my subject teaches me what is earnestness in the search of truth. Do you know where Sheba was? It was in Abyssinia, or some say in the southern part of Arabia Felix. In either case it was a great way off from Jerusalem. To get from there to Jerusalem she had to cross a country infested with bandits, and go across blistering deserts. Why did not the Queen of Sheba stay at home and send a committee to inquire about this new religion, and have the delegates report in regard to that religion and wealth of King Solomon? She wanted to see for herself, and hear for herself. She could not do this by work of committee. She felt she had a soul worth ten thousand kingdoms like Sheba, and she wanted a robe richer than any woven by Oriental shuttles, and she wanted a crown set with the jewels of eternity. Bring out the camels. Put on the spices. Gather up the jewels of the throne and put them on the caravan. Start now; no time to be lost.

Goad on the camels.   When I see that caravan, dust-covered, weary, and exhausted, trudging on across the desert and among the bandits until it reaches Jerusalem, I say: "There is an earnest seeker after the truth."

But there are a great many of you, my friends, who do not act in that way.   You all want to get the truth, but you want the truth to come to you; you do not want to go to it.   There are people who fold their arms and say: "I am ready to become a Christian at any time; if I am to be saved I shall be saved, and if I am to be lost I shall be lost."   A man who says that and keeps on saying it, will be lost.   Jerusalem will never come to you; you must go to Jerusalem.   The religion of the Lord Jesus Christ will not come to you; you must go and get religion. Bring out the camels; put on all the sweet spices, all the treasures of the heart's affection.   Start for the throne. Go in and hear the waters of salvation dashing in fountains all around about the throne.   Sit down at the banquet—the wine pressed from the grapes of the heavenly Eschol, the angels of God the cup-bearers.   Goad on the camels; Jerusalem will never come to you; you must go to Jerusalem.   The Bible declares it: "The Queen of the South"—that is, this very woman I am speaking of— "the Queen of the South shall rise up in judgment against this generation and condemn it; for she came from the uttermost parts of the earth to hear the wisdom of Solomon: and. behold! a greater than Solomon is here."   God help me to break up the infatuation of those people who are sitting down in idleness expecting to be saved. "Strive to enter in at the strait gate.   Ask, and it shall be given you; seek, and ye shall find; knock, and it shall be opened to you." Take the Kingdom of Heaven by violence. Urge on the camels!

Again, my subject impresses me with the fact that religion is a surprise to any one that gets it. This story of the new religion in Jerusalem, and of the glory of King Solomon, who was a type of Christ—that story rolls on and on, and is told by every traveler coming back from Jerusalem. The news goes on the wing of every ship and with every caravan, and you know a story enlarges as it is retold, and by the time that story gets down into the southern part of Arabia Felix, and the Queen of Sheba hears it, it must be a tremendous story. And yet this queen declares in regard to it, although she had heard so much and had her anticipations raised so high, the half—the half was not told her.

So religion is always a surprise to any one that gets it. The story of grace—an old story. Apostles preached it with rattle of chain; martyrs declared it with arm of fire; death-beds have affirmed it with visions of glory, and ministers of religion have sounded it through the lanes, and the highways, and the chapels, and the cathedrals. It has been cut into stone with chisel, and spread on the canvas with pencil; and it has been recited in the doxology of great congregations. And yet when a man first comes to look on the palace of God's mercy, and to see the royalty of Christ, and the wealth of this banquet, and the luxuriance of His attendants, and the loveliness of His face, and the joy of His service, he exclaims with prayers, with tears, with sighs, with triumphs: "The half—the half was not told me!"

I appeal to those in this house who are Christians.
Compare the idea you had of the joy of the Christian life
before you became a Christian with the appreciation of
that joy you have now since you have become a Christian,
and you are willing to attest before angels and men that
you never in the days of your spiritual bondage had any
appreciation of what was to come.   You are ready to-day
to answer, and if I gave you an opportunity in the midst
of this assemblage, you would speak out and say in regard
to the discoveries you have made of the mercy and the
grace and the goodness of God: " The half—the half was
not told me!"

Well, we hear a great deal about the good time that is
coming to this world, when it is to be girded with salvation.   Holiness on the bells of the horses.   The lion's
mane patted by the hand of a babe.   Ships of Tarshish
bringing cargoes for Jesus, and the hard, dry, barren,
winter-bleached, storm-scarred, thunder-split rock breaking into floods of bright water.   Deserts into which drome-
daries thrust their nostrils, because they were afraid of the
simoom—deserts blooming into carnation roses and silver-
tipped lilies.

It is the old story.   Everybody tells it.   Isaiah told it,
John told it, Paul told it, Ezekiel told it, Luther told it,
Calvin told it, John Milton told it—everybody tells it; and
yet—and yet when the midnight shall fly the hills, and
Christ shall marshal His great army, and China, dashing
her idols into the dust, shall hear the voice of God and
wheel into line; and India, destroying her Juggernaut and
snatching up her little children from the Ganges, shall

hear the voice of God and wheel into line; and vine-covered Italy, and wheat-crowned Russia, and all the nations of the earth shall hear the voice of God and fall into line; then the Church, which has been toiling and struggling through the centuries, robed and garlanded like a bride adorned for her husband, shall put aside her veil and look up into the face of her Lord the King, and say: "The half—the half was not told me!"

Well, there is coming a greater surprise to every Christian—a greater surprise than anything I have depicted. Heaven is an old story. Everybody talks about it. There is hardly a hymn in the hymn-book that does not refer to it. Children read about it in their Sabbath-school book. Aged men put on their spectacles to study it. We say it is a harbor from the storm. We call it our home. We say it is the house of many mansions. We weave together all sweet, beautiful, delicate, exhilarant words; we weave them into letters, and then we spell it out in rose and lily and amaranth. And yet that place is going to be a surprise to the most intelligent Christian. Like the Queen of Sheba, the report has come to us from the far country, and many of us have started. It is a desert march, but we urge on the camels. What though our feet be blistered with the way? We are hastening to the palace. We take all our loves and hopes and Christian ambitions, as frankincense and myrrh and cassia, to the great King. We must not rest. We must not halt. The night is coming on, and it is not safe out here in the desert. Urge on the camels. I see the domes against the sky, and the houses of Lebanon, and the temples and the gardens. See the fountains dance in the sun, and the gates flash as they open to let in the poor pilgrims.

Send the word up to the palace that we are coming, and that we are weary of the march of the desert. The King will come out and say: "Welcome to the palace; bathe in these waters, recline on these banks. Take this cinnamon and frankincense and myrrh and put it upon a censer and swing it before the altar." And yet, my friends, when heaven bursts upon us it will be a greater surprise than that—Jesus on the throne, and we made like Him! All our Christian friends surrounding us in glory! All our sorrows and tears and sins gone by forever! The thousands of thousands, the one hundred and forty-and-four thousand, the great multitudes that no man can number, will cry, world without end: "The half—the half was not told us!"

VICARIOUS SUFFERING.

" Without shedding of blood is no remission."—HEB. ix: 22.

JOHN G. WHITTIER, the last of the great school of American poets that made the last quarter of a century brilliant, asked me in the White Mountains, one morning after prayers, in which I had given out Cowper's famous hymn about "The Fountain Filled with Blood," "Do you really believe there is a literal application of the blood of Christ to the soul?" My negative reply then is my negative reply now. The Bible statement agrees with all physicians, and all physiologists, and all scientists, in saying that the blood is the life, and in the Christian religion it means simply that Christ's life was given for our life. Hence all this talk of men who say the Bible story of blood is disgusting, and that they don't want what they call a "slaughter-house religion," only shows their incapacity or unwillingness to look through the figure of speech toward the thing signified. The blood that, on the darkest Friday the world ever saw, oozed, or trickled, or poured from the brow, and the side, and the hands, and the feet of the illustrious sufferer, back of Jerusalem, in a few hours coagulated and dried up, and forever disappeared; and if man had depended on the application of the literal blood of Christ, there would not have been a soul saved for the last eighteen centuries.

In order to understand this red word of my text, we only have to exercise as much common sense in religion as we do in everything else. Pang for pang, hunger for hunger, fatigue for fatigue, tear for tear, blood for blood, life for life, we see every day illustrated. The act of substitution is no novelty, although I hear men talk as though the idea of Christ's suffering substituted for our suffering were something abnormal, something distressingly odd, something wildly eccentric, a solitary episode in the world's history; when I could take you out into this city, and before sundown point you to five hundred cases of substitution and voluntary suffering of one in behalf of another.

At two o'clock to-morrow afternoon go among the places of business or toil. It will be no difficult thing for you to find men who, by their looks, show you that they are overworked. They are prematurely old. They are hastening rapidly toward their decease. They have gone through crises in business that shattered their nervous system, and pulled on the brain. They have a shortness of breath, and a pain in the back of the head, and at night an insomnia that alarms them. Why are they drudging at business early and late? For fun? No; it would be difficult to extract any amusement out of that exhaustion. Because they are avaricious? In many cases no. Because their own personal expenses are lavish? No; a few hundred dollars would meet all their wants. The simple fact is, the man is enduring all that fatigue and exasperation, and wear and tear, to keep his home prosperous. There is an invisible line reaching from that store, from that bank, from that shop, from that scaffolding, to a quiet scene a few blocks, a few miles away, and there is the secret of that business endurance. He is simply the champion of a homestead, for which he wins bread, and wardrobe, and education, and prosperity, and in such battle ten thousand men fall. Of ten business men whom I bury, nine die of overwork for others. Some sudden disease finds them with no power of resistance, and they are gone. Life for life. Blood for blood. Substitution!

At one o'clock to-morrow morning, the hour when slumber is most uninterrupted and most profound, walk amid the dwelling-houses of the city. Here and there you will find a dim light, because it is the household custom to keep a subdued light burning: but most of the houses from base to top are as dark as though uninhabited. A merciful God has sent forth the archangel of sleep, and he puts his wings over the city. But yonder is a clear light burning, and outside on the window casement a glass or pitcher containing food for a sick child; the food is set in the fresh air. This is the sixth night that mother has sat up with that sufferer. She has to the last point obeyed the physician's prescription, not giving a drop too much or too little, or a moment too soon or too late. She is very anxious, for she has buried three children with the same disease, and she prays and weeps, each prayer and sob ending with a kiss of the pale cheek. By dint of kindness she gets the little one through the ordeal. After it is all over, the mother is taken down. Brain or nervous fever sets in, and one day she leaves the convalescent child with a mother's blessing, and goes up to join the three in the kingdom of heaven. Life for life. Substitution! The fact is that there are an uncounted number of mothers who, after they have navigated a large family of children through all the diseases of infancy, and got them fairly started up the flowering slope of boyhood and girlhood, have only strength enough left to die. They fade away. Some call it consumption; some call it nervous prostration; some call it intermittent or malarial disposition; but I call it martyrdom of the domestic circle. Life for life. Blood for blood. Substitution!

Or perhaps the mother lingers long enough to see a son get on the wrong road, and his former kindness becomes rough reply when she expresses anxiety about him. But she goes right on, looking carefully after his apparel, remembering his every birthday with some memento, and when he is brought home worn out with dissipation, nurses him till he gets well and starts him again, and hopes, and expects, and prays, and counsels, and suffers, until her strength gives out and she fails. She is going, and attendants, bending over her pillow, ask her if she has any message to leave, and she makes great effort to say something, but out of three or four minutes of indistinct utterance they can catch but three words: " My poor boy!" The simple fact is she died for him. Life for life. Substitution!

About twenty-four years ago there went forth from our homes hundreds of thousands of men to do battle for their country. All the poetry of war soon vanished, and left them nothing but the terrible prose. They waded knee-deep in mud. They slept in snow-banks. They marched till their cut feet tracked the earth. They were swindled out of their honest rations, and lived on meat not fit for a dog. They had jaws all fractured, and eyes extinguished, and limbs shot away. Thousands of them cried for water as they lay dying on the field the night after the battle, and got it not. They were homesick, and received no message from their loved ones. They died in barns, in bushes, in ditches, the buzzards of the summer heat the only attendants on their obsequies. No one but the infinite God who knows everything, knows the ten thousandth part of the length, and breadth, and depth, and height of anguish of the Northern and Southern battle-fields. Why did these fathers leave their children and go to the front, and why did these young men, postponing the marriage-day, start out into the probabilities of never coming back? For the country they died. Life for life. Blood for blood. Substitution!

But we need not go so far. What is that monument in Greenwood? It is to the doctors who fell in the Southern epidemics. Why go? Were there not enough sick to be attended in these Northern latitudes? Oh, yes; but the doctor puts a few medical books in his valise, and some vials of medicine, and leaves his patients here in the hands of other physicians, and takes the rail-train. Before he gets to the infected regions he passes crowded rail-trains, regular and extra, taking the flying and affrighted populations. He arrives in a city over which a great horror is brooding. He goes from couch to couch, feeling of pulse and studying symptoms, and prescribing day after day, night after night, until a fellow-physician says: " Doctor, you had better go home and rest; you look miserable." But he can not rest while so many are suffering. On and on, until some morning finds him in a delirium, in which he talks of home, and then rises and says he must go and look after those patients. He is told to lie down; but he fights his attendants until he falls back, and is weaker and weaker, and dies for people with whom he had no kinship, and far away from his own family, and is hastily put away in a stranger's tomb, and only the fifth part of a newspaper line tells us of his sacrifice—his name just mentioned among five. Yet he has touched the furthest height of sublimity in that three weeks of humanitarian service. He goes straight as an arrow to the bosom of Him who said: " I was sick and ye visited Me." Life for life. Blood for blood. Substitution!

In the legal profession I see the same principle of self-sacrifice. In 1846, William Freeman, a pauperized and idiotic negro, was at Auburn, N. Y., on trial for murder. He had slain the entire Van Nest family. The foaming wrath of the community could be kept off him only by armed constables. Who would volunteer to be his counsel? No attorney wanted to sacrifice his popularity by such an ungrateful task. All were silent save one, a young lawyer with feeble voice, that could hardly be heard outside the bar, pale and thin and awkward. It was William H. Seward, who saw that the prisoner was idiotic and irresponsible, and ought to be put in an asylum rather than put to death, the heroic counsel uttering these beautiful words:

"I speak now in the hearing of a people who have pre-judged prisoner and condemned me for pleading in his behalf. He is a convict, a pauper, a negro, without intellect, sense, or emotion. My child with an affectionate smile disarms my care-worn face of its frown whenever I cross my threshold. The beggar in the street obliges me to give because he says, ' God bless you!' as I pass. My dog caresses me with fondness if I will but smile on him. My horse recognizes me when I fill his manger. What reward, what gratitude, what sympathy and affection can I expect here? There the prisoner sits. Look at him. Look at the assemblage around you. Listen to their ill-suppressed censures and their excited fears, and tell me where among my neighbors or my fellow-men, where, even in his heart, I can expect to find a sentiment, a thought, not to say of reward or of acknowledgment, or even of recognition? Gentlemen, you may think of this evidence what you please, bring in what verdict you can, but I asseverate before Heaven and you, that, to the best of my knowledge and belief, the prisoner at the bar does not at this moment know why it is that my shadow falls on you instead of his own."

The gallows got its victim, but the post-mortem examination of the poor creature showed to all the surgeons and to all the world that the public were wrong, and William H. Seward was right, and that hard, stony step of obloquy in the Auburn court-room was the first step of the stairs of fame up which he went to the top, or to within one step of the top, that last denied him through the treachery of American politics. Nothing sublimer was ever seen in an

American court-room than William H. Seward, without reward, standing between the fury of the populace and the loathsome imbecile.   Substitution!

In the realm of the fine arts there was as remarkable an instance.   A brilliant but hypercriticised painter, Joseph William Turner, was met by a volley of abuse from all the art galleries of Europe.   His paintings, which have since won the applause of all civilized nations, " The Fifth Plague of Egypt," " Fishermen on a Lee Shore in Squally Weather," " Calais Pier," " The Sun Rising Through Mist," and " Dido Building Carthage," were then targets for critics to shoot at.   In defense of this outrageously abused man, a young author of twenty-four years, just one year out of college, came forth with his pen, and wrote the ablest and most famous essays on art that the world ever saw, or ever will see—John Ruskin's " Modern Painters."   For seventeen years this author fought the battles of the mal-treated artist, and after, in poverty and broken-hearted-ness, the painter had died, and the public tried to undo their cruelties toward him by giving him a big funeral and burial at St. Paul's Cathedral, his old-time friend took out of a tin box nineteen thousand pieces of paper containing drawings by the old painter, and through many weary and uncompensated months assorted and arranged them for public observation.   People say John Ruskin in his old days is cross, misanthropic, and morbid.   Whatever he may do that he ought not to do, and whatever he may say that he ought not to say between now and his death, he will leave this world insolvent as far as it has any capacity to pay this author's pen for its chivalric and Christian defense of a poor painter's pencil.   John Ruskin for William Turner.   Blood for blood.   Substitution!

What an exalting principle this which leads one to suffer for another!   Nothing so kindles enthusiasm or awakens eloquence, or chimes poetic canto, or moves nations.   The principle is the dominant one in our religion—Christ the Martyr, Christ the celestial Hero, Christ the Defender, Christ the Substitute.   No new principle, for it was as old as human nature; but now on a grander, wider, higher, deeper, and more world-resounding scale!   The shepherd boy as a champion for Israel with a sling toppled the giant of Philistine braggadocio in the dust; but here is another David who, for all the armies of churches militant and triumphant, hurls the Goliath of perdition into defeat, the crash of his brazen armor like an explosion at Hell Gate.   Abraham had at God's command agreed to sacrifice his son Isaac, and the same God just in time had provided a ram of the thicket as a substitute; but here is another Isaac bound to the altar, and no hand arrests the sharp edges of laceration and death, and the universe shivers and quakes and recoils and groans at the horror.

All good men have for centuries been trying to tell whom this Substitute was like, and every comparison, inspired and uninspired, evangelistic, prophetic, apostolic, and human, falls short, for Christ was the Great Unlike. Adam a type of Christ, because he came directly from God; Noah a type of Christ, because he delivered his own family from deluge; Melchisedec a type of Christ, because he had no predecessor or successor; Joseph a type of Christ, because he was cast out by his brethren; Moses a type of Christ, because he was a deliverer from bondage; Joshua a type of Christ, because he was a conqueror; Samson a type of Christ, because of his strength to slay the lions and carry off the iron gates of impossibility; Solomon a type of Christ, in the affluence of his dominion; Jonah a type of Christ, because of the stormy sea in which he threw himself for the rescue of others; but put together Adam and Noah and Melchisedec and Joseph and Moses and Joshua and Samson and Solomon and Jonah, and they would not make a fragment of a Christ, a quarter of a Christ, the half of a Christ, or the millionth part of a Christ.

He forsook a throne and sat down on His own footstool. He came from the top of glory to the bottom of humiliation, and changed a circumference seraphic for a circumference diabolic. Once waited on by angels, now hissed at by brigands. From afar and high up He came down; past meteors swifter than they; by starry thrones, Himself more lustrous; past larger worlds to smaller worlds; down stairs of firmaments, and from cloud to cloud, and through tree-tops and into the camel's stall, to thrust His shoulder under our burdens and take the lances of pain through His vitals, and wrapped himself in all the agonies which we deserve for our misdoings, and stood on the splitting decks of a foundering vessel, amid the drenching surf of the sea, and passed midnights on the mountains amid wild beasts of prey, and stood at the point where all earthly and infernal hostilities charged on Him at once with their keen sabers—our Substitute!

When did attorney ever endure so much for a pauper

client, or physician for the patient in the lazaretto, or mother for the child in membranous croup, as Christ for us, and Christ for you, and Christ for me? Shall any man or woman or child in this audience who has ever suffered for another find it hard to understand this Christly suffering for us? Shall those whose sympathies have been wrung in behalf of the unfortunate have no appreciation of that one moment which was lifted out of all the ages of eternity as most conspicuous, when Christ gathered up all the sins of those to be redeemed under His one arm, and all their sorrows under His other arm, and said: " I will atone for these under my right arm, and will heal all those under my left arm. Strike me with all thy glittering shafts, O Eternal Justice! Roll over me with all thy surges, ye oceans of sorrow "? And the thunderbolts struck Him from above, and the seas of trouble rolled up from beneath, hurricane after hurricane, and cyclone after cyclone, and then and there in presence of heaven and earth and hell, yea, all worlds witnessing, the price, the bitter price, the transcendent price, the awful price, the glorious price, the infinite price, the eternal price, was paid that sets us free.

That is what Paul means, that is what I mean, that is what all those who have ever had their heart changed mean by " blood." I glory in this religion of blood! I am thrilled as I see the suggestive color in sacramental cup, whether it be of burnished silver set on cloth immaculately white, or rough-hewn from wood set on table in log-hut meeting-house of the wilderness. Now I am thrilled as I see the altars of ancient sacrifice crimson with the blood of the slain lamb, and Leviticus is to me not so much the Old Testament as the New. Now I see why the destroying angel passing over Egypt in the night spared all those houses that had blood sprinkled on their door-posts. Now I know what Isaiah means when he speaks of " one in red apparel coming with dyed garments from Bozrah;" and whom the Apocalypse means when it describes a heavenly chieftain whose " vesture was dipped in blood;" and what Peter, the apostle, means when he speaks of the " precious blood that cleanseth from all sin;" and what the old, worn-out, decrepit missionary Paul means when, in my text, he cries, " Without shedding of blood is no remission." By that blood you and I will be saved—or never saved at all. In all the ages of the world God has not once pardoned a single sin except through the Saviour's expiation, and He never will. Glory be to God that the hill back of Jerusalem was the battle-field on which Christ achieved our liberty!

The most exciting and overpowering day of last summer was the day I spent on the battle-field of Waterloo. Starting out with the morning train from Brussels, Belgium, we arrived in about an hour on that famous spot. A son of one who was in the battle, and who had heard from his father a thousand times the whole scene recited, accompanied us over the field. There stood the old Hougomont Château, the walls dented, and scratched, and broken, and shattered by grape-shot and cannon-ball. There is the well in which three hundred dying and dead were pitched. There is the chapel with the head of the infant Christ shot off. There are the gates at which, for many hours, En-

glish and French armies wrestled. Yonder were the one
hundred and sixty guns of the English, and the two
hundred and fifty guns of the French. Yonder the
Hanoverian Hussars fled for the woods. Yonder was the
ravine of Ohain, where the French cavalry, not knowing
there was a hollow in the ground, rolled over and down,
troop after troop, tumbling into one awful mass of suffering, hoof of kicking horses against brow and breast of captains and colonels and private soldiers, the human and the
beastly groan kept up until, the day after, all was shoveled
under because of the malodor arising in that hot month of
June.

"There," said our guide, " the Highland regiments lay
down on their faces waiting for the moment to spring
upon the foe. In that orchard twenty-five hundred men
were cut to pieces. Here stood Wellington with white
lips, and up that knoll rode Marshal Ney on his sixth
horse, five having been shot under him. Here the ranks
of the French broke, and Marshal Ney, with his boot
slashed of a sword, and his hat off, and his face covered
with powder and blood, tried to rally his troops as he
cried: ' Come and see how a marshal of French dies on
the battle-field.' From yonder direction Grouchy was expected for the French re-enforcement, but he came not.
Around those woods Blucher was looked for to re-enforce
the English, and just in time he came up. Yonder is the
field where Napoleon stood, his arm through the reins of
the horse's bridle, dazed and insane, trying to go back."
Scene of a battle that went on from twenty-five minutes to
twelve o'clock, on the eighteenth of June, until four

o'clock, when the English seemed defeated, and their commander cried out; "Boys, can you think of giving way? Remember old England!" and the tides turned, and at eight o'clock in the evening the man of destiny, who was called by his troops Old Two Hundred Thousand, turned away with broken heart, and the fate of centuries was decided.

No wonder a great mound has been reared there, hundreds of feet high—a mound at the expense of millions of dollars and many years in rising, and on the top is the great Belgian lion of bronze, and a grand old lion it is. But our great Waterloo was in Palestine. There came a day when all hell rode up, led by Apollyon, and the Captain of our salvation confronted them alone. The Rider on the white horse of the Apocalypse going out against the black horse cavalry of death, and the battalions of the demoniac, and the myrmidons of darkness. From twelve o'clock at noon to three o'clock in the afternoon the greatest battle of the universe went on. Eternal destinies were being decided. All the arrows of hell pierced our Chieftain, and the battle-axes struck Him, until brow and cheek and shoulder and hand and foot were incarnadined with oozing life; but He fought on until He gave a final stroke with sword from Jehovah's buckler, and the commander-in-chief of hell and all his forces fell back in everlasting ruin, and the victory is ours. And on the mound that celebrates the triumph we plant this day two figures, not in bronze or iron or sculptured marble, but two figures of living light, the Lion of Judah's tribe and the Lamb that was slain.

POSTHUMOUS OPPORTUNITY.

"If the tree fall toward the south or toward the north, in the place where the tree falleth there it shall be."—ECCLES. xi: 3.

THERE is a hovering hope in the minds of a vast multitude that there will be an opportunity in the next world to correct the mistakes of this; that, if we do make complete shipwreck of our earthly life, it will be on a shore up which we may walk to a palace; that, as a defendant may lose his case in the Circuit Court, and carry it up to the Supreme Court or Court of Chancery and get a reversal of judgment in his behalf, all the costs being thrown over on the other party, so, if we fail in the earthly trial, we may in the higher jurisdiction of eternity have the judgment of the lower court set aside, all the costs remitted, and we may be victorious defendants forever.

My object in this sermon is to show that common sense, as well as my text, declares that such an expectation is chimerical. You say that the impenitent man, having got into the next world and seeing the disaster, will, as a result of that disaster, turn, the pain the cause of his reformation. But you can find ten thousand instances in this world of men who have done wrong and distress overtook them suddenly. Did the distress heal them? No; they went right on.

That man was flung of dissipations. "You must stop

drinking," said the doctor, " and quit the fast life you are leading, or it will destroy you." The patient suffers paroxysm after paroxysm; but, under skillful medical treatment, he begins to sit up, begins to walk about the room, begins to go to business. And, lo! he goes back to the same grog-shops for his morning dram, and his even dram, and the drams between. Flat down again! Same doctor. Same physical anguish. Same medical warning.

Now, the illness is more protracted; the liver is more stubborn, the stomach more irritable, and the digestive organs are more rebellious. But after awhile he is out again, goes back to the same dram-shops, and goes the same round of sacrilege against his physical health.

He sees that his downward course is ruining his household, that his life is a perpetual perjury against his marriage vow, that that broken-hearted woman is so unlike the roseate young wife that he married, that her old school-mates do not recognize her; that his sons are to be taunted for a life-time by the father's drunkenness, that the daughters are to pass into life under the scarification of a disreputable ancestor. He is drinking up their happiness, their prospects for this life, and, perhaps, for the life to come. Sometimes an appreciation of what he is doing comes upon him. His nervous system is all a tangle. From crown of head to sole of foot he is one aching, rasping, crucifying, damning torture. Where is he? In hell on earth. Does it reform him?

After awhile he has delirium tremens, with a whole jungle of hissing reptiles let out on his pillow, and his screams horrify the neighbors as he dashes out of his bed, crying: "Take these things off me!" As he sits, pale and convalescent, the doctor says: "Now I want to have a plain talk with you, my dear fellow. The next attack of this kind you will have you will be beyond all medical skill, and you will die." He gets better and goes forth into the same round again. This time medicine takes no effect. Consultation of physicians agree in saying there is no hope. Death ends the scene.

That process of inebriation, warning, and dissolution is going on within stone's throw of this church, going on in all the neighborhoods of Christendom. Pain does not correct. Suffering does not reform. What is true in one sense is true in all senses, and will forever be so, and yet men are expecting in the next world purgatorial rejuvenation. Take up the printed reports of the prisons of the United States, and you will find that the vast majority of the incarcerated have been there before, some of them four, five, six times. With a million illustrations all working the other way in this world, people are expecting that distress in the next state will be salvatory. You can not imagine any worse torture in any other world than that which some men have suffered here, and without any salutary consequence.

Furthermore, the prospect of a reformation in the next world is more improbable than a reformation here. In this world the life started with innocence of infancy. In the case supposed the other life will open with all the accumulated bad habits of many years upon him. Surely, it is easier to build a strong ship out of new timber than out of an old hulk that has been ground up in the breakers. If with innocence to start with in this life a man does not become godly, what prospect is there that in the next world, starting with sin, there would be a seraph evoluted? Surely the sculptor has more prospect of making a fine statue out of a block of pure white Parian marble than out of an old black rock seamed and cracked with the storms of a half century. Surely upon a clean, white sheet of paper it is easier to write a deed or a will than upon a sheet of paper all scribbled and blotted and torn from top to bottom. Yet men seem to think that, though the life that began here comparatively perfect turned out badly, the next life will succeed, though it starts with a dead failure.

"But," says some one, "I think we ought to have a chance in the next life, because this life is so short it allows only small opportunity. We hardly have time to turn around between cradle and tomb, the wood of the one almost touching the marble of the other." But do you know what made the ancient deluge a necessity? It was the longevity of the antediluvians. They were worse in the second century of their life-time than in the first hundred years, and still worse in the third century, and still worse all the way on to seven, eight, and nine hundred years, and the earth had to be washed, and scrubbed, and soaked, and anchored, clear out of sight for more than a month before it could be made fit for decent people to live in. Longevity never cures impenitency. All the pictures of Time represent him with a scythe to cut, but I never saw any picture of Time with a case of medicines to heal.

Seneca says that Nero for the first five years of his public
life was set up for an example of clemency and kindness,
but his path all the way descended until at sixty-eight he
became a suicide. If eight hundred years did not make
antediluvians any better, but only made them worse, the
ages of eternity could have no effect except prolongation of
depravity.

"But," says some one, "in the future state evil surroundings will be withdrawn and elevated influences substituted, and hence expurgation, and sublimation, and
glorification." But the righteous, all their sins forgiven,
have passed on into a beatific state, and consequently the
unsaved will be left alone. It can not be expected that
Doctor Duff, who exhausted himself in teaching Hindoos
the way to heaven, and Doctor Abeel, who gave his life in
the evangelization of China, and Adoniram Judson, who
toiled for the redemption of Borneo, should be sent down
by some celestial missionary society to educate those who
wasted all their earthly existence. Evangelistic and missionary efforts are ended. The entire kingdom of the
morally bankrupt by themselves, where are the salvatory
influences to come from? Can one speckled and bad apple
in a barrel of diseased apples turn the other apples good?
Can those who are themselves down help others up? Can
those who have themselves failed in the business of the soul
pay the debts of their spiritual insolvents? Can a million
wrongs make one right?

Poneropolis was a city where King Philip of Thracia
put all the bad people of his kingdom. If any man had
opened a primary school at Poneropolis I do not think the

parents from other cities would have sent their children there. Instead of amendment in the other world, all the associations, now that the good are evolved, will be degenerating and down. You would not want to send a man to a cholera or yellow fever hospital for his health; and the great lazaretto of the next world, containing the diseased and plague-struck, will be a poor place for moral recovery. If the surroundings in this world were crowded of temptation, the surroundings of the next world, after the righteous have passed up and on, will be a thousand per cent. more crowded of temptation.

The Count of Chateaubriand made his little son sleep at night at the top of a castle turret, where the winds howled and where specters were said to haunt the place; and while the mother and sisters almost died with fright, the son tells us that the process gave him nerves that could not tremble and a courage that never faltered. But I don't think that towers of darkness and the spectral world swept by Sirocco and Euroclydon will ever fit one for the land of eternal sunshine. I wonder what is the curriculum of that college of Inferno, where, after proper preparation by the sins of this life, the candidate enters, passing on from freshman class of depravity to sophomore of abandonment, and from sophomore to junior, and from junior to senior, and day of graduation comes, and with diploma signed by Satan, the president, and other professorial demoniacs, attesting that the candidate has been long enough under their drill, he passes up to enter heaven! Pandemonium a preparative course for heavenly admission! Ah, my friends, Satan and his cohorts have fitted uncounted multitudes for ruin, but never fitted one soul for happiness.

Furthermore, it would not be safe for this world if men had another chance in the next. If it had been announced that, however wickedly a man might act in this world, he could fix it up all right in the next, society would be terribly demoralized, and the human race demolished in a few years. The fear that, if we are bad and unforgiven here, it will not be well for us in the next existence, is the chief influence that keeps civilization from rushing back to semi-barbarism, and semi-barbarism from rushing into midnight savagery, and midnight savagery from extinction; for it is the astringent impression of all nations, Christian and heathen, that there is no future chance for those who have wasted this.

Multitudes of men who are kept within bounds would say, " Go to, now! Let me get all out of this life there is in it. Come, gluttony, and inebriation, and uncleanness, and revenge, and all sensualities, and wait upon me! My life may be somewhat shortened in this world by dissoluteness, but that will only make heavenly indulgence on a larger scale the sooner possible. I will overtake the saints at last, and will enter the Heavenly Temple only a little later than those who behaved themselves here. I will on my way to heaven take a little wider excursion than those who were on earth pious, and I shall go to heaven *via* Gehenna and *via* Sheol." Another chance in the next world means free license and wild abandonment in this.

Suppose you were a party in an important case at law, and you knew from consultation with judges and attorneys that it would be tried twice, and the first trial would be of little importance, but that the second would decide everything; for which trial would you make the most preparation, for which retain the ablest attorneys, for which be most anxious about the attendance of witnesses? You would put all the stress upon the second trial, all the anxiety, all the expenditure, saying, "The first is nothing, the last is everything." Give the race assurance of a second and more important trial in the subsequent life, and all the preparation for eternity would be *post-mortem*, post-funeral, post-sepulchral, and the world with one jerk be pitched off into impiety and godlessness.

Furthermore, let me ask why a chance should be given in the next world if we have refused innumerable chances in this? Suppose you give a banquet, and you invite a vast number of friends, but one man declines to come, or treats your invitation with indifference. You in the course of twenty years give twenty banquets, and the same man is invited to them all, and treats them all in the same obnoxious way. After awhile you remove to another house, larger and better, and you again invite your friends, but send no invitation to the man who declined or neglected the other invitations. Are you to blame? Has he a right to expect to be invited after all the indignities he has done you? God in this world has invited us all to the banquet of His grace. He invited us by His Providence and His Spirit three hundred and sixty-five days of every year since we knew our right hand from our left. If we declined it every time, or treated the invitation with indifference, and gave twenty or forty or fifty years of indignity on our part toward the Banqueter, and at last He spreads the banquet in a more luxurious and kingly place, amid the heavenly gardens, have we a right to expect Him to invite us again, and have we a right to blame Him if He does not invite us?

If twelve gates of salvation stood open twenty years or fifty years for our admission, and at the end of that time they are closed, can we complain of it and say, "These gates ought to be open again. Give us another chance"? If the steamer is to sail for Hamburg, and we want to get to Germany by that line, and we read in every evening and every morning newspaper that it will sail on a certain day, for two weeks we have that advertisement before our eyes, and then we go down to the docks fifteen minutes after it has shoved off into the stream and say: "Come back. Give me another chance. It is not fair to treat me in this way. Swing up to the dock again, and throw out planks, and let me come on board." Such behavior would invite arrest as a madman.

And if, after the Gospel ship has lain at anchor before our eyes for years and years, and all the benign voices of earth and heaven have urged us to get on board, as she might sail away at any moment, and after awhile she sails without us, is it common sense to expect her to come back? You might as well go out on the Highlands at Neversink and call to the "Aurania" after she has been three days out, and expect her to return, as to call back an opportunity for heaven when it once has sped away. All heaven offered us as a gratuity, and for a life-time we refuse to take it, and then rush on the bosses of Jehovah's buckler demanding another chance. There ought to be, there can be, there will be no such thing as posthumous opportunity. Thus, our common sense agrees with my text—"If the tree fall toward the south, or toward the north, in the place where the tree falleth, there it shall be."

You see that this idea lifts this world up from an unimportant way-station to a platform of stupendous issues, and makes all eternity whirl around this hour. But one trial for which all the preparation must be made in this world, or never made at all. That piles up all the emphases and all the climaxes and all the destinies into life here. No other chance! Oh, how that augments the value and the importance of this chance!

Alexander with his army used to surround a city, and then would lift a great light in token to the people that, if they surrendered before that light went out, all would be well; but if once the light went out, then the battering-rams would swing against the wall, and demolition and disaster would follow. Well, all we need do for our present and everlasting safety is to make surrender to Christ, the King and Conqueror—surrender of our hearts, surrender of our lives, surrender of everything. And He keeps a great light burning, light of Gospel invitation, light kindled with the wood of the cross and flaming up against the dark night of our sin and sorrow. Surrender while that great light continues to burn, for after it goes out there will be no other opportunity of making peace with God through our Lord Jesus Christ. Talk of another chance! Why, this is a supernal chance!

In the time of Edward the Sixth, at the battle of Mus-selburgh, a private soldier, seeing that the Earl of Hunt-ley had lost his helmet, took off his own helmet and put it upon the head of the earl; and the head of the private soldier uncovered, he was soon slain, while his commander rode safely out of the battle. But in our case, instead of a private soldier offering helmet to an earl, it is a King putting His crown upon an unworthy subject, the King dying that we might live. Tell it to all points of the compass. Tell it to night and day. Tell it to all earth and heaven. Tell it to all centuries, all ages, all millen-niums, that we have such a magnificent chance in this world that we need no other chance in the next.

I am in the burnished Judgment Hall of the Last Day. A great white throne is lifted, but the Judge has not yet taken it. While we are waiting for His arrival I hear im-mortal spirits in conversation. " What are you waiting here for?" says a soul that went up from Madagascar to a soul that ascended from America. The latter says: " I came from America, where forty years I heard the Gospel preached, and Bible read, and from the prayer that I learned in infancy at my mother's knee until my last hour I had Gospel advantage, but, for some reason, I did not make the Christian choice, and I am here waiting for the Judge to give me a new trial and another chance." " Strange!" says the other; " I had but one Gospel call in Madagascar, and I accepted it, and I do not need an-other chance."

" Why are you here?" says one who on earth had feeblest intellect to one who had great brain, and silvery tongue, and scepters of influence. The latter responds: "Oh, I knew more than my fellows. I mastered libraries, and had learned titles from colleges, and my name was a synonym for eloquence and power. And yet I neglected my soul, and I am here waiting for a new trial." "Strange," says the one of the feeble earthly capacity; "I knew but little of worldly knowledge, but I knew Christ, and made Him my partner, and I have no need of another chance."

Now the ground trembles with the approaching chariot. The great folding-doors of the Hall swing open. "Stand back!" cry the celestial ushers. "Stand back, and let the Judge of quick and dead pass through!" He takes the throne, and, looking over the throng of nations, He says: "Come to judgment, the last judgment, the only judgment!" By one flash from the throne all the history of each one flames forth to the vision of himself and all others. "Divide!" says the Judge to the assembly. "Divide!" echo the walls. "Divide!" cry the guards angelic.

And now the immortals separate, rushing this way and that, and after awhile there is a great aisle between them, and a great vacuum widening and widening, and the Judge, turning to the throng on one side, says: "He that is righteous, let him be righteous still, and he that is holy, let him be holy still;" and then, turning toward the throng on the opposite side, He says: "He that is unjust, let him be unjust still, and he that is filthy, let him be filthy still;" and then, lifting one hand toward each group, He declares: "If the tree fall toward the south or toward the north, in the place where the tree falleth, there it shall be.'' And then I hear something jar with a great sound. It is the closing of the Book of Judgment. The Judge ascends the stairs behind the throne. The hall of the last assize is cleared and shut. The high court of eternity is adjourned forever.

THE LORD'S RAZOR.

***

"In the same day shall the Lord shave with a razor that is hired, namely, by them beyond the river, by the King of Assyria."— ISAIAH vii: 20.

THE Bible is the boldest book ever written. There are no similitudes in Ossian or the Iliad or the Odyssey so daring. Its imagery sometimes seems on the verge of the reckless, but only seems so. The fact is that God would startle and arouse and propel men and nations. A tame and limping similitude would fail to accomplish the object. While there are times when He employs in the Bible the gentle dew and the morning cloud and the dove and the daybreak in the presentation of truth, we often find the iron chariot, the lightning, the earthquake, the spray, the sword, and, in my text, the razor.

This keen-bladed instrument has advanced in usefulness with the ages. In Bible times and lands the beard remained uncut save in the seasons of mourning and humiliation, but the razor was always a suggestive symbol. David says of Doeg, his antagonist: "Thy tongue is a sharp razor working deceitfully;" that is, it pretends to clear the face, but is really used for deadly incision. In this morning's text the weapon of the toilet appears under the following circumstances: Judea needed to have some of its prosperities cut off, and God sends against it three Assyrian kings—first Sennacherib, then Esrahaddon, and afterward Nebuchadnezzar. These three sharp invasions, that cut down the glory of Judea, are compared to so many sweeps of the razor across the face of the land. And these circumstances were called a hired razor because God took the kings of Assyria, with whom He had no sympathy, to do the work, and paid them in palaces and spoils and annexations. These kings were hired to execute the divine behests. And now the text, which on its first reading may have seemed trivial or inapt, is charged with momentous import: " In the same day shall the Lord shave with a razor that is hired—namely, by them beyond the river, by the King of Assyria. "

Well, if God's judgments are razors, we had better be careful how we use them on other people. In careful sheath these domestic weapons are put away, where no one by accident may touch them, and where the hands of children may not reach them. Such instruments must be carefully handled or not handled at all. But how reck-lessly some people wield the judgments of God! If a man meet with business misfortune, how many there are ready to cry out: " That is a judgment of God upon him be-cause he was unscrupulous, or arrogant, or overreaching, or miserly. I thought he would get cut down! What a clean sweep of everything! His city house and country house gone! His stables emptied of all the fine bays and sorrels and grays that used to prance by his door! All his resources overthrown, and all that he prided himself on tumbled into demolition! Good for him!" Stop, my brother. Don't sling around too freely the judgments of God, for they are razors.

Some of the most wicked business men succeed, and they live and die in prosperity, and some of the most honest and conscientious are driven into bankruptcy. Perhaps his manner was unfortunate, and he was not really as proud as he looked to be. Some of those who carry their head erect and look imperial are humble as a child, while many a man in seedy coat and slouch hat and unblacked shoes is as proud as Lucifer. You can not tell by a man's look. Perhaps he was not unscrupulous in business, for there are two sides to every story, and everybody that accomplishes anything for himself or others gets industriously lied about. Perhaps his business misfortune was not a punishment, but the fatherly discipline to prepare him for heaven, and God may love him far more than He loves you, who can pay dollar for dollar, and are put down in the commercial catalogues as A1. Whom the Lord loveth He gives four hundred thousand dollars and lets die on embroidered pillows? No: whom the Lord loveth He chasteneth. Better keep your hand off the Lord's razors, lest they cut and wound people that do not deserve it. If you want to shave off some of the bristling pride of your own heart do so; but be very careful how you put the sharp edge on others.

How I do dislike the behavior of those persons who, when people are unfortunate, say: " I told you so—getting punished—served him right." If those I-told-you-so's got their desert they would long ago have been pitched over the battlements. The mote in their neighbor's eyes

—so small that it takes a microscope to find it—gives them more trouble than the beam which obscures their own optics. With air sometimes supercilious and sometimes Pharisaical, and always blasphemous, they take the razor of the divine judgment and sharpen it on the hone of their own hard hearts, and then go to work on men sprawled out at full length under disaster, cutting mercilessly. They begin by soft expressions of sympathy and pity and half praise, and, lather the victim all over before they put on the sharp edge.

Let us be careful how we shoot at others lest we take down the wrong one, remembering the servant of King William Rufus who shot at a deer, but the arrow glanced against a tree and killed the king. Instead of going out with shafts to pierce, and razors to cut, we had better imitate the friend of Richard Cœur de Lion, who, in the war of the Crusades, was captured and imprisoned, but none of his friends knew where. So his loyal friend went around the land from stronghold to stronghold, and sung at each window a snatch of song that Richard Cœur de Lion had taught him in other days. And one day, coming before a jail where he suspected his king might be incarcerated, he sung two lines of song, and immediately King Richard responded from his cell with the other two lines, and so his whereabouts were discovered, and immediately a successful movement was made for his liberation. So let us go up and down the world with the music of kind words and sympathetic hearts, serenading the unfortunate, and trying to get out of trouble men who had noble natures, but, by unforeseen circumstances, have been incarcerated, thus liberating kings.   More hymn-book and less razor.

Especially ought we to be apologetic and merciful toward those who, while they have great faults, have also great virtues. Some people are barren of virtues. No weeds verily, but no flowers. I must not be too much enraged at a nettle along the fence if it be in a field containing forty acres of ripe Michigan wheat. At the present time, naturalists tell us, there is on the sun a spot twenty thousand miles long, but from the brightness and warmth I conclude it is a good deal of a sun yet.

Again, when I read in my text that the Lord shaves with the hired razor of Assyria the land of Judea, I bethink myself of the precision of God's providence. A razor swung the tenth part of an inch out of the right line means either failure or laceration, but God's dealings never slip, and they do not miss by the thousandth part of an inch the right direction. People talk as though things in this world were at loose ends. Cholera sweeps across Marseilles and Madrid and Palermo, and we watch anxiously. Will the epidemic sweep Europe and America? People say, " That will entirely depend on whether inoculation is a successful experiment; that will depend entirely on quarantine regulations; that will depend on the early or late appearance of frost; that epidemic is pitched into the world, and it goes blundering across the continents, and it is all guess-work and an appalling perhaps."

My friends, I think, perhaps, that God had something to do with it, and that His mercy may have in some way protected us—that He may have done as much for us as the quarantine and the health officers. It was right and a necessity that all caution should be used, but there has come enough macaroni from Italy, and enough grapes from the south of France, and enough rags from tatter-demalions, and hidden in these articles of transportation enough choleraic germs to have left by this time all Brooklyn mourning at Greenwood, and all Philadelphia at Laurel Hill, and all Boston at Mount Auburn. I thank all the doctors and quarantines; but, more than all, and first of all, and last of all, and all the time, I thank God. In all the six thousand years of the world's existence there has not one thing merely " happened so." God is not an anarchist, but a King, a Father.

When little Tod, the son of President Lincoln, died, all the land sympathized with the sorrow in the White House. He used to rush into the room where the cabinet was in session, and while the most eminent men of the land were discussing the questions of national existence. But the child had no care about those questions. Now God the Father, and God the Son, and God the Holy Ghost are in perpetual session in regard to this world and kindred worlds. Shall you, His child, rush in to criticise or arraign or condemn the divine government? No; the Cabinet of the Eternal Three can govern and will govern in the wisest and best way, and there never will be a mistake, and like razor skillfully swung, shall cut that which ought to be cut, and avoid that which ought to be avoided. Precision to the very hair-breadth. Earthly time-pieces may get out of order and strike wrong, saying that it is one o'clock when it is two, or two when it is three. God's clock is always right, and when it is one it strikes one, and when it is twelve it strikes twelve, and the second hand is as accurate as the minute hand.

Further, my text tells us that God sometimes shaves nations: "In the same day shall the Lord shave with the razor that is hired." With one sharp sweep He went across Judea and down went its pride and its power. In 1861 God shaved our nation. We had allowed to grow Sabbath desecration, and oppression, and blasphemy, and fraud, and impurity, and all sorts of turpitude. The South had its sins, and the North its sins, and the East its sins, and the West its sins. We had been warned again and again, and we did not heed. At length the sword of war cut from the St. Lawrence to the Gulf, and from Atlantic seaboard to Pacific seaboard. The pride of the land, not the cowards, but the heroes, on both sides went down. And that which we took for the sword of war was the Lord's razor.

In 1862, again, it went across the land. In 1863 again. In 1864 again. Then the sharp instrument was incased and put away. Never in the history of the ages was any land more thoroughly shaved than during those four years of civil combat; and, my brethren, if we do not quit some of our individual sins, national sins, the Lord will again take us in hand. He has other razors within reach besides war: epidemics, droughts, deluges, plagues—grasshopper and locust; or our overtowering success may so far excite the jealousy of other lands that, under some pretext, the great nations of Europe and Asia may combine to put us down. This nation, so easily approached on north and south and from both oceans, might have on hand at once more hostilities than were ever arrayed against any power.

We have recently been told by skillful engineers that all our fortresses around New York harbor could not keep the shells from being hurled from the sea into the heart of these great cities. Insulated China, the wealthiest of all nations, as will be realized when her resources are developed, will have adopted all the modes of modern warfare, and at the Golden Gate may be discussing whether Americans must go. If the combined jealousies of Europe and Asia should come upon us, we should have more work on hand than would be pleasant. I hope no such combination against us will ever be formed, but I want to show that, as Assyria was the hired razor against Judea, and Cyrus the hired razor against Babylon, and the Huns the hired razor against the Goths, there are now many razors that the Lord could hire if, because of our national sins, He should undertake to shave us. In 1870, Germany was the razor with which the Lord shaved France. England is the razor with which very shortly the Lord will shave Russia. But nations are to repent in a day. May a speedy and world-wide coming to God hinder, on both sides the sea, all national calamity. But do not let us, as a nation, either by unrighteous law at Washington, or bad lives among ourselves, defy the Almighty.

One would think that our national symbol of the eagle might sometimes suggest another eagle, that which ancient Rome carried. In the talons of that eagle were clutched at one time Britain, France, Spain, Italy, Dalmatia, Rhactia, Noricum, Pannonia, Mœsia, Dacia, Thrace,

Macedonia, Greece, Asia Minor, Syria, Phœnicia, Palestine, Egypt, and all Northern Africa, and all the islands of the Mediterranean, indeed, all the world that was worth having, an hundred and twenty millions of people under the wings of that one eagle. Where is she now? Ask Gibbon, the historian, in his prose poem, the "Decline and Fall of the Roman Empire." Ask her gigantic ruins straggling their sadness through the ages, the screech owl at windows out of which world-wide conquerors looked. Ask the day of judgment when her crowned debauchees, Commodus and Pertinax, and Caligula and Diocletian, shall answer for their infamy? As men and as nations let us repent, and have our trust in a pardoning God, rather than depend on former successes for immunity! Out of thirteen greatest battles of the world, Napoleon had lost but one before Waterloo. Pride and destruction often ride in the same saddle.

But notice once more, and more than all in my text, that God is so kind and loving, that when it is necessary for Him to cut, He has to go to others for the sharp-edged weapon. "In the same day shall the Lord shave with a razor that is hired." God is love. God is pity. God is help. God is shelter. God is rescue. There are no sharp edges about Him, no thrusting points, no instruments of laceration. If you want balm for wounds, He has that. If you want salve for divine eyesight, He has that. But if there is sharp and cutting work to do which requires a razor, that He hires. God has nothing about Him that hurts, save when dire necessity demands, and then He has to go clear off to some one else to get the instrument.

This divine geniality will be no novelty to those who have pondered the Calvarean massacre, where God submerged Himself in human tears, and crimsoned Himself from punctured arteries, and let the terrestrial and infernal worlds maul Him until the chandeliers of the sky had to be turned out, because the universe could not endure the indecency. Illustrious for love He must have been to take all that as our substitute, paying out of His own heart the price of our admission at the gates of heaven.

King Henry II., of England, crowned his son as king, and on the day of coronation put on a servant's garb and waited, he, the king, at the son's table, to the astonishment of all the princes. But we know of a more wondrous scene, the King of heaven and earth offering to put on you, His child, the crown of life, and in the form of a servant waiting on you with blessing. Extol that love, all painting, all sculpture, all music, all architecture, all worship! In Dresdenian gallery let Raphael hold Him up as a child, and in Antwerp Cathedral let Rubens hand Him down from the cross as a martyr, and Handel make all his oratorio vibrate around that one chord—" He was wounded for our transgressions, bruised for our iniquity." But not until all the redeemed get home, and from the countenances of all the piled-up galleries of the ransomed shall be revealed the wonders of redemption, shall either man or seraph or archangel know the height, and depth, and length, and breadth of the love of God.

At our national capital, a monument in honor of him who did more than any one to achieve our American Independence, was for scores of years in building, and most of us were discouraged and said it never would be completed. And how glad we all were when in the presence of the highest officials of the nation, the work was done! But will the monument to Him who died for the eternal liberation of the human race ever be completed? For ages the work has been going up; evangelists and apostles and martyrs have been adding to the heavenly pile, and every one of the millions of the redeemed going up from earth, has made to it contribution of gladness, and weight of glory is swung to the top of other weight of glory, higher and higher as the centuries go by, higher and higher as the whole millenniums roll, sapphire on the top of jasper, sardonyx on the top of chalcedony, and chryso-prasus above topaz, until, far beneath shall be the walls and towers and domes of the great capitol, a monument forever and forever rising, and yet never done. "Unto Him who hath loved us and washed us from our sins in His own blood, and made us kings and priests forever."

Allelujah, amen.

WINDOWS TOWARD JERUSALEM.

"His windows being open and his chamber toward Jerusalem."
DAN. vi: 10.

THE scoundrelly princes of Persia, urged on by political jealousy against Daniel, have succeeded in getting a law passed that whosoever prays to God shall be put under the paws and teeth of the lions, who are lashing themselves in rage and hunger up and down the stone cage, or putting their lower jaws on the ground, bellowing till the earth trembles. But the leonine threat did not hinder the devotion of Daniel, the Cœur-de-Lion of the ages. His enemies might as well have a law that the sun should not draw water or that the south wind should not sweep across a garden of magnolias or that God should be abolished. They could not scare him with the red-hot furnaces, and they can not now scare him with the lions. As soon as Daniel hears of this enactment he leaves his office of Secretary of State, with its upholstery of crimson and gold, and comes down the white marble steps and goes to his own house. He opens his window and puts the shutters back and pulls the curtain aside so that he can look toward the sacred city of Jerusalem, and then prays.

I suppose the people in the street gathered under and before his window, and said: "Just see that man defying the law; he ought to be arrested." And the constabulary of the city rush to the police head-quarters and report that Daniel is on his knees at the wide-open window. "You are my prisoner," says the officer of the law, dropping a heavy hand on the shoulder of the kneeling Daniel. As the constables open the door of the cavern to thrust in their prisoner, they see the glaring eyes of the monsters. But Daniel becomes the first lion-tamer, and they lick his hand and fawn at his feet, and that night he sleeps with the shaggy mane of a wild beast for his pillow, while the king that night, sleepless in the palace, has on him the paw and teeth of a lion he can not tame—the lion of a remorseful conscience.

What a picture it would be for some artist: Darius, in the early dusk of morning, not waiting for footmen or chariot, hastening to the den, all flushed and nervous and in dishabille, and looking through the crevices of the cage to see what had become of his prime-minister! "What, no sound!" he says: "Daniel is surely devoured, and the lions are sleeping after their horrid meal, the bones of the poor man scattered across the floor of the cavern." With trembling voice Darius calls out, "Daniel!" No answer, for the prophet is yet in profound slumber. But a lion, more easily awakened, advances, and, with hot breath blown through the crevice, seems angrily to demand the cause of this interruption, and then another wild beast lifts his mane from under Daniel's head, and the prophet, waking up, comes forth to report himself all unhurt and well.

But our text stands us at Daniel's window, open toward Jerusalem. Why in that direction open? Jerusalem was his native land, and all the pomp of his Babylonish suc-

cesses could not make him forget it.   He came there from
Jerusalem at eighteen years of age, and he never visited it,
though he lived to be eighty-five years.   Yet, when he
wanted to arouse the deepest emotions and grandest aspirations of his heart, he had his window open toward his
native Jerusalem.   There are many of you to-day who
understand that without any exposition.   This is getting
to be a nation of foreigners.   They have come into all occupations and professions.   They sit in all churches.   It
may be twenty years ago since you got your naturalization
papers, and you may be thoroughly Americanized, but you
can't forget the land of your birth, and your warmest sympathies go out toward it.   Your windows are open toward
Jerusalem.   Your father and mother are buried there.   It
may have been a very humble home in which you were
born, but your memory often plays around it, and you
hope some day to go and see it—the hill, the tree, the
brook, the house, the place so sacred, the door from which
you started off with parental blessing to make your own
way in the world; and God only knows how sometimes you
have longed to see the familiar places of your childhood,
and how in awful crises of life you would like to have
caught a glimpse of the old, wrinkled face that bent over
you as you lay on the gentle lap twenty or forty or fifty
years ago.   You may have on this side of the sea risen in
fortune, and, like Daniel, have become great, and may
have come into prosperities which you never could have
reached if you had stayed there, and you may have many
windows to your house—bay-windows, and sky-light-win-
dows, and windows of conservatory, and windows on all

sides—but you have at least one window open toward Jerusalem.

When the foreign steamer comes to the wharf, you see the long line of sailors, with shouldered mail-bags, coming down the planks, carrying as many letters as you might suppose would be enough for a year's correspondence, and this repeated again and again during the week. Multitudes of them are letters from home, and at all the post-offices of the land people will go to the window and anxiously ask for them, hundreds of thousands of persons finding that window of foreign mails the open window toward Jerusalem. Messages that say: " When are you coming home to see us? Brother has gone into the army. Sister is dead. Father and mother are getting very feeble. We are having a great struggle to get on here. Would you advise us to come to you, or will you come to us? All join in love, and hope to meet you, if not in this world, then in a better. Good-bye."

Yes, yes; in all these cities, and amid the flowering western prairies, and on the slopes of the Pacific, and amid the Sierras, and on the banks of the lagoon, and on the ranches of Texas there is an uncounted multitude who, this hour, stand and sit and kneel with their windows open toward Jerusalem. Some of them played on the heather of the Scottish hills. Some of them were driven out by Irish famine. Some of them, in early life, drilled in the German army. Some of them were accustomed at Lyons or Marseilles or Paris to see on the street Victor Hugo and Gambetta. Some chased the chamois among the Alpine precipices. Some plucked the ripe clusters from Italian vineyard. Some lifted their faces under the midnight sun of Norway. It is no dishonor to our land that they remember the place of their nativity. Miscreants would they be if, while they have some of their windows open to take in the free air of America and the sunlight of an atmosphere which no kingly despot has ever breathed, they forgot sometime to open the window toward Jerusalem.

No wonder that the son of the Swiss, when far away from home, hearing the national air of his country sung, the malady of home-sickness comes on him so powerfully as to cause his death. You have the example of the heroic Daniel of my text for keeping early memories fresh. Forget not the old folks at home. Write often; and, if you have surplus of means and they are poor, make practical contribution, and rejoice that America is bound to all the world by ties of sanguinity as is no other nation. Who can doubt but it is appointed for the evangelization of other lands? What a stirring, melting, gospelizing theory that all the doors of other nations are open toward us, while our windows are open toward them!

But Daniel, in the text, kept this port-hole of his domestic fortress unclosed because Jerusalem was the capital of sacred influences. There had smoked the sacrifice. There was the Holy of Holies. There was the Ark of the Covenant. There stood the temple. We are all tempted to keep our windows open on the opposite side, toward the world, that we may see and hear and appropriate its advantages. What does the world say? What does the world think? What does the world do? Worshipers of the world instead of worshipers of God. Windows open toward Babylon. Windows open toward Corinth. Windows open toward Athens. Windows open toward Sodom. Windows open toward the flats, instead of windows open toward the hills. Sad mistake, for this world as a god is like something I saw the other day in the museum of Strasburg, Germany—the figure of a virgin in wood and iron. The victim in olden time was brought there, and this figure would open its arms to receive him, and, once infolded, the figure closed with a hundred knives and lances upon him, and then let him drop one hundred and eighty feet sheer down. So the world first embraces its idolaters, then closes upon them with many tortures, and then lets them drop forever down. The highest honor the world could confer was to make a man Roman emperor; but, out of sixty-three emperors, it allowed only six to die peacefully in their beds.

The dominion of this world over multitudes is illustrated by the names of coins of many countries. They have their pieces of money which they call sovereigns and half sovereigns, crowns and half crowns, Napoleons and half Napoleons, Fredericks and double Fredericks, and ducats, and Isabellinos, all of which names mean not so much usefulness as dominion. The most of our windows open toward the exchange, toward the salon of fashion, toward the god of this world. In olden times the length of the English yard was fixed by the length of the arm of King Henry I., and we are apt to measure things by a variable standard and by the human arm that in the great crises of life can give us no help. We need, like Daniel, to open our windows toward God and religion.

But, mark you, that good lion-tamer is not standing at the window, but kneeling, while he looks out. Most photographs are taken of those in standing or sitting posture. I now remember but one picture of a man kneeling, and that was David Livingstone, who in the cause of God and civilization sacrificed himself; and in the heart of Africa his servant, Majwara, found him in the tent by the light of a candle, stuck on the top of a box, his head in his hands upon the pillow, and dead on his knees. But here is a great lion-tamer, living under the dash of the light, and his hair disheveled of the breeze, praying. The fact is, that a man can see further on his knees than standing on tiptoe. Jerusalem was about five hundred and fifty statute miles from Babylon, and the vast Arabian Desert shifted its sands between them. Yet through that open window Daniel saw Jerusalem, saw all between it, saw beyond, saw time, saw eternity, saw earth, and saw heaven. Would you like to see the way through your sins to pardon, through your troubles to comfort, through temptation to rescue, through dire sickness to immortal health, through night to day, through things terrestrial to things celestial, you will not see them till you take Daniel's posture. No cap of bone to the joints of the fingers, no cap of bone to the joints of the elbow, but cap of bone to the knees, made so because the God of the body was the God of the soul, and especial provision for those who want to pray, and physiological structure joins with spiritual necessity in bidding us pray, and pray, and pray.

In olden time the Earl of Westmoreland said he had no need to pray, because he had enough pious tenants on his estate to pray for him; but all the prayers of the church universal amount to nothing unless, like Daniel, we pray for ourselves. Oh, men and women, bounded on one side by Shadrach's red-hot furnace, and the other side by devouring lions, learn the secret of courage and deliverance by looking at that Babylonish window open toward the south-west! "Oh," you say, "that is the direction of the Arabian Desert!" Yes; but on the other side of the desert is God, is Christ, is Jerusalem, is heaven.

The Brussels lace is superior to all other lace, so beautiful, so multiform, so expensive—four hundred francs a pound. All the world seeks it. Do you know how it is made? The spinning is done in a dark room, the only light admitted through a small aperture, and that light falling directly on the pattern. And the finest specimens of Christian character I have ever seen or ever expect to see are those to be found in lives all of whose windows have been darkened by bereavement and misfortune save one, but under that one window of prayer the interlacing of divine workmanship went on until it was fit to deck a throne, a celestial embroidery which angels admired and God approved.

But it is another Jerusalem toward which we now need to open our windows. The exiled evangelist of Ephesus saw it one day as the surf of the Icarian sea foamed and splashed over the bowlders at his feet, and his vision reminded me of a wedding-day when the bride by sister and maid was having garlands twisted for her hair and jewels strung for her neck just before she puts her betrothed hand into the hand of her affianced: "I, John, saw the Holy

City, New Jerusalem, coming down from God out of heaven prepared as a bride adorned for her husband.'' Toward that bridal Jerusalem are our windows opened?

We would do well to think more of heaven. It is not a mere annex of earth. It is not a desolate outpost. As Jerusalem was the capital of Judae, and Babylon the capital of the Babylonian monarchy, and London is the capital of Great Britain, and Washington is the capital of our own republic, the New Jerusalem is the capital of the universe. The king lives there, and the royal family of the redeemed have their palaces there, and there is a congress of many nations and the parliament of all the worlds. Yea, as Daniel had kindred in Jerusalem of whom he often thought, though he had left home when a very young man, perhaps father and mother and brothers and sisters still living, and was homesick to see them, and they belonged to the high circles of royalty, Daniel himself having royal blood in his veins, so we have in the New Jerusalem a great many kindred, and we are sometimes homesick to see them, and they are all princes and princesses, in them the blood imperial, and we do well to keep our windows open toward their eternal residence.

It is a joy for us to believe that while we are interested in them they are interested in us. Much thought of heaven makes one heavenly. The airs that blow through that open window are charged with life, and sweep up to us aromas from gardens that never wither, under skies that never cloud, in a spring-tide that never terminates. Compared with it all other heavens are dead failures.

Homer's heaven was an elysium which he describes as a

plain at the end of the earth or beneath, with no snow nor rainfall, and the sun never goes down, and Rhadamanthus, the justest of men, rules. Hesiod's heaven is what he calls the islands of the blessed, in the midst of the ocean, three times a year blooming with most exquisite flowers, and the air is tinted with purple, while games and music and horse-races occupy the time. The Scandinavian's heaven was the hall of Walhalla, where the god Odin gave unending wine-suppers to earthly heroes and heroines. The Mohammedan's heaven passes its disciples in over the bridge Al-Sirat, which is finer than a hair and sharper than a sword, and then they are let loose into a riot of everlasting sensuality.

The American aborigines look forward to a heaven of illimitable hunting-ground, partridge and deer and wild duck more than plentiful, and the hounds never off the scent, and the guns never missing fire. But the geographer has followed the earth round, and found no Homer's elysium. Voyagers have traversed the deep in all directions, and found no Hesiod's islands of the blessed. The Mohammedan's celestial debauchery and the Indian's eternal hunting-ground for vast multitudes have no charm. But here rolls in the Bible heaven. No more sea—that is, no wide separation. No more night—that is, no insomnia. No more tears—that is, no heart-break. No more pain— that is, dismissal of lancet and bitter draught and miasma, and banishment of neuralgias and catalepsies and consumptions. All colors in the wall except gloomy black; all the music in the major-key, because celebrative and jubilant. River crystalline, gate crystalline, and skies crystalline, because everything is clear and without doubt. White robes, and that means sinlessness. Vials full of odors, and that means pure regalement of the senses. Rainbow, and that means the storm is over. Marriage supper, and that means gladdest festivity. Twelve manner of fruits, and that means luscious and unending variety. Harp, trumpet, grand march, anthem, amen, and hallelujah in the same orchestra. Choral meeting solo, and overture meeting antiphon, and strophe joining dithyramb, as they roll into the ocean of doxologies. And you and I may have all that, and have it forever through Christ, if we will let Him with the blood of one wounded hand rub out our sin, and with the other wounded hand swing open the shining portals.

Day and night keep your window open toward that Jerusalem. Sing about it. Pray about it. Think about it. Talk about it. Dream about it. Do not be inconsolable about your friends who have gone into it. Do not worry if something in your heart indicates that you are not far off from its ecstasies. Do not think that when a Christian dies he stops, for he goes on.

An ingenious man has taken the heavenly furlongs as mentioned in Revelation, and has calculated that there will be in heaven one hundred rooms sixteen feet square for each ascending soul, though this world should lose a hundred millions yearly. But all the rooms of heaven will be ours, for they are family rooms; and as no room in your house is too good for your children, so all the rooms of all the palaces of the heavenly Jerusalem will be free to God's children and even the throne-room will not be denied, and you may run up the steps of the throne, and put your hand on the side of the throne, and sit down beside the king according to the promise: "To him that overcometh will I grant to sit with me in my throne."

But you can not go in except as conquerors. Many years ago the Turks and Christians were in battle, and the Christians were defeated, and with their commander Stephen fled toward a fortress where the mother of this commander was staying. When she saw her son and his army in disgraceful retreat, she had the gates of the fortress rolled shut, and then from the top of the battlement cried out to her son, "You can not enter here except as conqueror!" Then Stephen rallied his forces and resumed the battle and gained the day, twenty thousand driving back two hundred thousand. For those who are defeated in the battle with sin and death and hell nothing but shame and contempt; but for those who gain the victory through our Lord Jesus Christ the gates of the New Jerusalem will hoist, and there shall be an abundant entrance into the everlasting kingdom of our Lord, toward which you do well to keep your windows open.

STORMED AND TAKEN.

"And Abimelech gat him up to Mount Zalmon, he and all the people that were with him; and Abimelech took an ax in his hand, and cut down a bough from the trees, and took it, and laid it on his shoulder. . . . . And all the people likewise cut down every man his bough, and followed Abimelech, and put them to the hold, and set the hold on fire upon them; so that all the men of the tower of Shechem died also, about a thousand men and women."—JUDGES ix: 48, 49.

ABIMELECH is a name malodorous in Bible history, and yet full of profitable suggestion. Buoys are black and uncomely, but they tell where the rocks are. The snake's rattle is hideous, but it gives timely warning. From the piazza of my summer home, night by night I saw a lighthouse fifteen miles away, not placed there for adornment, but to tell mariners to stand off from that dangerous point. So all the iron-bound coast of moral danger is marked with Saul, and Herod, and Rehoboam, and Jezebel, and Abimelech. These bad people are mentioned in the Bible, not only as warnings, but because there were sometimes flashes of good conduct in their lives worthy of imitation. God sometimes drives a very straight nail with a very poor hammer.

The city of Shechem had to be taken, and Abimelech and his men were to do it. I see the dust rolling up from their excited march. I hear the shouting of the captains and the yell of the besiegers. The swords clack sharply on the parrying shields, and the vociferation of two armies in death-grapple is horrible to hear. The battle goes on all day, and as the sun is setting Abimelech and his army cry " Surrender!" to the beaten foe. And, unable longer to resist, the city of Shechem falls; and there are pools of blood, and dissevered limbs, and glazed eyes looking up beggingly for mercy that war never shows, and dying soldiers with their head on the lap of mother, or wife, or sister, who have come out for the last offices of kindness and affection: and a groan rolls across the city, stopping not, because there is no spot for it to rest, so full is the place of other groans. A city wounded! A city dying! A city dead! Wail for Shechem, all ye who know the horrors of a sacked town!

As I look over the city I can find only one building standing, and that is the temple of the god Berith. Some soldiers outside of the city, in a tower, finding that they can no longer defend Shechem, now begin to look out for their own personal safety, and they fly to this temple of Berith. They get within the door, shut it, and they say, " Now we are safe. Abimelech has taken the whole city, but he can not take this temple of Berith. Here we shall be under the protection of the gods." Oh, Berith, the god! do your best now for these refugees. If you have eyes, pity them. If you have hands, help them. If you have thunderbolts, strike for them.

But how shall Abimelech and his army take this temple of Berith and the men who are there fortified? Will they do it with sword? Nay. Will they do it with spear? Nay. With battering-ram, rolled up by hundred-armed strength, crashing against the walls? Nay. Abimelech marches his men to a wood in Zalmon. With his ax he hews off a limb of a tree, and puts that limb upon his own shoulder, and then he says to his men, "You do the same." They are obedient to their commander.

Oh, what a strange army, with what strange equipment! They come to the foot of the temple of Berith, and Abimelech takes his limb of a tree and throws it down; and the first platoon of soldiers come up and they throw down their branches; and the second platoon, and the third, until all around about the temple of Berith there is a pile of tree-branches. The Shechemites look out from the windows of the temple upon what seems to them childish play on the part of their enemies. But soon the flints are struck, and the spark begins to kindle the brush, and the flame comes up all through the pile, and the red elements leap to the casement, and the woodwork begins to blaze, and one arm of flame is thrown up on the right side of the temple, and another arm of flame is thrown up on the left side of the temple, until they clasp their lurid palms under the wild night sky, and the cry of "Fire!" within, and "Fire!" without announces the terror, and the strangulation, and the doom of the Shechemites, and the complete overthrow of the temple of the god Berith. Then there went up a shout, long and loud, from the stout lungs and swarthy chests of Abimelech and his men, as they stood amid the ashes and the dust, crying: "Victory! Victory!"

Now, I learn first from this subject the folly of depend-

4

ing upon any one form of tactics in anything we have to do for this world or for God. Look over the weaponry of olden times—javelins, battle-axes, habergeons—and show me a single weapon with which Abimelech and his men could have gained such complete victory. It is no easy thing to take a temple thus armed. I saw a house where, during revolutionary times, a man and his wife kept back a whole regiment hour after hour, because they were inside the house, and the assaulting soldiers were outside the house. Yet here Abimelech and his army come up, they surround this temple, and they capture it without the loss of a single man on the part of Abimelech, although I suppose some of the old Israelitish heroes told Abimelech: "You are only going up there to be cut to pieces." Yet you are willing to testify to-day that by no other mode—certainly not by ordinary modes—could that temple so easily, so thoroughly have been taken. Fathers and mothers, brethren and sisters in Jesus Christ, what the Church most wants to learn this day is that any plan is right, is lawful, is best, which helps to overthrow the temple of sin, and capture this world for God. We are very apt to stick to the old modes of attack.

We put on the old-style coat of mail. We come up with the sharp, keen, glittering steel spear of argument, expecting in that way to take the castle, but they have a thousand spears where we have ten. And so the castle of sin stands. Oh, my friends, we will never capture this world for God by any keen saber of sarcasm, by any glittering lances of rhetoric, by any sapping and mining of profound disquisition, by any gunpowdery explosions of indignation, by sharp shootings of wit, by howitzers of mental strength made to swing shell five miles, by cavalry horses gorgeously caparisoned pawing the air. In vain all the attempts on the part of these ecclesiastical foot soldiers, light horsemen, and grenadiers.

My friends, I propose this morning a different style of tactics. Let each one go to the forest of God's promise and invitation, and hew down a branch and put it on his shoulder, and let us all come around these obstinate iniquities, and then, with this pile, kindled by the fires of a holy zeal and the flames of a consecrated life, we will burn them out. What steel can not do, fire may. And I, this morning, announce myself in favor of any plan of religious attack that succeeds—any plan of religious attack, however radical, however odd, however unpopular, however hostile to all the conventionalities of Church and State. We want more heart in our song, more heart in our alms-giving, more heart in our prayers, more heart in our preaching. Oh, for less of Abimelech's sword, and more of Abimelech's conflagration! I have often heard

"There is a fountain filled with blood"

sung artistically by four birds perched on their Sunday roost in the gallery, until I thought of Jenny Lind, and Nilsson, and Sontag, and all the other warblers; but there came not one tear to my eye, nor one master emotion to my heart. But one night I went down to the African Methodist meeting-house in Philadelphia, and at the close of the service a black woman, in the midst of the audience, began to sing that hymn, and all the audience joined in, and we were floated some three or four miles nearer heaven

than I have ever been since. I saw with my own eyes that
" fountain filled with blood "—red, agonizing, sacrificial,
redemptive—and I heard the crimson plash of the wave as
we all went down under it:

> "For sinners plunged beneath that flood
> Lose all their guilty stains."

Oh, my friends, the Gospel is not a syllogism; it is not
casuistry, it is not polemics, or the science of squabble.
It is blood-red fact; it is warm-hearted invitation; it is
leaping, bounding, flying good news; it is efflorescent with
all light; it is rubescent with all glow; it is arborescent
with all sweet shade. I have seen the sun rise on Mount
Washington, and from the Tip-top House; but there was
no beauty in that compared with the day-spring from on
high when Christ gives light to a soul. I have heard
Parepa sing; but there was no music in that compared
with the voice of Christ when He said: " Thy sins are forgiven thee; go in peace." Good news! Let every one cut
down a branch of this tree of life and wave it. Let him
throw it down and kindle it. Let all the way from Mount
Zalmon to Shechem be filled with the tossing joy. Good
news! This bonfire of the Gospel shall consume the last
temple of sin, and will illumine the sky with apocalyptic
joy that Jesus Christ came into the world to save sinners.
Any new plan that makes a man quit his sin, and that
prostrates a wrong, I am as much in favor of as though all
the doctors, and the bishops, and the archbishops, and the
synods, and the academical gownsmen of Christianity sanc-
tioned it. The temple of Berith must come down, and I
do not care how it comes.

Still further, I learn from this subject the power of example. If Abimelech had sat down on the grass and told his men to go and get the boughs, and go out to the battle, they would never have gone at all, or, if they had, it would have been without any spirit or effective result; but when Abimelech goes with his own ax and hews down a branch, and with Abimelech's arm puts it on Abimelech's shoulder, and marches on—then, my text says, all the people did the same. How natural that was! What made Garibaldi and Stonewall Jackson the most magnetic commanders of this century? They always rode ahead. Oh, the overcoming power of example! Here is a father on the wrong road; all his boys go on the wrong road. Here is a father who enlists for Christ; his children enlist.

I saw, in some of the picture-galleries of Europe, that before many of the great works of the masters—the old masters—there would be sometimes four or five artists taking copies of the pictures. These copies they were going to carry with them, perhaps to distant lands; and I have thought that your life and character are a masterpiece, and it is being copied, and long after you are gone it will bloom or blast in the homes of those who knew you, and be a Gorgon or a Madonna. Look out what you say. Look out what you do. Eternity will hear the echo. The best sermon ever preached is a holy life. The best music ever chanted is a consistent walk.

I saw, near the beach, a wrecker's machine. It was a cylinder with some holes at the side, made for the thrusting in of some long poles with strong leverage; and when there is a vessel in trouble or going to pieces out in the offing, the wreckers shoot a rope out to the suffering men. They grasp it, and the wreckers turn the cylinder, and the rope winds around the cylinder, and those who are shipwrecked are saved. So at your feet to-day there is an influence with a tremendous leverage. The rope attached to it swings far out into the billowy future. Your children, your children's children, and all the generations that are to follow, will grip that influence and feel the long-reaching pull long after the figures on your tombstone are so near worn out that the visitor can not tell whether it was in 1885, or 1775, or 1675 that you died.

Still further, I learn from this subject the advantages of concerted action. If Abimelech had merely gone out with a tree-branch the work would not have been accomplished, or if ten, twenty, or thirty men had gone; but when all the axes are lifted, and all the sharp edges fall, and all these men carry each his tree-branch down and throw it about the temple, the victory is gained—the temple falls. My friends, where there is one man in the Church of God at this day shouldering his whole duty there are a great many who never lift an ax or swing a blow.

Oh, we all want our boat to get over to the golden sands, but the most of us are seated either in the prow or in the stern, wrapped in our striped shawl, holding a big-handled sunshade, while others are blistered in the heat, and pull until the oar-locks groan, and the blades bend till they snap. Oh, religious sleepy-heads, wake up! While we have in our church a great many who are toiling for God, there are some too lazy to brush the flies off their heavy eyelids.

Suppose, in military circles, on the morning of battle the roll is called, and out of a thousand men only a hundred men in the regiment answered. What excitement there would be in the camp! What would the colonel say? What high talking there would be among the captains, and majors, and the adjutants! Suppose word came to head-quarters that these delinquents excused themselves on the ground that they had overslept themselves, or that the morning was damp and they were afraid of getting their feet wet, or that they were busy cooking rations. My friends, this is the morning of the day of God Almighty's battle! Do you not see the troops? Hear you not all the trumpets of heaven and all the drums of hell? Which side are you on? If you are on the right side, to what cavalry troop, to what artillery service, to what garrison duty do you belong? In other words, in what Sabbath-school do you teach? in what prayer-meeting do you exhort? to what penitentiary do you declare eternal liberty? to what alms-house do you announce the riches of heaven? What broken bone of sorrow have you ever set? Are you doing nothing? Is it possible that a man or woman sworn to be a follower of the Lord Jesus Christ is doing nothing? Then hide the horrible secret from the angels. Keep it away from the book of judgment. If you are doing nothing do not let the world find it out, lest they charge your religion with being a false-face. Do not let your cowardice and treason be heard among the martyrs about the throne, lest they forget the sanctity of the place and curse your betrayal of that cause for which they agonized and died.

May the eternal God rouse us all to action! As for my-

self, I feel I would be ashamed to die now and enter
heaven until I have accomplished something more decisive
for the Lord that bought me. I would like to join with
you in an oath, with hand high uplifted to heaven, swearing new allegiance to Jesus Christ, and to work more for
His kingdom. Are you ready to join with me in some
new work for Christ? I feel that there is such a thing as
claustral piety, that there is such a thing as insular work,
but it seems to me that what we want now is concerted
action. The temple of Berith is very broad, and it is very
high. It has been going up by the hands of men and
devils, and no human enginery can demolish it; but if the
fifty thousand ministers of Christ in this country should
each take a branch of the tree of life, and all their congregations should do the same, and we should march on and
throw these branches around the great temples of sin, and
worldliness and folly, it would need no match, or coal, or
torch of ours to touch off the pile; for, as in the days of
Elijah, fire would fall from heaven and kindle the bonfire
of Christian victory over demolished sin. It is kindling
now! Huzzah! The day is ours!

Still further, I learn from this subject the danger of
false refuges. As soon as these Shechemites got into the
temple they thought they were safe. They said: "Berith
will take care of us. Abimelech may batter down everything else; he can not batter down this temple where we
are now hid." But very soon they heard the timbers
crackling, and they were smothered with smoke, and they
miserably died. And you and I are just as much tempted
to false refuges. The mirror this morning may have per-

suaded you that you have a comely cheek; your best friends may have persuaded you that you have elegant manners. Satan may have told you that you are all right; but bear with me if I tell you that, if unpardoned, you are all wrong. I have no clinometer by which to measure how steep is the inclined plane you are descending, but I know it is very steep. "Well," you say, "if the Bible is true I am a sinner. Show me some refuge; I will step right into it."

I suppose every person in this audience this moment is stepping into some kind of refuge. Here you step in the tower of good works. You say: "I shall be safe here in this refuge." The battlements are adorned; the steps are varnished; on the wall are pictures of all the suffering you have alleviated, and all the schools you have established, and all the fine things you have ever done. Up in that tower you feel you are safe. But hear you not the tramp of your unpardoned sins all around the tower? They each have a match. They are kindling the combustible material. You feel the heat and the suffocation. Oh, may you leap in time, the Gospel declaring: "By the deeds of the law shall no flesh living be justified."

"Well," you say, "I have been driven out of that tower; where shall I go?" Step into this tower of indifference. You say: "If this tower is attacked, it will be a great while before it is taken." You feel at ease. But there is an Abimelech, with ruthless assaults, coming on. Death and his forces are gathering around, and they demand that you surrender everything, and they clamor for your immortal overthrow, and they throw their skeleton arms in the windows, and with their iron fists they beat against the door; and while you are trying to keep them out you see the torches of judgment kindling, and every forest is a torch, and every mountain a torch, and every sea a torch; and while the Alps, the Pyrenees, and Himalayas turn into a live coal, blown redder and redder by the whirlwind breath of a God omnipotent, what will become of your refuge of lies?

"But," says some one, "you are engaged in a very mean business, driving us from tower to tower." Oh, no. I want to tell you of a Gibraltar that never has been and never will be taken; of a wall that no satanic assault can scale; of a bulwark that the judgment earthquakes can not budge. The Bible refers to it when it says: "In God is thy refuge, and underneath thee are the everlasting arms." Oh, fling yourself into it! Tread down unceremoniously everything that intercepts you. Wedge your way there. There are enough hounds of death and peril after you to make you hurry. Many a man has perished just outside the tower, with his foot on the step, with his hand on the latch. Oh, get inside! Not one surplus second have you to spare. Quick, quick, quick!

Great God, is life such an uncertain thing? If I bear a little too hard with my right foot on the earth, does it break through into the grave? Is this world, which swings at the speed of thousands of miles an hour around the sun, going with tenfold more speed toward the judgment-day? Oh, I am overborne with the thought; and in the conclusion I cry to one and I cry to the other: "Oh, time! Oh, eternity! Oh, the dead! Oh, the judgment-day! Oh,

Jesus! Oh, God!" But, catching at the last apostrophe, I feel that I have something to hold on to: for " in God is thy refuge, and underneath thee are the everlasting arms." And, exhausted with my failure to save myself, I throw my whole weight of body, mind, and soul on this divine promise, as a weary child throws itself into the arms of its mother; as a wounded soldier throws himself on the hospital pillow; as a pursued man throws himself into the refuge; for " in God is thy refuge, and underneath thee are the everlasting arms." Oh, for a flood of tears with which to express the joy of this eternal rescue!

ALL THE WORLD AKIN.

"And hath made of one blood all nations of men."--ACTS xvii: 26.

SOME have supposed that God originally made an Asiatic Adam and a European Adam and an African Adam and an American Adam, but that theory is entirely overthrown by my text, which says that all nations are blood relatives, having sprung from one and the same stock. A difference in climate makes much of the difference in national temper.

An American goes to Europe and stays there a long while, and finds his pulse moderating and his temper becoming more calm. The air on this side the ocean is more tonic than on the other side. An American breathes more oxygen than a European. A European coming to America finds a great change taking place in himself. He walks with more rapid strides, and finds his voice becoming keener and shriller. The Englishman who walks in London Strand at the rate of three miles the hour, coming to America and residing for a long while here, walks Broadway at the rate of four miles the hour. Much of the difference between an American and a European, between an Asiatic and an African, is atmospheric. The lack of the warm sunlight pales the Greenlander. The full dash of the sunlight darkens the African.

Then, ignorance or intelligence makes its impression on the physical organism—in the one case ignorance flattening the skull, as with the Egyptian; in the other case intelligence building up the great dome of the forehead, as with the German. Then the style of god that the nation worships decides how much it shall be elevated or debased, so that those nations that worship reptiles are themselves only a superior form of reptile, while those nations that worship the natural sun in the heavens are the noblest style of barbaric people. But whatever be the difference of physiognomy, and whatever the difference of temperament, the physiologist tells us that after careful analysis he finds out that the plasma and the disk in the human blood have the same characteristics: so that if you should put twenty men from twenty nationalities abreast in line of battle, and a bullet should fly through the hearts of the twenty men, the blood flowing forth would, through analysis, prove itself to be the same blood in every instance. In other words, the science of the day confirming the truth of my text that " God hath made of one blood all nations of men."

I have thought, my friends, it might be profitable this morning if I gave you some of the moral and religious impressions which I received when, through your indulgence, I had transatlantic absence. First, I observe that the majority of people in all lands are in a mighty struggle for bread. While in nearly all lands there are only a few cases of actual starvation reported, there is a vast population in every country I visited who have a limited supply of food, or such food as is incompetent to sustain physical vigor. This struggle in some lands is becoming more agonizing, while here and there it is lightened. I have joy in reporting that Ireland, about the sufferings of which we have heard so much, has far better prospects than I have seen there in previous visits. In 1879, coming home from that land, I prophesied the famine that must come upon, and did come upon, the deluged fields of that country. This year the crops are large, and both parties—those who like the English Government and those who don't like it— are expecting relief. I said to one of the intelligent men of Ireland: "Tell me in a few words what are the sufferings of Ireland, and what is the Land Relief enactment?" He replied: "I will tell you. Suppose I am a landlord and you a tenant. You rent from me a place for ten pounds a year. You improve it. You turn it from a bog into a garden. You put a house upon it. After awhile I, the landlord, come around, and I say to my agent: 'How much rent is this man paying;' He answers, 'Ten pounds.' 'Is that all? Put his rent up to twenty pounds.' The tenant goes on improving his property, and after awhile I come around and I say to my agent, 'How much rent is this man paying?' He says, 'Twenty pounds.' 'Put his rent up to twenty-five pounds.' The tenant protests and says, 'I can't pay it.' Then I, the landlord, say, 'Pay it or get out;' and the tenant is helpless, and, leaving the place, the property in its improved condition turns over to the landlord. Now, to stop that outrage the Relief Enactment comes in and appoints commissioners who shall see that if the tenant is turned out he shall receive the difference of value between the farm as he got it and the farm as he surrenders it. Moreover, the government loans money to the tenant, so that he may buy the property out and out if the landlord will sell.'' Mighty advancement toward the righting of a great wrong! But there and in all lands, not excepting our own, there is a far-reaching distress. And let those who broke their fast this morning, and those who shall dine to-day, remember those who are in want, and by prayer and practical beneficence do all they can to alleviate the hunger swoon of nations.

Another impression was—indeed the impression carried with me all the summer—the thought already suggested, the brotherhood of man. The fact is that the differences are so small between nations that they may be said to be all alike. Though I spent the most of the summer in silence, I spoke a few times and to people of different nations, and how soon I noticed that they were very much alike! If a man knows how to play the piano, it does not make any difference whether he finds it in New Orleans or San Francisco or Boston or St. Petersburg or Moscow or Madras; it has so many keys, and he puts his fingers right on them. And the human heart is a divine instrument, with just so many keys in all cases, and you strike some of them and there is joy, and you strike some of them and there is sorrow. Plied by the same motives, lifted up by the same success, depressed by the same griefs. The cabmen of London have the same characteristics as the cabmen of New York, and are just as modest and retiring. The gold and silver drive Piccadilly and the Boulevards just as they drive Wall Street. If there be a great political excitement in Europe, the Bourse in Paris howls just as loudly as ever did the American gold-room.

The same grief that we saw in our country in 1864 you may find now in the military hospitals of England containing the wounded and sick from the Egyptian wars. The same widowhood and orphanage that sat down in despair after the battles of Shiloh and South Mountain poured their grief in the Shannon and the Clyde and the Dee and the Thames. Oh, ye men and women who know how to pray, never get up from your knees until you have implored God in behalf of the fourteen hundred millions of the race just like yourselves, finding life a tremendous struggle! For who knows but that as the sun to-day draws up drops of water from the Caspian and the Black seas and from the Amazon and the Mississippi, after a while to distill the rain, these very drops on the fields— who knows but that the sun of righteousness may draw up the tears of your sympathy, and then rain them down in distillation of comfort o'er all the world?

Who is that poor man, carried on a stretcher to the Afghan ambulance? He is your brother. If in the Pantheon at Paris you smite your hand against the wall among the tombs of the dead, you will hear a very strange echo coming from all parts of the Pantheon just as soon as you smite the wall. And I suppose it is so arranged that every stroke of sorrow among the tombs of bereavement ought to have loud, long, and oft-repeated echoes of sympathy all around the world. Oh, what a beautiful theory it is—and it is a Christian theory—that Englishman, Scotchman, Irishman, Norwegian, Frenchman, Italian, Russian, are all akin. Of one blood all nations. That is a very beautiful inscription that I saw a few days ago over the door in Edinburgh, the door of the house where John Knox used to live. It is getting somewhat dim now, but there is the inscription, fit for the door of any household—" Love God above all, and your neighbor as yourself."

I was also impressed in journeying on the other side the sea with the difference the Bible makes in countries. The two nations of Europe that are the most moral to-day and that have the least crime are Scotland and Wales. They have by statistics, as you might find, fewer thefts, fewer arsons, fewer murders. What is the reason? A bad book can hardly live in Wales. The Bible crowds it out. I was told by one of the first literary men in Wales: " There is not a bad book in the Welsh language." He said: " Bad books come down from London, but they can not live here." It is the Bible that is dominant in Wales. And then in Scotland just open your Bible to give out your text, and there is a rustling all over the house almost startling to an American. What is it? The people opening their Bibles to find the text, looking at the context, picking out the referenced passages, seeing whether you make right quotation. Scotland and Wales Bible-reading people. That accounts for it. A man, a city, a nation that reads God's Word must be virtuous. That Book is the foe of all wrong-doing. What makes Edinburgh better than Constantinople? The Bible.

Oh, I am afraid in America we are allowing the good book to be covered up with other good books! We have our ever-welcome morning and evening newspapers, and

we have our good books on all subjects—geological subjects, botanical subjects, physiological subjects, theological
subjects—good books, beautiful books, and so many good
books that we have not time to read the Bible. Oh, my
friends, it is not a matter of very great importance that
you have a family Bible on the center-table in your parlor!
Better have one pocket New Testament, the passages
marked, the leaves turned down, the binding worn smooth
with much usage, than fifty pictorial family Bibles too
handsome to read! Oh, let us take a whisk-broom and
brush the dust off our Bibles! Do you want poetry? Go
and hear Job describe the war-horse, or David tell how the
mountains skipped like lambs. Do you want logic? Go
and hear Paul reason until your brain aches under the
spell of his mighty intellect. Do you want history? Go
and see Moses put into a few pages stupendous information which Herodotus, Thucydides, and Prescott never
preached after. And, above all, if you want to find how
a nation struck down by sin can rise to happiness and to
heaven, read of that blood which can wash away the pollution of a world. There is one passage in the Bible of vast
tonnage: "God so loved the world that He gave His only
begotten Son, that whosoever believeth in Him should not
perish, but have everlasting life." Oh, may God fill this
country with Bibles and help the people to read them!

I was also impressed in my transatlantic journeys with
the wonderful power that Christ holds among the nations.
The great name in Europe to-day is not Victoria, not
Marquis of Salisbury, not William the Emperor, not Bis-
marck; the great name in Europe to-day is Christ. You

find the crucifix on the gate-post, you find it in the hay-field, you find it at the entrance of the manor, you find it by the side of the road.

The greatest pictures in all the galleries of Italy, Germany, France, England, and Scotland are Bible pictures. What were the subjects of Raphael's great paintings? "The Transfiguration," "The Miraculous Draught of Fishes," "The Charge to Peter," "The Holy Family," "The Massacre of the Innocents," "Moses at the Burning Bush," "The Nativity," "Michael the Archangel," and the four or five exquisite "Madonnas." What are Tintoretto's great pictures? "Fall of Adam," "Cain and Abel," "The Plague of the Fiery Serpent," "Paradise," "Agony in the Garden," "The Temptation," "The Adoration of the Magi," "The Communication," "Baptism," "Massacre of the Innocents," "The Flight into Egypt," "The Crucifixion," "The Madonna." What are Titian's great pictures? "The Flagellation of Christ," "The Supper at Emmaus," "The Death of Abel," "The Assumption," "The Entombment," "Faith," "The Madonna." What are Michael Angelo's great pictures? "The Annunciation," "The Spirits in Prison," "At the feet of Christ," "The Infant Christ," "The Crucifixion," "The Last Judgment." What are Paul Veronese's great pictures? "Queen of Sheba," "The Marriage in Cana," "Magdalen Washing the Feet of Christ," "The Holy Family." Who has not heard of Da Vinci's "Last Supper"? Who has not heard of Turner's "Pools of Solomon"? Who has not heard of Claude's "Marriage of Isaac and Rebecca"? Who has not heard of Dürer's "Dragon of the Apocalypse"? The mightiest picture on this planet is Rubens' "Scourging of Christ." Painter's pencil loves to sketch the face of Christ. Sculptor's chisel loves to present the form of Christ. Organs love to roll forth the sorrows of Christ.

The first time you go to London go into the Doré picture gallery. As I went and sat down before "Christ Descending the Steps of the Prætorium," at the first I was disappointed. I said: "There isn't enough majesty in that countenance, not enough tenderness in that eye;" but as I sat and looked at the picture it grew upon me until I was overwhelmed with its power, and I staggered with emotion as I went out into the fresh air, and said; "Oh, for that Christ I must live, and for that Christ I must be willing to die!" Make that Christ your personal friend, my sister, my brother. You may never go to Milan to see Da Vinci's "Last Supper;" but, better than that, you can have Christ come and sup with you. You may never get to Antwerp to see Rubens' "Descent of Christ from the Cross," but you can have Christ come down from the mountain of His suffering into your heart and abide there forever. Oh, you must have Him! We are all so diseased with sin that we want that which hurts us, and we won't have that which cures us. The best thing for you and for me to do to-day is to get down on our bended knees before God and say: "Oh, Almighty Son of God, I am blind! I want to see. My arms are palsied. I want to take hold of thy cross. Have mercy on me, O Lord Jesus!" Why will you live on husks when you may sit down to this white bread of heaven? Oh, with such a God, and with such a Christ, and with such a Holy Spirit, and with such an immortal nature, wake up!

Once more, I was impressed greatly on the other side the sea with the wonderful triumphs of the Christian religion. The tide is rising, the tide of moral and spiritual prosperity in the world. I think that any man who keeps his eyes open, traveling in foreign lands, will come to that conclusion. More Bibles than ever before, more churches, more consecrated men and women, more people ready to be martyrs now than ever before, if need be; so that instead of there being, as people sometimes say, less spirit of martyrdom now than ever before, I believe where there was once one martyr there would be a thousand martyrs if the fires were kindled—men ready to go through flood and fire for Christ's sake. Oh, the signs are promising! The world is on the way to millennial brightness. All art, all invention, all literature, all commerce will be the Lord's.

These ships that you see going up and down New York harbor are to be brought into the service of God. All those ships I saw at Liverpool, at Southampton, at Glasgow, are to be brought into the service of Christ. What is that passage, " Ships of Tarshish shall bring presents "? That is what it means. Oh, what a goodly fleet when the vessels of the sea come into the service of God! No guns frowning through the port-holes, no pikes hung in the gangway, nothing from cut-water to taffrail to suggest atrocity. Those ships will come from all parts of the seas. Great flocks of ships that never met on the high sea but in wrath, will cry, " Ship ahoy!" and drop down beside each other in calmness, the flags of Emmanuel streaming from the top-gallants. The old slaver, with decks scrubbed and washed and glistened and burnished—the old slaver will wheel into line; and the Chinese junk and the Venetian gondola, and the miners' and the pirates' corvette, will fall into line, equipped, readorned, beautified, only the small craft of this grand flotilla which shall float out for the truth—a flotilla mightier than the armada of Xerxes moving in the pomp and pride of Persian insolence; mightier than the Carthaginian navy rushing with forty thousand oarsmen upon the Roman galleys, the life of nations dashed out against the gunwales.

Rise, O sea! and shine, O heavens! to greet this squadron of light and victory! On the glistening decks are the feet of them that bring good tidings, and songs of heaven float among the rigging. Crowd on all the canvas. Line-of-battle ship and merchantmen wheel into the way. It is noon. Strike eight bells. From all the squadron the sailors' songs arise. "Surely the isles shall wait for thee, and the ships of Tarshish to bring thy sons from afar, their silver and their gold with them, to the name of the Lord thy God, and the Holy One of Israel."

A MOMENTOUS QUEST.

'Seek ye the Lord while he may be found."—ISA. lv: 6.

ISAIAH stands head and shoulders above the other Old Testament authors in vivid descriptiveness of Christ. Other prophets give an outline of our Saviour's features. Some of them present, as it were, the side face of Christ; others a bust of Christ; but Isaiah gives us the full-length portrait of Christ. Other Scripture writers excel in some things. Ezekiel more weird, David more pathetic, Solomon more epigrammatic, Habakkuk more sublime; but when you want to see Christ coming out from the gates of prophecy in all His grandeur and glory, you involuntarily turn to Isaiah. So that if the prophecies in regard to Christ might be called the "Oratorio of the Messiah," the writing of Isaiah is the "Hallelujah Chorus," where all the batons wave and all the trumpets come in. Isaiah was not a man picked up out of insignificance by inspiration. He was known and honored. Josephus, and Philo, and Sirach extolled him in their writings. What Paul was among the apostles, Isaiah was among the prophets.

My text finds him standing on a mountain of inspiration, looking out into the future, beholding Christ advancing and anxious that all men might know Him; his voice rings down the ages: "Seek ye the Lord while He may

be found." "Oh," says some one: "that was for olden
times." No, my hearer. If you have traveled in other
lands you have taken a circular letter of credit from some
banking-house in New York, and in St. Petersburg, or
Venice, or Rome, or Antwerp, or Brussels, or Paris; you
presented that letter and got financial help immediately.
And I want you to understand that the text, instead of being appropriate for one age, or for one land, is a circular
letter for all ages and for all lands, and wherever it is presented for help, the help comes: "Seek ye the Lord while
He may be found."

I come, to-day, with no hair-spun theories of religion,
with no nice distinctions, with no elaborate disquisition;
but with a plain talk on the matters of personal religion.
I feel that the sermon I preach this morning will be the
savor of life unto life, or of death unto death. In other
words, the Gospel of Christ is a powerful medicine: it
either kills or cures. There are those who say: "I would
like to become a Christian. I have been waiting a good
while for the right kind of influences to come;" and still
you are waiting. You are wiser in worldly things than
you are in religious things. If you want to get to Albany,
you go to the Grand Central Depot, or to the steam-boat
wharf, and, having got your ticket, you do not sit down on
the wharf or sit in the depot; you get aboard the boat or
train. And yet there are men who say they are waiting to
get to heaven—waiting, waiting, but not with intelligent
waiting, or they would get on board the line of Christian
influences that would bear them into the kingdom of God.

Now you know very well that to seek a thing is to search

for it with earnest endeavor. If you want to see a certain
man in New York, and there is a matter of $10,000 con-
nected with your seeing him, and you can not at first find
him, you do not give up the search. You look in the
directory, but can not find the name; you go in circles
where you think, perhaps, he may mingle, and, having
found the part of the city where he lives, but perhaps not
knowing the street, you go through street after street, and
from block to block, and you keep on searching for weeks
and for months.

You say: "It is a matter of $10,000 whether I see him
or not." Oh, that men were as persistent in seeking for
Christ! Had you one half that persistence you would long
ago have found Him who is the joy of the forgiven spirit.
We may pay our debts, we may attend church, we may
relieve the poor, we may be public benefactors, and yet all
our life disobey the text, never seek God, never gain
heaven. Oh, that the Spirit of God would help this morning while I try to show you, in carrying out the idea of my
text, first, how to seek the Lord, and in the next place,
when to seek Him. "Seek ye the Lord while He may be
found."

I remark, in the first place, you are to seek the Lord
through earnest and believing prayer. God is not an
autocrat or a despot seated on a throne, with His arms
resting on brazen lions, and a sentinel pacing up and down
at the foot of the throne. God is a father seated in a
bower, waiting for His children to come and climb on His
knee, and get His kiss and His benediction. Prayer is the
cup with which we go to the "fountain of living water,"

and dip up refreshment for our thirsty soul. Grace does not come to the heart as we set a cask at the corner of the house to catch the rain in the shower. It is a pulley fastened to the throne of God, which we pull, bringing the blessing.

I do not care so much what posture you take in prayer, nor how large an amount of voice you use. You might get down on your face before God, if you did not pray right inwardly, and there would be no response. You might cry at the top of your voice, and unless you had a believing spirit within, your cry would not go further up than the shout of a plow-boy to his oxen. Prayer must be believing, earnest, loving. You are in your house some summer day, and a shower comes up, and a bird, affrighted, darts into the window, and wheels about the room. You seize it. You smooth its ruffled plumage. You feel its fluttering heart. You say, " Poor thing, poor thing!" Now, a prayer goes out of the storm of this world into the window of God's mercy, and He catches it, and He feels its fluttering pulse, and He puts it in His own bosom of affection and safety. Prayer is a warm, ardent, pulsating exercise. It is the electric battery which, touched, thrills to the throne of God! It is the diving-bell in which we go down into the depths of God's mercy and bring up " pearls of great price." There was an instance where prayer made the waves of the Gennesaret solid as Russ pavement. Oh, how many wonderful things prayer has accomplished! Have you ever tried it? In the days when the Scotch Covenanters were persecuted, and the enemies were after them, one of the head men among the Covenanters prayed: "Oh, Lord, we be as dead men unless Thou shalt help us! Oh, Lord, throw the lap of Thy cloak over these poor things!" And instantly a Scotch mist enveloped and hid the persecuted from their persecutors — the promise literally fulfilled: "While they are yet speaking I will hear."

Oh, impenitent soul, have you ever tried the power of prayer? God says: "He is loving, and faithful, and patient." Do you believe that? You are told that Christ came to save sinners. Do you believe that? You are told that all you have to do to get the pardon of the Gospel is to ask for it. Do you believe that? Then come to Him and say: "Oh, Lord! I know Thou canst not lie. Thou hast told me to come for pardon, and I could get it. I come, Lord. Keep Thy promise, and liberate my captive soul."

Oh, that you might have an altar in the parlor, in the kitchen, in the store, in the barn, for Christ will be willing to come again to the manger to hear prayer. He would come in your place of business, as He confronted Matthew, the tax commissioner. If a measure should come before Congress that you thought would ruin the nation, how you would send in petitions and remonstrances! And yet there has been enough sin in your heart to ruin it forever, and you have never remonstrated or petitioned against it. If your physical health failed, and you had the means, you would go and spend the summer in Germany, and the winter in Italy, and you would think it a very cheap outlay if you had to go all round the earth to get back your physical health. Have you made any effort, any expenditure, any exertion for your immortal and spiritual health? No, you have not taken one step.

O that you might now begin to seek after God with earnest prayer. Some of you have been working for years and years for the support of your families. Have you given one half day to the working out of your salvation with fear and trembling? You came here this morning with an earnest purpose, I take it, as I have come hither with an earnest purpose, and we meet face to face, and I tell you, first of all, if you want to find the Lord, you must pray, and pray, and pray.

I remark again, you must seek the Lord through Bible study. The Bible is the newest book in the world. "Oh," you say, "it was made hundreds of years ago, and the learned men of King James translated it hundreds of years ago." I confute that idea by telling you it is not five minutes old, when God, by His blessed Spirit, retranslates it into the heart. If you will, in the seeking of the way of life through Scripture study, implore God's light to fall upon the page, you will find that these promises are not one second old, and that they drop straight from the throne of God into your heart.

There are many people to whom the Bible does not amount to much. If they merely look at the outside beauty, why it will no more lead them to Christ than Washington's farewell address or the Koran of Mohammed or the Shaster of the Hindoos. It is the inward light of God's Word you must get or die. I went up to the church of the Madeleine, in Paris, and looked at the doors which were the most wonderfully constructed I ever saw, and I could have stayed there for a whole week; but I had only a little time, so, having glanced at the wonderful carving on the doors, I passed in and looked at the radiant altars, and the sculptured dome. Alas, that so many stop at the outside door of God's Holy Word, looking at the rhetorical beauties, instead of going in and looking at the altars of sacrifice and the dome of God's mercy and salvation that hovers over penitent and believing souls!

O my friends! if you merely want to study the laws of language, do not go to the Bible. It was not made for that. Take "Howe's Elements of Criticism"—it will be better than the Bible for that. If you want to study metaphysics, better than the Bible will be the writings of William Hamilton. But if you want to know how to have sin pardoned, and at last to gain the blessedness of Heaven, search the Scriptures, "for in them ye have eternal life."

When people are anxious about their souls—and there are some such here to-day—there are those who recommend good books. That is all right. But I want to tell you that the Bible is the best book under such circumstances. Baxter wrote "A Call to the Unconverted," but the Bible is the best call to the unconverted. Philip Doddridge wrote "The Rise and Progress of Religion in the Soul," but the Bible is the best rise and progress. John Angell James wrote "Advice to the Anxious Inquirer," but the Bible is the best advice to the anxious inquirer.

O, the Bible is the very book you need, anxious and inquiring soul! A dying soldier said to his mate: "Comrade, give me a drop!" The comrade shook up the canteen, and said: "There isn't a drop of water in the canteen." "Oh," said the dying soldier, "that's not what I want; feel in my knapsack for my Bible," and his comrade found the Bible, and read him a few of the gracious promises, and the dying soldier said: "Ah, that's what I want. There isn't anything like the Bible for a dying soldier, is there, my comrade?" O blessed book while we live! Blessed book when we die!

I remark, again, we must seek God through church ordinances. "What," say you, "can't a man be saved without going to church?" I reply, there are men, I suppose, in glory, who have never seen a church: but the church is the ordained means by which we are to be brought to God; and if truth affects us when we are alone, it affects us more mightily when we are in the assembly—the feelings of others emphasizing our own feelings. The great law of sympathy comes into play, and a truth that would take hold only with the grasp of a sick man, beats mightily against the soul with a thousand heart-throbs.

When you come into the religious circle, come only with one notion, and only for one purpose—to find the way to Christ. When I see people critical about sermons, and critical about tones of voice, and critical about sermonic delivery, they make me think of a man in prison. He is condemned to death, but an officer of the government brings a pardon and puts it through the wicket of the prison, and says: "Here is your pardon. Come and get it." "What! Do you expect me to take that pardon offered with such a voice as you have, with such an awkward manner as you have? I would rather die than so compromise my rhetorical notions!" Ah, the man does not say that; he takes it! It is his life. He does not care how it is handed to him. And if, this morning, that pardon from the throne of God is offered to our souls, should we not seize it, regardless of all criticism, feeling that it is a matter of heaven or hell?

But I come now to the last part of my text. It tells us when we are to seek the Lord. "While He may be found." When is that? Old age? You may not see old age. To-morrow? You may not see to-morrow. To-night? You may not see to-night. Now! O if I could only write on every heart in three capital letters, that word N-O-W—Now!

Sin is an awful disease. I hear people say with a toss of the head and with a trivial manner: "Oh, yes, I'm a sinner." Sin is an awful disease. It is leprosy. It is dropsy. It is consumption. It is all moral disorders in one. Now you know there is a crisis in a disease. Perhaps you have had some illustration of it in your family. Sometimes the physician has called, and he has looked at the patient and said: "That case was simple enough; but the crisis has passed. If you had called me yesterday, or this morning, I could have cured the patient. It is too late now; the crisis has passed." Just so it is in the spiritual treatment of the soul—there is a crisis. Before that, life! After that, death! O my dear brother, as you love your soul do not let the crisis pass unattended to!

There are some here who can remember instances in life when, if they had bought a certain property, they would have become very rich. A few acres that would have cost them almost nothing were offered them. They refused them. Afterward a large village or city sprung up on those acres of ground, and they see what a mistake they made in not buying the property. There was an opportunity of getting it. It never came back again. And so it is in regard to a man's spiritual and eternal fortune. There is a chance; if you let that go, perhaps it never comes back. Certainly, that one never comes back.

A gentleman told me that at the battle of Gettysburg he stood upon a height looking off upon the conflicting armies. He said it was the most exciting moment of his life; now one army seeming to triumph, and now the other. After awhile the host wheeled in such a way that he knew in five minutes the whole question would be decided. He said the emotion was almost unbearable. There is just such a time to-day with you, O impenitent soul!—the forces of light on the one side, and the siege-guns of hell on the other side, and in a few moments the matter will be settled for eternity.

There is a time which mercy has set for leaving port. If you are on board before that, you will get a passage for heaven. If you are not on board, you miss your passage for heaven. As in law courts a case is sometimes adjourned from term to term, and from year to year till the bill of costs eats up the entire estate, so there are men who are adjourning the matter of religion from time to time, and from year to year, until heavenly bliss is the bill of costs the man will have to pay for it.

Why defer this matter, oh, my dear hearer? Have you any idea that sin will wear out? that it will evaporate?

that it will relax its grasp? that you may find religion as a
man accidentally finds a lost pocket-book? Ah, no! No
man ever became a Christian by accident, or by the relax-
ing of sin. The embarrassments are all the time increas-
ing. The hosts of darkness are recruiting, and the longer
you postpone this matter the steeper the path will become.
I ask those men who are before me this morning, whether,
in the ten or fifteen years they have passed in the post-
ponement of these matters, they have come any nearer
God or heaven?

I would not be afraid to challenge this whole audience,
so far as they may not have found the peace of the Gospel,
in regard to the matter. Your hearts, you are willing
frankly to tell me, are becoming harder and harder, and
that if you come to Christ it will be more of an undertaking now than it ever would have been before. Oh, fly for
refuge! The avenger of blood is on the track! The
throne of judgment will soon be set; and, if you have anything to do toward your eternal salvation, you had better
do it now, for the redemption of your soul is precious, and
it ceaseth forever!

Oh, if men could only catch just one glimpse of Christ,
I know they would love Him! Your heart leaps at the
sight of a glorious sunrise or sunset. Can you be without
emotion as the Sun of Righteousness rises behind Calvary,
and sets behind Joseph's sepulcher? He is a blessed
Saviour! Every nation has its type of beauty. There is
German beauty, and Swiss beauty, and Italian beauty,
and English beauty; but I care not in what land a man
first looks at Christ, he pronounces Him " chief among ten

thousand, and the One altogether lovely." O my blessed Jesus! Light in darkness! The Rock on which I build! The Captain of Salvation! My joy! My strength! How strange it is that men can not love Thee!

The diamond districts of Brazil are carefully guarded, and a man does not get in there except by a pass from the government; but the love of Christ is a diamond district we may all enter, and pick up treasures for eternity. Oh, cry for mercy! "To-day, if ye will hear His voice, harden not your hearts." There is a way of opposing the mercy of God too long, and then there remaineth no more sacrifice for sin, but a fearful looking for judgment and fiery indignation, which shall devour the adversary. My friends, my neighbors, what can I say to induce you to attend to this matter—to attend to it now? Time is flying, flying—the city clock joining my voice this moment, seeming to say to you, "Now is the time! Now is the time!" Oh, put it not off!

Why should I stand here and plead, and you sit there? It is your immortal soul. It is a soul that shall never die. It is a soul that must soon appear before God for review. Why throw away your chance for heaven? Why plunge off into darkness when all the gates of glory are open? Why become a castaway from God when you can sit upon the throne? Why will ye die miserably when eternal life is offered you, and it will cost you nothing but just willingness to accept it? " Come, for all things are now ready." Come, Christ is ready, pardon is ready! The Church is ready. Heaven is ready. You will never find a more convenient season, if you should live fifty years more, than this very one. Reject this, and you may die in your sins. Why do I say this? Is it to frighten your soul? Oh, no! It is to persuade you. I show you the peril. I show you the escape. Would I not be a coward beyond all excuse, if, believing that this great audience must soon be launched into the eternal world, and that all who believe in Christ shall be saved, and that all who reject Christ will be lost—would I not be the veriest coward on earth to hide that truth or to stand before you with a cold, or even a placid manner? My dear brethren, now is the day of your redemption.

It is very certain that you and I must soon appear before God in judgment. We can not escape it. The Bible says: "Every eye shall see Him, and they also which pierced Him, and all the kindreds of the earth shall wail because of Him." On that day all our advantages will come up for our glory or for our discomfiture—every prayer, every sermon, every exhortatory remark, every reproof, every call of grace; and while the heavens are rolling away like a scroll, and the world is being destroyed, your destiny and my destiny will be announced. Alas! alas! if on that day it is found that we have neglected these matters. We may throw them off now. We can not then. We will all be in earnest then. But no pardon then. No offer of salvation then. No rescue then. Driven away in our wickedness—banished, exiled, forever!

Have you ever imagined what will be the soliloquy of the soul on that day unpardoned, as it looks back upon its past life? "Oh," says the soul, "I had glorious Sabbaths!

There was one Sabbath in autumn when I was invited to Christ. There was a Sabbath morning when Jesus stood and spread out His arm and invited me to His holy heart. I refused Him. I have destroyed myself. I have no one else to blame. Ruin complete! Darkness unpitying, deep, eternal! I am lost! Notwithstanding all the opportunities I have had of being saved, I am lost! O Thou long-suffering Lord God Almighty, I am lost! O day of judgment, I am lost! O father, mother, brother, sister, child in glory, I am lost!" And then as the tide goes out, your soul goes out with it—further from God, further from happiness, and I hear your voice fainter, and fainter, and fainter: "Lost! Lost! Lost! Lost! Lost!" O ye dying, yet immortal men, "seek the Lord while He may be found."

But I want you to take the hint of the text that I have no time to dwell on—the hint that there is a time when He can not be found. There is a man in New York, eighty years of age, who said to a clergyman who came in, "Do you think that a man at eighty years of age can get pardoned?" "Oh, yes," said the clergyman. The old man said: "I can't; when I was twenty years of age —I am now eighty years—the Spirit of God came to my soul, and I felt the importance of attending to these things, but I put it off. I rejected God, and since then I have had no feeling." "Well," said the minister, "wouldn't you like to have me pray with you?" "Yes," replied the old man, "but it will do no good. You can pray with me if you like to." The minister knelt down and prayed, and commended the man's soul to God. It seemed to have no effect upon him. After awhile the last hour of the man's life came, and through his delirium a spark of intelligence seemed to flash, and with his last breath he said; "I shall never be forgiven!" "O seek the Lord while He may be found."

THE GREAT ASSIZE.

DOCTOR TALMAGE'S SERMON, PREACHED AT CORK, IRELAND, SUNDAY MORNING, SEPT. 6th, 1885.

" When the Son of Man shall come in His glory, and all the holy angels with Him, then shall He sit upon the throne of His glory: and before Him shall be gathered all nations: and He shall separate them one from another, as a shepherd divideth his sheep from the goats."—MATTHEW xxv: 31, 32.

HALF-WAY between Chamouny, Switzerland, and Martigny, I reined in the horse on which I was riding, and looked off upon the most wonderful natural amphitheater of valley and mountain and rock, and I said to my companion, " What an appropriate place this would be for the last judgment. Yonder overhanging rock the place for the judgment seat. These galleries of surrounding hills occupied by attendant angels. This vast valley, sweeping miles this way and miles that, the audience-room for all nations." But sacred geography does not point out the place. Yet we know that somewhere, some time, somehow, an audience will be gathered together stupendous beyond all statistics, and just as certainly as you and I make up a part of this audience to-day, we will make up a part of that audience on that day."

A common sense of justice in every man's heart demands that there shall be some great winding-up day, in which that which is now inexplicable shall be explained.

Why did that good man suffer, and that bad man prosper? You say, " I don't know, but I must know." Why is that good Christian woman dying of what is called a spider cancer, while that daughter of folly sits wrapped in luxury, ease, and health? You say, " I don't know, but I must know." There are so many wrongs to be righted that if there were not some great righting-up day in the presence of all ages, there would be an outcry against God from which His glory would never recover. If God did not at last try the nations, the nations would try Him. We are, therefore, ready for the announcement of the text. The world never saw Christ except in disguise. If once when He was on earth He had let out His glory, instead of the blind eyes being healed, all visions would have been extinguished. No human eye could have endured it. And instead of bringing the dead to life, all around about him would have been the slain under that overpowering effulgence. Disguise of human flesh. Disguise of seamless robe. Disguise of sandal. Disguise of voice. From Bethlehem caravansary to mausoleum in the rock, a complete disguise.

But on the day of which I speak the Son of Man will come in His glory. No hiding of luster. No sheathing of strength. No suppression of grandeur. No wrapping out of sight of the Godhead. Any fifty of the most brilliant sunsets that you ever saw on land or sea would be dim as compared with the cerulean appearance on that day when

Christ rolls through, and rolls on, and rolls down in His glory. The air will be all abloom with His presence, and everything from horizon to horizon aflame with His splendor.

Elijah rode up the sky-steep in a chariot, the wheels of whirling fire and the horses of galloping fire, and the charioteer drawing reins of fire on bits of fire; but Christ will need no such equipage, for the law of gravitation will be laid aside, and the natural elements will be laid aside, and Christ will descend swiftly enough to make speedy arrival, but slowly enough to allow the gaze of millions of spectators. In his glory! Glory of form, glory of omnipotence, glory of holiness, glory of justice, glory of love. In His glory! An unveiled, an uncovered God descending to meet the human race in an interview which will be prolonged only for a few hours, and yet which shall settle all the past and all the present and all the future, and be closed before the end of that day, which will close, not with setting sun, but with the destruction of the planet as a snuffers takes off the top of a burned wick.

It is a solemn time in a court-room when there is an important case on hand, and the judge of the Supreme Court enters, and he sits down, and with gavel strikes on the desk commanding bar and jury and witnesses and audience into silence. All voices are hushed, all heads are uncovered. But how much more impressive when Christ shall take the judgment seat on the last day of the last week of the last month of the last year of the world's existence, and with gavel of thunder-bolt shall smite the mountains. commanding all the land and all the sea into silence.

Can you have any doubt about who it is on the seat on the judgment day? Better make investigation, to see whether there are any scars about Him that reveal His person. Apparel may change. You can not always tell by apparel. But scars will tell the story after all else fails. I find under His left arm a scar, and on His right hand a scar, and on His left hand a scar, and on His right foot a scar, and on His left foot a scar. Oh, yes, He is the Son of Man in His glory. Every mark of wound now a badge of victory, every ridge showing the fearful gash now telling the story of pain and sacrifice which He suffered in behalf of the human race.

But what is all that commotion and flutter, and surging to and fro above Him and on either side of Him? It is a detailed regiment of heaven, a constabulary angelic, sent forth to take part in that scene, and to execute the mandates that shall be issued. Ten regiments, a hundred regiments, a thousand regiments of angels; for on that day all heaven will be emptied of its inhabitants to let them attend the scene. All the holy angels. From what a center to what a circumference. Widening out and widening out, and higher up and higher up. Wings interlocking wings. Galleries of cloud above galleries of cloud, all filled with the faces of angels come to listen and come to watch, and come to help on that day for which all other days were made. Who are those two taller and more conspicuous angels? The one is Michael, who is the commander of all those who come out to destroy sin. The other is Gabriel, who is announced as commander of all those who come forth to help the righteous. Who is that mighty angel near the throne? That is the resurrection angel, his lips still aquiver and his cheek aflush with the blast that shattered the cemeteries and woke the dead. Who is that other great angel, with dark and overshadowing brow? That is the one who in one night, by one flap of his wing, turned one hundred and eighty-five thousand of Sennacherib's host into corpses.

Who are those bright immortals near the throne, their faces partly turned toward each other as though about to sing? Oh, they are the Bethlehem chanters of the first Christmas night! Who are this other group standing so near the throne? They are the Saviour's especial body-guard, which hovered over Him in the wilderness and administered to Him in the hour of martyrdom, and heaved away the rock of His sarcophagus, and escorted Him upward on Ascension Day, now appropriately escorting Him down. Divine glory flanked on both sides by angelic radiance.

But now lower your eye from the divine and angelic to the human. The entire human race is present. All nations, says my text. Before that time the American Republic, the English Government, the French Republic, all modern modes of government may be obliterated for something better; but all nations, whether dead or alive, will be brought up into that assembly. Thebes and Tyre and Babylon and Greece and Rome as wide awake in that assembly as though they had never slumbered amid the dead nations. Europe, Asia, Africa, North and South America, and all the nineteenth century, the eighteenth century, the twelfth century, the tenth century, the fourth century—all centuries present. Not one being that ever drew the breath of life but will be in that assembly.

No other audience a thousandth part as large. No other audience a millionth part as large. No human eye could look across it. Wing of albatross and falcon and eagle not strong enough to fly over it. A congregation, I verily believe, not assembled on any continent, because no continent would be large enough to hold it. But, as the Bible intimates, in the air. The law of gravitation unanchored, the world moved out of its place. As now sometimes on earth a great tent is spread for some great convention, so over that great audience of the judgment shall be lifted the blue canopy of the sky, and underneath it for floor the air made buoyant by the hand of Almighty God. An architecture of atmospheric galleries strong enough to hold up worlds. Surely the two arms of God's almightiness are two pillars strong enough to hold up any auditorium.

But that audience is not to remain in session long. Most audiences on earth after an hour or two adjourn. Sometimes in court-rooms an audience will tarry four or five hours, but then it adjourns. So this audience spoken of in the text will adjourn. My text says, " He will separate them one from another as a shepherd divideth the sheep from the goats."

" No," says my Universalist friend, " let them all stay together." But the text says, " He shall separate them." " No," say the kings of this world, " let men have their choice, and if they prefer monarchical institutions, let them go together, and if they prefer republican institutions, let them go together." " No," say the conventionalities of this world, " let all those who moved in what are called high circles go together, and all those who on earth moved in low circles go together. The rich together, the poor together, the wise together, the ignorant together." Ah! no. Do you not notice in that assembly the king is without his scepter, and the soldier without his uniform, and the bishop without his pontifical ring, and the millionaire without his certificates of stock, and the convict without his chain, and the beggar without his rags, and the illiterate without his bad orthography, and all of us without any distinction of earthly inequality? So I take it from that as well as from my text that the mere accident of position in this world will do nothing toward deciding the questions of that very great day.

" He will separate them as a shepherd divideth the sheep from the goats." The sheep, the cleanliest of creatures, here made a symbol of those who have all their sins washed away in the fountain of redeeming mercy. The goat, one of the filthiest of creatures, here a type of those who in the last judgment will be found never to have had any divine ablution. Division according to character. Not only character outside, but character inside. Character of heart, character of choice, character of allegiance, character of affection, character inside as well as character outside.

In many cases it will be a complete and immediate reversal of all earthly conditions. Some who in this world wore patched apparel will take on raiment lustrous as a summer noon. Some who occupied a palace will take a dungeon. Division regardless of all earthly caste, and some who were down will be up, and some who were up will be down. Oh, what a shattering of conventionalities! What an upheaval of all social rigidities, what a turning of the wheel of earthly condition, a thousand revolutions in a second! Division of all nations, of all ages, not by the figure 9, nor the figure 8, nor the figure 7, nor the figure 6, nor the figure 5, nor the figure 4; but by the figure 2.

Two! Two characters, two destinies, two estates, two dominions, two eternities, a tremendous, an all-comprehensive, an all-decisive, and everlasting two!

I sometimes think that the figure of the book that shall be opened allows us to forget the thing signified by the symbol. Where is the book-binder that could make a volume large enough to contain the names of all the people who have ever lived? Besides that, the calling of such a roll would take more than fifty years, more than a hundred years, and the judgment is to be consummated in less time than passes between sunrise and sunset. Ah! my friends, the leaves of that book of judgment are not made out of paper, but of memory. One leaf in every human heart. You have known persons who were near drowning, but they were afterward resuscitated, and they have told you that in the two or three minutes between the accident and the resuscitation, all their past life flashed before them —all they had ever thought, all they had ever done, all they had ever seen, in an instant came to them. The memory never loses anything. It is only a folded leaf. It is only a closed book.

Though you be an octogenarian, though you be a nonagenarian, all the thoughts and acts of your life are in your mind, whether you recall them now or not, just as Macaulay's history is in two volumes, although the volumes may be closed, and you can not see a word of them, and will not until they are opened. As in the case of the drowning man, the volume of memory was partly open, or the leaf partly unrolled; in the case of the judgment the entire book will be opened, so that everything will be displayed from preface to appendix.

You have seen self-registering instruments which recorded how many revolutions they had made and what work they had done, so the manufacturer could come days after and look at the instrument and find just how many revolutions had been made, or how much work had been accomplished. So the human mind is a self-registering instrument, and it records all its past movements. Now that leaf, that all-comprehensive leaf in your mind and mine this moment, the leaf of judgment, brought out under the flash of the judgment throne, you can easily see how all the past of our lives in an instant will be seen. And so great and so resplendent will be the light of that throne that not only this leaf in my heart and that leaf in your heart will be revealed at a flash, but all the leaves will be opened, and you will read not only your own character and your own history, but the character and history of others.

In a military encampment the bugle sounded in one way means one thing, and sounded in another way it means another thing. Bugle sounded in one way means, "Prepare for sudden attack." Bugle sounded in another way means, "To your tents, and let all the lights be put out." I have to tell you, my brother, that the trumpet of the Old

Testament, the trumpet that was carried in the armies of olden times, and the trumpet on the walls in olden times, in the last great day will give significant reverberation. Old, worn-out, and exhausted Time, having marched across decades and centuries and ages, will halt, and the sun and the moon and the stars will halt with it. The trumpet! the trumpet!

Peal the first: Under its power the sea will stretch itself out dead, the white foam on the lip, in its crystal sarcophagus, and the mountains will stagger and reel and stumble, and fall into the valleys never to rise. Under one puff of that last cyclone all the candles of the sky will be blown out. The trumpet! the trumpet!

Peal the second: The alabaster halls of the air will be filled with those who will throng up from all the cemeteries of all the ages—from Greyfriar's Churchyard and Roman Catacomb, from Westminster Abbey and from the coral crypts of oceanic cave, and some will rend off the bandage of Egyptian mummy, and others will remove from their brow the garland of green sea-weed. From the north and the south and the east and the west they come. The dead! The trumpet! the trumpet!

Peal the third: Amid surging clouds and the roar of attendant armies of heaven, the Lord comes through, and there are lightnings and thunder-bolts, and an earthquake, and a hallelujah, and a wailing. The trumpet! the trumpet!

Peal the fourth: All the records of human life will be revealed. The leaf containing the pardoned sin, the leaf containing the unpardoned sin. Some clapping hands with joy, some grinding their teeth with rage, and all the forgotten past becomes a vivid present. The trumpet! the trumpet!

Peal the last: The audience breaks up. The great trial is ended. The high court of heaven adjourns. The audience hie themselves to their two termini. They rise, they rise! They sink, they sink! Then the blue tent of the sky will be lifted and folded up and put away. Then the auditorium of atmospheric galleries will be melted. Then the folded wings of attendant angels will be spread for upward flight. The fiery throne of judgment will become a dim and a vanishing cloud. The conflagration of divine and angelic magnificence will roll back and off. The day for which all other days are made has closed, and the world has burned down, and the last cinder has gone out, and an angel flying on errand from world to world will poise long enough over the dead earth to chant the funeral litany as he cries, "Ashes to ashes!"

That judgment leaf in your heart I seize hold of this moment for cancellation. In your city halls the great book of mortgages has a large margin, so that when the mortgagor has paid the full amount to the mortgagee, the officer of the law comes, and he puts down on that margin the payment and the cancellation; and though that mortgage demanded vast thousands before, now it is null and void. So I have to tell you that that leaf in my heart and in your heart, that leaf of judgment, that all-comprehensive leaf, has a wide margin for cancellation.

There is only one hand in all the universe that can touch that margin. That hand this moment lifted to make the record null and void forever. It may be a trembling hand, for it is a wounded hand, the nerves were cut and the muscles were lacerated. That record on that leaf was made in the black ink of condemnation; but if cancellation take place, it will be made in the red ink of sacrifice. O judgment-bound brother and sister! let Christ this moment bring to that record complete and glorious cancellation. This moment, in an outburst of impassioned prayer, ask for it. You think it is the fluttering of your heart. Oh, no! it is the fluttering of that leaf, that judgment leaf.

I ask you not to take from your iron safe your last will and testament, but I ask for something of more importance than that. I ask you not to take from your private papers that letter so sacred that you have put it away from all human eyesight, but I ask you for something of more meaning than that. That leaf, that judgment leaf in my heart, that judgment leaf in your heart, which will decide our condition after this world shall have five thousand million years been swept out the heavens, an extinct planet, and time itself will be so long past that on the ocean of eternity it will seem only as now seems a ripple on the Atlantic.

When the goats in vile herd start for the barren mountains of death, and the sheep in fleeces of snowy whiteness and bleating with joy move up the terraced hills to join the lambs already playing in the high pastures of celestial altitude, oh, may you and I be close by the Shepherd's crook! "When the Son of Man shall come in His glory, and all the holy angels with Him, then shall He sit upon the throne of His glory; and before Him shall be gathered all nations; and He shall separate them one from another, as a shepherd divideth the sheep from the goats.''   `      `

Oh, that leaf, that one leaf in my heart, that one leaf in your heart! That leaf of judgment! Oh, those two tremendous words at the last, '' Come!'' '' Go!'' As though the overhanging heavens were the cup of a great bell, and all the stars were welded into a silvery tongue and swung from side to side until it struck, '' Come!'' As though all the great guns of eternal disaster were discharged at once, and they boomed forth in one resounding cannonade of '' Go!'' Arithmetical sum in simple division. Eternity the dividend. The figure two the divisor. Your unalterable destiny the quotient.

THE ROAD TO THE CITY.

"And an highway shall be there, and a way, and it shall be called the way of holiness; the unclean shall not pass over it; but it shall be for those: the wayfaring men, though fools, shall not err therein. No lion shall be there, nor any ravenous beast shall go up thereon, it shall not be found there; but the redeemed shall walk there; and the ransomed of the Lord shall return, and come to Zion with songs and everlasting joy upon their heads: they shall obtain joy and gladness, and sorrow and sighing shall flee away."— ISAIAH xxxv: 8–10.

THERE are hundreds of people in this house this morning who want to find the right road. You sometimes see a person halting at cross roads, and you can tell by his looks that he wishes to ask a question as to what direction he had better take. And I stand in your presence this morning conscious of the fact that there are many of you here who realize that there are a thousand wrong roads, but only one right one; and I take it for granted that you have come in to ask which one it is. Here is one road that opens widely, but I have not much faith in it. There are a great many expensive toll-gates scattered all along that way. Indeed at every rod you must pay in tears, or pay in genuflexions, or pay in flagellations. On that road, if you get through it at all, you have to pay your own way; and since this differs so much from what I have heard in regard to the right way, I believe it is the wrong way.

Here is another road. On either side of it are houses of sinful entertainment, and invitations to come in, and dine and rest; but, from the looks of the people who stand on the piazza I am very certain that it is the wrong house and the wrong way. Here is another road. It is very beautiful and macadamized. The horses' hoofs clatter and ring, and they who ride over it spin along the highway, until suddenly they find that the road breaks over an embankment, and they try to halt, and they saw the bit in the mouth of the fiery steed, and cry "Ho! ho!" But it is too late, and—crash!—they go over the embankment. We shall turn, this morning, and see if we can not find a different kind of a road.

You have heard of the Appian Way. It was three hundred and fifty miles long. It was twenty-four feet wide, and on either side the road was a path for foot passengers. It was made out of rocks cut in hexagonal shape and fitted together. What a road it must have been! Made of smooth, hard rock, three hundred and fifty miles long. No wonder that in the construction of it the treasures of a whole empire were exhausted. Because of invaders, and the elements, and time—the old conqueror who tears up a road as he goes over it—there is nothing left of that structure excepting a ruin. But I have this morning to tell you of a road built before the Appian Way, and yet it is as good as when first constructed. Millions of souls have gone over it. Millions more will come.

> " The prophets and apostles, too,
> Pursued this road while here below;
> We therefore will, without dismay
> Still walk in Christ, the good old way."

" An highway shall be there, and a way, and it shall be called the way of holiness; the unclean shall not pass over it; but it shall be for those: the wayfaring men, though fools, shall not err therein. No lion shall be there, nor any ravenous beast shall go up thereon, it shall not be found there; but the redeemed shall walk there; and the ransomed of the Lord shall return, and come to Zion with songs and everlasting joy upon their heads; they shall obtain joy and gladness, and sorrow and sighing shall flee away!"

I. First, this road of the text is the King's highway. In the diligence you dash over the Bernard pass of the Alps, mile after mile, and there is not so much as a pebble to jar the wheels. You go over bridges which cross chasms that make you hold your breath; under projecting rock; along by dangerous precipices; through tunnels adrip with the meltings of the glaciers; and, perhaps for the first time, learn the majesty of a road built and supported by government authority. Well, my Lord the King decided to build a highway from earth to heaven. It should span all the chasms of human wretchedness; it should tunnel all the mountains of earthly difficulty; it should be wide enough and strong enough to hold fifty thousand millions of the human race, if so many of them should ever be born. It should be blasted out of the " Rock of Ages," and cemented with the blood of the Cross, and be lifted amid the shouting of angels and the execration of devils.

The King sent His Son to build that road. He put head and hand and heart to it, and, after the road was completed, waved His blistered hand over the way, crying, "It is finished!" Napoleon paid fifteen million francs for the building of the Simplon Road, that his cannon might go over for the devastation of Italy; but our King, at a greater expense, has built a road for a different purpose, that the banners of heavenly dominion might come down over it, and all the redeemed of earth travel up over it.

Being a King's highway, of course it is well built. Bridges splendidly arched and buttressed have given way and crushed the passengers who attempted to cross them. But Christ, the King, would build no such thing as that. The work done, He mounts the chariot of His love, and multitudes mount with Him, and He drives on and up the steep of heaven amid the plaudits of gazing worlds! The work is done—well done—gloriously done—magnificently done.

II. Still further: this road spoken of is a clean road.

Many a fine road has become miry and foul because it has not been properly cared for; but my text says the unclean shall not walk on this one. Room on either side to throw away your sins. Indeed, if you want to carry them along, you are not on the right road. That bridge will break, those overhanging rocks will fall, the night will come down, leaving you at the mercy of the mountain bandits, and at the very next turn of the road you will perish. But if you are really on this clean road of which I have been speaking, then you will stop ever and anon to wash in the water that stands in the basin of the eternal rock. Ay, at almost every step of the journey you will be crying out: "Create within me a clean heart!" If you have no such aspirations as that, it proves that you have mistaken your way; and if you will only look up and see the finger-board above your head, you may read upon it the words: "There is a way that seemeth right unto a man, but the end thereof is death." Without holiness no man shall see the Lord; and if you have any idea that you can carry along your sins, your lusts, your worldliness, and yet get to the end of the Christian race, you are so awfully mistaken that, in the name of God, this morning I shatter the delusion.

III. Still further, the road spoken of is a plain road. "The wayfaring men, though fools, shall not err therein." That is, if a man is three fourths an idiot, he can find this road just as well as if he were a philosopher. The imbecile boy, the laughing-stock of the street, and followed by a mob hooting at him, has only just to knock once at the gate of heaven, and it swings open: while there has been many a man who can lecture about pneumatics, and chemistry, and tell the story of Farraday's theory of electrical polarization, and yet has been shut out of heaven. There has been many a man who stood in an observatory and swept the heavens with his telescope, and yet has not been able to see the Morning Star. Many a man has been familiar with all the higher branches of mathematics, and yet could not do the simple sum, "What shall it profit a man if he gain the whole world and lose his own soul?" Many a man has been a fine reader of tragedies and poems, and yet could not " read his title clear to mansions in the skies." Many a man has botanized across the continent, and yet not know the " Rose of Sharon and the Lily of the Valley." But if one shall come in the right spirit, crying the way to heaven, he will find it a plain way. The pardon is plain. The peace is plain. Everything is plain.

He who tries to get on the road to heaven through the New Testament teaching will get on beautifully. He who goes through philosophical discussion will not get on at all. Christ says: " Come to Me, and I will take all your sins away, and I will take all your troubles away." Now what is the use of my discussing it any more? Is not that plain? If you wanted to go to Albany, and I pointed you out a highway thoroughly laid out, would I be wise in detaining you by a geological discussion about the gravel you will pass over, or a physiological discussion about the muscles you will have to bring into play? No. After this Bible has pointed you the way to heaven, is it wise for me to detain you with any discussion about the nature of the human will, or whether the atonement is limited or unlimited? There is the road—go on it. It is a plain way.

" This is a faithful saying, and worthy of all acceptation, that Christ Jesus came into the world to save sinners." And that is you and that is me. Any little child here can understand this as well as I can. " Unless you become as a little child, you can not see the kingdom of God." If you are saved, it will not be as a philosopher, it will be as a little child. " Of such is the kingdom of

Heaven." Unless you get the spirit of little children, you will never come out at their glorious destiny.

IV. Still further: this road to heaven is a safe road. Sometimes the traveler in those ancient highways would think himself perfectly secure, not knowing there was a lion by the way, burying his head deep between his paws, and then, when the right moment came, under the fearful spring the man's life was gone, and there was a mauled carcass by the roadside. But, says my text, "No lion shall be there." I wish I could make you feel, this morning, your entire security. I tell you plainly that one minute after a man has become a child of God, he is as safe as though he had been ten thousand years in heaven. He may slip, he may slide, he may stumble; but he can not be destroyed. Kept by the power of God, through faith, unto complete salvation. Everlastingly safe.

The severest trial to which you can subject a Christian man is to kill him, and that is glory. In other words, the worst thing that can happen a child of God is heaven. The body is only the old slippers that he throws aside just before putting on the sandals of light. His soul, you can not hurt it. No fires can consume it. No floods can drown it. No devils can capture it.

> "Firm and unmoved are they
>   Who rest their souls on God;
>   Fixed as the ground where David stood,
>   Or where the ark abode."

His soul is safe. His reputation is safe. Everything is safe. "But," you say, "suppose his store burns up?"

Why, then, it will be only a change of investments from earthly to heavenly securities. "But," you say, "suppose his name goes down under the hoof of scorn and contempt?" The name will be so much brighter in glory. "Suppose his physical health fails?" God will pour into him the floods of everlasting health, and it will not make any difference. Earthly subtraction is heavenly addition. The tears of earth are the crystals of heaven. As they take rags and tatters and put them through the paper-mill, and they come out beautiful white sheets of paper, so, often, the rags of earthly destitution, under the cylinders of death, come out a white scroll upon which shall be written eternal emancipation.

There was one passage of Scripture, the force of which I never understood until one day at Chamounix, with Mont Blanc on one side, and Montanvent on the other, I opened my Bible and read: "As the mountains are around about Jerusalem, so the Lord is around about them that fear Him." The surroundings were an omnipotent commentary.

> "Though troubles assail, and dangers affright;
> Though friends should all fail, and foes all unite;
> Yet one thing secures us, whatever betide,
> The Scriptures assure us the Lord will provide."

V. Still further: the road spoken of is a pleasant road. God gives a bond of indemnity against all evil to every man that treads it. "All things work together for good to those who love God." No weapon formed against them can prosper. That is the bond, signed, sealed, and de-

livered by the President of the whole universe. What is
the use of your fretting, O child of God, about food?
" Behold the fowls of the air: for they sow not, neither do
they reap, nor gather into barns; yet your heavenly Father
feedeth them." And will He take care of the sparrow,
will He take care of the hawk, and let you die? What is
the use of your fretting about clothes? " Consider the
lilies of the field. Shall He not much more clothe you, O
ye of little faith?" What is the use worrying for fear
something will happen to your home? " He blesseth the
habitation of the just." What is the use of your fretting
lest you will be overcome of temptations? " God is faithful, who will not suffer you to be tempted above that ye
are able; but will with the temptation also make a way to
escape, that ye may be able to bear it."

O this King's highway! Trees of life on either side,
bending over until their branches interlock and drop mid-
way their fruit and shade. Houses of entertainment on
either side the road for poor pilgrims. Tables spread with
a feast of good things, and walls adorned with apples of
gold in pictures of silver. I start out on this King's highway, and I find a harper, and I say: " What is your
name?" The harper makes no response, but leaves me to
guess, as, with his eyes toward heaven and his hand upon
the trembling strings this tune comes rippling on the air:
" The Lord is my light and my salvation. Whom shall I
fear? The Lord is the strength of my life; of whom shall
I be afraid?" I go a little further on the same road and
meet a trumpeter of heaven, and I say: " Haven't you
got some music for a tired pilgrim?" And wiping his lip

and taking a long breath, he puts his mouth to the trumpet and pours forth this strain: " They shall hunger no more, neither shall they thirst any more, neither shall the sun light on them, nor any heat, for the Lamb which is in the midst of the throne shall lead them to living fountains of water, and God shall wipe away all tears from their eyes." I go a little distance further on the same road, and I meet a maiden of Israel. She has no harp, but she has cymbals. They look as if they had rusted from seaspray; and I say to the maiden of Israel: " Have you no song for a tired pilgrim?" And like the clang of victors' shields the cymbals clap as Miriam begins to discourse: " Sing ye to the Lord, for He hath triumphed gloriously; the horse and the rider hath He thrown into the sea." And then I see a white-robed group. They come bounding toward me, and I say: " Who are they? The happiest, and the brightest, and the fairest in all heaven—who are they?" And the answer comes: " These are they who came out of great tribulations, and had their robes washed and made white with the blood of the Lamb."

I pursue this subject only one step further. What is the terminus? I do not care how fine a road you may put me on, I want to know where it comes out. My text declares it: " The redeemed of the Lord come to Zion." You know what Zion was. That was the King's palace. It was a mountain fastness. It was impregnable. And so heaven is the fastness of the universe. No howitzer has long enough range to shell those towers. Let all the batteries of earth and hell blaze away; they can not break in those gates. Gibraltar was taken, Sebastopol was taken,

Babylon fell; but these walls of heaven shall never surrender either to human or Satanic besiegement. The Lord God Almighty is the defense of it. Great capital of the universe! Terminus of the King's highway!

Doctor Dick said that, among other things, he thought in heaven we should study chemistry, and geometry, and conic sections. Southey thought that in heaven he would have the pleasure of seeing Chaucer and Shakespeare. Now, Doctor Dick may have his mathematics for all eternity, and Southey his Shakespeare. Give me Christ and my old friends—that is all the heaven I want, that is heaven enough for me. O garden of light, whose leaves never wither, and whose fruits never fail! O banquet of God, whose sweetness never palls the taste, and whose guests are kings forever! O city of light, whose walls are salvation, and whose gates are praise! O palace of rest, where God is the monarch and everlasting ages the length of His reign! O song louder than the surf-beat of many waters, yet soft as the whisper of cherubim!

O my heaven! When my last wound is healed, when the last heart-break is ended, when the last tear of earthly sorrow is wiped away, and when the redeemed of the Lord shall come to Zion, then let all the harpers take down their harps, and all the trumpeters take down their trumpets, and all across heaven there be chorus of morning stars, chorus of white-robed victors, chorus of martyrs from under the throne, chorus of ages, chorus of worlds, and there be but one song sung, and but one name spoken, and but one throne honored—that of Jesus only.

THE RANSOMLESS.

"Beware lest He take thee away with His stroke: then a great ransom can not deliver thee."—Job xxxvi: 18.

Trouble makes some men mad. It was so with Job. He had lost his property, he had lost his physical health, he had lost his dear children, and the losses had led to exasperation instead of any spiritual profit. I suppose that he was in the condition that many are now in who sit before me. There are those here whose fortunes have begun to flap their wings, as though to fly away. There is a hollow cough in some of your dwellings. There is a subtraction of comfort and happiness, and you feel disgusted with the world, and impatient with many events that are transpiring in your history, and you are in the condition in which Job was when the words of my text accosted him: "Beware lest He take thee away with His stroke: and then a ransom can not deliver thee."

I propose to show you that sometimes God suddenly removes from us our gospel opportunities, and that, when He has done so, our case is ransomless. "Beware lest He take thee away with His stroke: then a great ransom can not deliver thee."

I. Sometimes the stroke comes in the removal of the intellect.

" Oh," says some man, " as long as I keep my mind I can afford to adjourn religion." But suppose you do not keep it? A fever, the hurling of a missile, the falling of a brick from a scaffolding, the accidental discharge of a gun —and your mind is gone. If you have ever been in an anatomical room, and have examined the human brain, you know what a delicate organ it is. And can it be possible that our eternity is dependent upon the healthy action of that which can be so easily destroyed?

" Oh," says some one, " you don't know how strong a mind I have." I reply: Losses, accident, bereavement, and sickness may shipwreck the best physical or mental condition. There are those who have been ten years in lunatic asylums who had as good a mind as you. While they had their minds they neglected God, and when their intellect went, with it went their last opportunity for heaven. Now they are not responsible for what they do, or for what they say; but in the last day they will be held responsible for what they did when they were mentally well; and if, on that day, a soul should say: " Oh, God, I was demented, and I had no responsibility," God will say: " Yes, you were demented; but there were long years when you were not demented. That was your chance for heaven, and you missed it." Oh, better be, as the Scotch say, a little " daft," nevertheless having grace in the heart; better be like poor Richard Hampson, the Cornish fool, whose biography has just appeared in England—a silly man he was, yet bringing souls to Jesus Christ by scores and scores—giving an account of his own conversion, when he said: " The mob got after me, and I lost my hat, and climbed up by a meat-stand, in order that I might not be trampled under foot, and while I was there, my heart got on fire with love toward those who were chasing me, and, springing to my feet, I began to exhort and to pray." Oh, my God, let me be in the last, last day the Cornish fool, rather than have the best intellect God ever created unillumined by the Gospel of Jesus Christ!

Consider what an uncertain possession you have in your intellect, when there are so many things around to destroy it; and beware, lest before you use it in making the religious choice, God takes it away with a stroke. I know a good many of my friends who are putting off religion until the last hour. They say when they get sick they will attend to it, but generally the intellect is beclouded; and oh; what a doleful thing it is to stand by a dying bed, and talk to a man about his soul, and feel, from what you see of the motion of his head, and the glare of his eye, and from what you hear of the jargon of his lips, that he does not understand what you are saying to him. I have stood beside the death-bed of a man who had lived a sinful life, and was as unprepared for eternity as it is possible for a man to be, and I tried to make him understand my pastoral errand; but all in vain. He could not understand it, and so he died.

Oh! ye who are putting off until the sick hour preparation for eternity, let me tell you that in all probability, you will not be able in your last hour to attend to it at all. There are a great many people who say they will repent on the death-bed.

I have no doubt there are many who have repented on the death-bed, but I think it is the exception. Albert Barnes, who was one of the coolest of men, and gave no rash statistics, said thus: that in a ministry of nearly half a century—he was over seventy when he went up to glory—he had known a great many people who said they repented on the dying bed, but, unexpectedly to themselves, got well; and he says, How many of those, do you suppose, who thought it was their dying bed, and who, after they repented on that dying bed, having got well, lived consistently, showing that it was real repentance, and not mock repentance—how many? not one! not one!

II. Again: this stroke may come to you in the withdrawal of God's spirit.

I see people before me who were, twenty years ago, serious about their souls. They are not now. They have no interest in what I am saying. They will never have any anxiety in what any minister of the Gospel says about their souls. Their time seems to have passed. I know a man, seventy-five years of age, who, in early life, became almost a Christian, but grieved away the spirit of God, and he has never thought earnestly since, and he can not be roused. I do not believe he will be roused until eternity flashes on his astonished vision.

It does seem as if sometimes, in quite early life, the Holy Spirit moves upon a heart, and being grieved away and rejected, never comes back. You say that is all imaginary? A letter, the address of which I will not give, dated last Monday morning, came to me on Tuesday, saying this: "Your sermon last night (that is, last Sabbath

6

night) did not fit my case, although I believe it did all others in the Academy; but your sermon of a week ago did fit my case, for I am 'past feeling.' I am not ashamed to be a Christian. I would as soon be known to be a Christian as anything else. Indeed, I wish I was, but I have not the least power to become one. Don't you know that with some persons there is a tide in their spiritual natures which, if taken at the flood, leads on to salvation? Such a tide I felt two years ago. I want you to pray for me, not that I may be led to Christ—for that prayer would not be answered—but that I may be kept from the temptation to suicide!"

What I had to say to the author of that I said in a private letter; but what I have to say to this audience is: Beware lest you grieve the Holy Ghost, and He be gone, and never return. Next Wednesday, at two or three o'clock, a Cunard steamer will put out from Jersey City wharf for Liverpool. After it has gone one hour, and the vessel is down by the Narrows, or beyond, go out on the Jersey City wharf, and wave your hand, and shout, and ask that steamer to come back to the wharf. Will it? Yes, sooner than the Holy Ghost will come back when once He has taken His final flight from thy soul. With that Holy Spirit some of you have been in treaty, my dear friends.

The Holy Spirit said: "Come, come to Christ." You said: "No, I won't." The Spirit said, more importunately: "Come to Christ." You said: "Well, I will after awhile, when I get my business fixed up; when my friends consent to my coming; when they won't laugh at me—

then I'll come." But the Holy Spirit more emphatically said: "Come now." You said: "No, I can't. I can't come now." And that Holy Spirit stands in your heart to-night, with His hand on the door of your soul, ready to come out. Will you let Him depart? If so, then, with a pen of light, dipped in ink of eternal blackness, the sentence may be now writing: "Ephraim is joined to his idols. Let him alone! Let him alone!" When that fatal record is made, you might as well brace yourselves up against the sorrows of the last day, against the anguish of an unforgiven death-bed, against the flame and the overthrow of an undone eternity; for though you might live thirty years after that in the world, your fate would be as certain as though you had already entered the gates of darkness. That is the dead line. Look out how you cross it!

> " 'There is a line by us unseen,
>   That crosses every path;
>   The hidden boundary between
>   God's patience and His wrath.' "

And some of you, to-night, have come up to that line. Ay, you have lifted your foot, and when you put it down, it will be on the other side! Look out how you cross it! Oh, grieve not the Spirit of God, lest He never come back!

III. This fatal stroke spoken of in the text may be our exit from this world. I hear aged people sometimes saying: "I can't live much longer." But do you know the fact that there are a hundred young people and middle-aged people who go out of this life to one aged person, for the simple reason that there are not many aged people to leave life? The aged seem to stand around like stalks—separate stalks of wheat at the corner of the field; but when death goes a-mowing, he likes to go down amid the thick of the harvest. What is more to the point: a man's going out of this world is never in the way he expects—it is never at the time he expects. The moment of leaving this world is always a surprise. If you expect to go in the winter, it may be in the summer; if in the summer, it may be in the winter; if in the night, it may be in the day-time; if you think to go in the day-time, it may be in the night. Suddenly the event will rush upon you, and you will be gone. Where? If a Christian—into joy. If not a Christian—into suffering.

The Gospel call stops outside of the door of the sepulcher. The sleeper within can not hear it. If that call should be sounded out with clarion voice louder than ever rang through the air, that sleeper could not hear it. I suppose every hour of the day, and now, while I am speaking, there are souls rushing into eternity unprepared. They slide from the pillow, or they slip from the pavement, and in an eye-twinkling they are gone. Elegant and eloquent funeral oration will not do them any good. Epitaph, cut on polished Scotch granite, will not do them any good. Wailing of beloved kindred can not call them back.

But, says some one: "I'll keep out of peril; I will not go on the sea, I will not go into battle—I'll keep out of all danger." That is no defense. Thousands of people, last night, on their couches, with the front door locked, and no armed assassin anywhere around, surrounded by all defended circumstances, slipped out of this life into the next. If time had been on one side of the shuttle and eternity on the other side of the shuttle, they could not have shot quicker across it. A man was saying: "My father was lost at sea, and my grandfather, and my great-grand-father. Wasn't it strange?" A man, talking to him, said: "You ought never to venture on the sea, lest you, yourself, be lost at sea." The man turned to the other, and said: "Where did your father die?" He replied: "In his bed." "Where did your grandfather die?" "In his bed." "Where did your great-grandfather die?" "In his bed." "Then," he said, "be careful, lest some night, while you are asleep on your couch, your time may come!"

Death alone is sure. Suddenly, you and I will go out of life. I am not saying anything to your soul that I am not going to say to my own soul. We have got to go suddenly out of this life. If I am prepared for that change, I do not care where my body is taken from—at what point I am taken out of this life. If I am ready, all is well. If I am not ready, though I might be at home, and though my loved ones might be standing around me, and though there might be the best surgical and medical ability in the room, I tell you, if I were not prepared, I would be frightened more than tongue can tell. It may seem like cowardice, but I am not ashamed to say that I should have the most indescribable horror about going out of this world if I thought I was unprepared for the next—if I had no Christ in my soul; for it would be a plunge compared with which a leap from the top of Mount Blanc would be nothing.

But this brings me to the most tremendous thought of my text. The text supposes that a man goes into ruin, and that an effort is made afterward for his rescue, and then says the thing can not be done. Is that so? After death seizes upon that soul, is there no resurrection? If a man topples off the edge of life, is there nothing to break his fall? If an impenitent man goes overboard, are there no grappling-hooks to hoist him into safety? The text says distinctly: "Then a great ransom can not deliver thee."

I know there are people who call themselves "Restorationists," and they say a sinful man may go down into the world of the lost; he stays there until he gets reformed, and then comes up into the world of light and blessedness. It seems to me to be a most unreasonable doctrine—as though the world of darkness were a place where a man could get reformed. Is there anything in the society of the lost world—the abandoned and the wretched of God's universe—to elevate a man's character and lift him at last to heaven? Can we go into companionship of the Neroes and the Herods, and the Jim Fisks, and spend a certain number of years in that lost world, and then by that society be purified and lifted up? Is that the kind of society that reforms a man and prepares him for heaven? Would you go to Shreveport or Memphis, with the yellow fever there, to get your physical health restored? Can it be that a man may go down into the diseased world—a world overwhelmed by an epidemic of transgressions—and by that process, and in that atmosphere, be lifted up to health and glory? Your common sense says: "No! no!"

In such society as that, instead of being restored, you would go down worse and worse, plunging every hour into deeper depths of suffering and darkness. What your common sense says the Bible reaffirms, when it says: " These shall go away into three months of punishment." I have quoted it wrong. " These shall go away into ten years of punishment." I have quoted it wrong. " These shall go into a thousand years of punishment." I have quoted it wrong. " These shall go into *everlasting* punishment." And now I have quoted it right; or, if you prefer, in the words of my text: " Then a great ransom can not deliver thee."

Now just suppose that a spirit should come down from heaven and knock at the gates of woe and say: " Let that man out! Let me come in and suffer in his stead. I will be the sacrifice. Let him come out." The grim jailer would reply: " No, you don't know what a place this is, or you would not ask to come in; besides that, this man had full warning and full opportunity of escape. He did not take the warning, and now a great ransom shall not deliver him."

Sometimes men are sentenced to imprisonment for life. There comes another judge on the bench, there comes another governor in the chair, and in three or four years you find the man who was sentenced for life in the street. You say: " I thought you were sentenced for life." " Oh!" he says, " politics are changed, and I am now a free man." But it will not be so for a soul at the last. There will be no new judge or new governor. If at the end of a century a soul might come out, it would not be so bad. If at the end of a thousand years it might come out, it would not be so bad. If there were any time in all the future, in quadrillions and quadrillions of years, that the soul might come out, it would not be so bad; but if the Bible be true, it is a state of unending duration.

Far on in the ages one lost soul shall cry out to another lost soul: "How long have you been here?" and the soul will reply: "The years of my ruin are countless. I estimated the time for thousands of years; but what is the use of estimating when all these rolling cycles bring us no nearer the terminus." Ages! Ages! Ages! Eternity! Eternity! Eternity! The wrath to come! The wrath to come! The wrath to come! No medicine to cure that marasmus of the soul. No hammer to strike off the handcuff of that incarceration. No burglar's key to pick the locks which the Lord hath fastened. Sir Francis Newport, in his last moment, caught just one glimpse of that world. He had lived a sinful life. Before he went into the eternal world he looked into it. The last words he ever uttered were, as he gathered himself up on his elbows in the bed: "Oh, the insufferable pangs of hell!" The lost soul will cry out: "I can not stand this! I can not stand this! Is there no way out?" and the echo will answer: "No way out." And the soul will cry: "Is this forever?" and the echo will answer: "Forever!"

Is it all true? "These shall go away into everlasting punishment, while the righteous go into life eternal." Are there two destinies? and must all this audience share one or the other? Shall I give an account for what I have told you to-night? Have I held back any truth, though it were plain, though it were unpalatable? Must I meet you there, oh, you dying but immortal auditory? I wish that my text, with all its uplifted hands of warning, could come upon your souls: "Beware lest He take thee away with His stroke: then a great ransom can not deliver thee."

Glory be to God, there is a ransom that can now deliver you, braver than Grace Darling putting out in a life-boat from Eddystone Light-house for the rescue of the crew of the Forfarshire steamer—Christ the Lord launched from heaven, amid the shouting of the angels. Thirty-three years afterward, Christ the Lord launched from earth to heaven, amid human and infernal execration; yet staying here long enough to save all who will believe in Him. Do you hear that? To save all who will believe in Him. Oh, that pierced side! Oh, that bleeding brow! Oh, that crushed foot! Oh, that broken heart! That is your hope, sinner. That is your ransom from sin, and death, and hell.

Why have I told you all these things to-night, plainly and frankly? It is because I know there is redemption for you, and I would have you now come and get it. Oh, men and women long prayed for, and striven with, and coaxed of the mercy of God—have you concentrated all your physical, mental, and spiritual energies in one awful determination to be lost? Is there nothing in the value of your soul, in the graciousness of Christ, in the thunders of the last day, in the blazing glories of heaven, and the surging wrath of an undone eternity to start you out of your indifference, and make you pray? Oh, must God come upon you in some other way? Must He take another

darling child from your household? Must He take
another installment from your worldly estate? Must He
come upon you with sorrow after sorrow, and smite you
down with sickness before you will be moved, and before
you will feel?

Oh, weep now, while Jesus will count the tears! Sigh
now in repentance, while Jesus will hear the grief. Now
clutch the cross of the Son of God before it be swept away.
Beware, lest the Holy Spirit leave thy heart. Beware,
lest this night thy soul be required of thee. "Beware, lest he take thee away with His stroke: then a great
ransom can not deliver thee." Oh, Lord God of Israel,
see these impenitent souls on the verge of death ready to
topple over! See them! Is there no help? Is this plea
all in vain? I can not believe it, blessed God. Oh, thou
mighty One, whose garments are red with the wine-press
of Thine own sufferings, in the greatness of Thy strength
ride through this audience, and may all this people fall
into line, the willing captives of Thy grace. Men and
women immortal! I lay hold of you to-night with both
hands of entreaty and of prayer, and I beg of you, prepare
for death, judgment, and eternity.

THE THREE GROUPS.

"And they sat down in ranks by hundreds and by fifties."—
MARK vi: 40.

THE sun was far down in the west, night was coming
on, and there were five thousand people tired, hungry,
shelterless. You know how Washington felt at Valley
Forge, when his army was starving and freezing. You
may imagine how any great-hearted general would feel
while his troops were suffering. Imagine, then, how
Christ, with His great heart, must have felt as He saw
these five thousand hunger-bitten people. Yes, I suppose
there were ten thousand there, for the Bible says there
were five thousand men, besides women and children.
The case is put in that way, not because the women and
children were of less importance than the men, but because they would eat less; and the whole force of the
miracle turns on the amount of food required.

How shall this great multitude be supplied? I see a self-
ish man in that crowd pulling a luncheon out of his own
pocket, and saying: "Let the people starve. They had
no business to come out here in the desert without any
provisions. They are improvident, and the improvident
ought to suffer." There is another man, not quite
so heartless, who says: "Go up into the village and

buy bread." What a foolish proposition! There is not
enough food in all the village for this crowd; besides that,
who has the money to pay for it? Xerxes' army, one
million strong, was fed by a private individual of great
wealth for only one day, but it broke him. Who, then,
shall feed this multitude?

I see a man rising in that great crowd and asking: " Is
there any one here who has bread or meat?" A kind of
moan goes through the whole throng. " No bread—no
meat." But just at that time a lad steps up. You know
when a great crowd goes off upon an excursion, there are
always men and boys to go along for the purpose of merchandise and to strike a bargain: and so, I suppose, this
boy had gone along for the purpose of merchandise; but
he was nearly all sold out, having only five loaves and two
fishes left. He is a generous boy, and he turns them over
to Christ.

But these loaves would not feed twenty people, how
much less ten thousand! Though the action was so generous on the part of the boy, so far as satisfying the multitude, it was a dead failure. Then Jesus comes to the
rescue. He is apt to come when there is a dead lift. He
commands the people that they sit down " in ranks, by
hundreds and by fifties," as much as to say: " Order!
order! so that none be missed." It was fortunate that
that arrangement was made; otherwise, at the very first
appearance of bread, the strong ones would have clutched
it, while the feeble and the modest would have gone un-
supplied.

I suppose it was no easy work to get that crowd seated,

for they all wanted to be in the front row, lest the bread give out before their turn come. No sooner are they seated than there comes a great hush over all the people. Jesus stands there, His light complexion and auburn locks illumined by the setting sun. Every eye is on Him. They wonder what He will do next. He takes one of the loaves that the boy furnished and breaks off it a piece, which immediately grows to as large a size as the original loaf, the original loaf staying as large as it was before the piece was broken off. And they leaned forward with intense scrutiny, saying: "Look! look!" When some one, anxious to see more minutely what is going on, rises in front, they cry: "Sit down in front! Let us look for ourselves."

And then, when the bread is passed around, they taste of it skeptically and inquiringly, as much as to say: "Is it bread? Really, is it bread?" Yes, the best bread that was ever made, for Christ made it. Bread for the first fifty and second fifty. Bread for the first hundred and the second hundred. Bread for the first thousand and the second thousand. Pass it all around the circle: there, where that aged man sits leaning on his staff, and where that woman sits with the child in her arms. Pass it all around. Are you all fed? "Ay! ay!" respond the ten thousand voices; "all fed." One basket would have held the loaves before the miracle; it takes twelve baskets now. Sound it through all the ages of earth and heaven, that Christ the Lord comes to our suffering race with the bread of this life in one hand, and the bread of eternal life in the other hand.

You have all immediately run out the analogy between that scene and this. There were thousands there; there are thousands here. They were in the desert; many of you are in the desert of trouble and sin. No human power could feed them; no human power can feed you. Christ appeared to them; Christ appears to you. Bread enough for all in the desert; bread enough for all who are here. And, as on that occasion, so in this: we have the people " sit down in ranks by hundreds and by fifties;" for the fact that many of you stand is no fault of ours, for we have tried to give you seats. As Christ divided that company into groups, so I divide this audience into three groups: the pardoned, the seeking, the careless.

I. And, first, I speak to the pardoned.

It is with some of you half past five in the morning, and some faint streaks of light. With others it is seven o'clock, and thus full dawn. With others it is twelve o'clock at noon, and you sit in full blaze of Gospel pardon. I bring you congratulation. Joseph delivered from Potiphar's dungeon; Daniel lifted from the lion's den; Saul arrested and unhorsed on the road to Damascus. Oh, you delivered captives, how your eyes should gleam, and your souls should bound, and your lips should sing in this pardon! From what land did you come? A land of darkness. What is to be your destiny? A land of light. Who got you out? Christ, the Lord. Can you sit so placidly and unmoved while all heaven comes to your soul with congratulation, and harps are strung, and crowns are lifted, and a great joy swings round the heavens at the news of your disinthrallment? If you could realize out of what a pit you have been dug, to what height you are to be raised, and to what glory you are destined, you would spring to your feet with "Hosanna!"

In 1808 there was a meeting of the emperors of France and Russia at Erfurt. There were distinguished men there also from other lands. It was so arranged that when any of the emperors arrived at the door of the reception-room, the drum should beat three times; but when a lesser dignitary should come, then the drum would sound but twice. After awhile the people in the audience-chamber heard two taps of the drum. They said: "A prince is coming." But after awhile there were three taps, and they cried: "The emperor!" Oh, there is a more glorious arrival at your soul to-night! The drum beats twice at the coming in of the lesser joys and congratulations of your soul; but it beats once, twice, thrice at the coming in of a glorious King—Jesus the Saviour, Jesus the God! I congratulate you. All are yours—things present and things to come.

II. I come now to speak of the second division—those who are seeking; some of you with more earnestness, some of you with less earnestness. But I believe that to-night, if I should ask all those who wish to find the way to heaven to rise, and the world did not scoff at you, and your own proud heart did not keep you down, there would be a thousand souls who would cry out as they rose up: "Show me the way to heaven!" That young man who smiled to the one next to him, as though he cared for none of these things, would be on his knees crying for mercy. Why this anxious look? Why this deep disquietude in the soul?

Why, at the beginning of this service, did you do what you have not done for years—bow your head in prayer? You are seeking.

" I am a gambler," says one man. There is mercy for you. " I am a libertine," says another. There is mercy for you. " I have plunged into every abomination." Mercy for you. The door of grace does not stand ajar to-night, nor half swung around on the hinges. It is wide, wide open; and there is nothing in the Bible, or in Christ, or God, or earth, or heaven, or hell, to keep you out of the door of safety, if you want to go in. Christ has borne your burdens, fought your battles, suffered for your sins. The debt is paid, and the receipt is handed to you, written in the blood of the Son of God—will you have it? Oh, decide the matter now! Decide it here! Fling your exhausted soul down at the feet of an all-compassionate, all-sympathizing, all-pitying, all-pardoning Jesus. The laceration on His brow, the gash in His side, the torn muscles and nerves of His feet beg you to come.

But remember that one inch outside the door of pardon, and you are in as much peril as though you were a thousand miles away. Many a shipwrecked sailor has got almost to the beach, but did not get on it. There are thousands in the world of the lost who came very near being saved—perhaps as near as you are to-night—but were not saved.

On the eastern coast of England, a few weeks ago, in a fishing-village, there was a good deal of excitement. While people were in church, the sailors and fishermen hearing the Gospel on the Sabbath, there was a cry: " To the beach!" and the minister closed the Bible, and with his congregation went out to help, and they saw in the offing a ship in trouble; but there was some disorder amid the fishing-smacks, and amid all the boats, and it was almost impossible to get anything launched. But after awhile they did, and they pulled away for the wreck, and came almost up, when suddenly the distressed bark in the offing capsized, and they all went down. Oh, if the life-boats had only been ten minutes quicker! And how many a life-boat has been launched from the Gospel shore! It has come almost up to the drowning, and yet, after all, they were not rescued. Somehow they did not get into it!

I suppose there are people who have asked for our prayers, and I suppose there were some in the side room, last Sabbath night, talking about their souls, who will miss heaven. They do not take the last step, and all the other steps go for nothing until you have taken the last step, for I have here, in the presence of God and this people, to announce the solemn truth, that to be almost saved is to be lost forever. That is all I have to say to the second division.

III. I come now to speak to the careless. You look in-different, and I suppose you are indifferent. You say: " I came in here because a friend invited me to see what is going on, but with no serious intentions about my soul. I have so much work, and so much pleasure on hand, don't bother me about religion." And yet you are gentlemanly, and you are lady-like, in your behavior, and, therefore, I know that you will listen respectfully if I talk courteously. Christian people are sometimes afraid to talk to men and

women of the world lest they be insulted. If they talk
courteously to people of the world, they will listen courteously. So now I try to come in that way, and in that
spirit, and talk to those of you who tell me that you are
careless about your soul.

Then you have a soul, have you? Yes, precious, with
infinite capacity for joy or suffering, winged for flight
somewhere. Beckoned upward, beckoned downward.
Fought after by angels and by fiends. Immortal!

> " The sun is but a spark of fire,
>   A transient meteor in the sky:
> The soul, immortal as its Sire,
>   Can never die."

Your body will soon be taken down, the castle will be destroyed, the tower will be in the dust, the windows will be
broken out, and the place where your body sleeps will be
forgotten; but your soul, after that, will be living, acting,
feeling, thinking—where? where? Oh, there must be
something of incomputable worth in that for which heaven
gave up its best inhabitant, and Christ went into martyrdom, and at the coming of which angels chant an eternal
litany and devils rush to the gate. When everything above
you, and beneath you, and around you, is intent upon that
soul, you can not afford to be careless, especially when I
think, this moment while I speak, there are thousands of
souls in heaven rejoicing that they attended to this matter
in time, while at this very instant there are souls in the
lost world mourning that they did not attend to it in time.
Hark to the howling of the damned!

Oh, if this room could be vacated of this audience, and you were all gone, and the wan spirits of the lost could come up and occupy this place, and I could stand before them with offers of pardon through Jesus Christ, and then ask them if they would accept it, there would come up an instantaneous, multitudinous, overwhelming cry: "Yes! yes! yes! yes!" No such fortune for them. They had their day of grace, and sacrificed it. You have yours; will you sacrifice it? I wish that I could have you see these things as you will one day see them.

Suppose, on your way home, a runaway horse should dash across the street, or between the dock and the boat you should accidentally slip, where would you be at twelve o'clock to-night or seven o'clock to-morrow morning? Or for all eternity where would you be? I do not answer the question. I just leave it to you to answer.

But suppose you escape fatal accident. Suppose you go out by the ordinary process of sickness. I will just suppose now that your last hour has come. The doctor says, as he goes out of the room: "Can't get well." There is something in the faces of those who stand around you that prophesies that you can not get well. You say within yourself: "I can't get well." Where are your comrades now? Oh, they are off to the gay party that very night! They dance as well as they ever did. They drink as much wine. They laugh as loud as though you were not dying. They destroyed your soul, but do not come to help you die.

Well, there are father and mother in the room. They are very quiet, but occasionally they go out into the next room and weep bitterly. The bed is very much disheveled.

They have not been able to make it up for two or three days. There are four or five pillows lying around, because they have been trying to make you as easy as they could. On the one side of your bed are all the past years of your life—the Bibles, the sermons, the communion-tables, the offers of mercy. You say: "Take them away." Your mother thinks you are delirious. She says: "There is nothing there, my dear, nothing there." There is something there! It is your wasted opportunities. It is your procrastinations. It is those years you gave to the world that you ought to have given to Christ. They are there; and some of them put their fingers on your aching temples, and some of them feel for the strings of your heart, and some put more thorns in your tumbled pillow, and you say: "Turn me over." And they turn you over, but, alas! there is a more appalling vision. You say: "Take that away!" They say: "There is nothing there, nothing there." There is—an open grave there! the judgment is there! a lost eternity is there! Take it away! They can not take it away.

You say: "How dark it is getting in the room!" Why, the burners are all lighted. Your family come up one by one, and tenderly kiss you good-bye. Your feet are cold, and the hands are cold, and the lips are cold, and they take a small mirror and they put it over your mouth to see if there is any breathing, and that mirror is taken away without a single blur upon it; and they whisper through the room: "She is gone." And then the door of the body opens and the soul flashes out. Make room for the destroyed spirit.

Push back that door! Lost! Let it come into its eternal residence. Woe! woe! No cup of merriment now, but cup of the wrath of Almighty God. The last chance for heaven gone. The door of mercy shut. The doom sealed. The blackness of darkness forever!

Voltaire is there. Herod is there. Robespierre is there. The debauchees are there. The murderers are there. All the rejectors of Jesus Christ are there. And you will be there unless you repent. You can not say, my dear brother, that you were not warned. This sermon would be a witness against you. You can not say that God's Holy Spirit never strove with your heart. He is striving now. You can not say that you had no chance for heaven, for the Omnipotent Son of God offers you His rescue. You can not say: " I had no warning about that world; I didn't know there was any such place," for the Bible distinctly rings in your ears to-day, saying: " At the end of the world the angels shall separate the wicked from among the just, and shall cast them into a furnace of fire." And again that book says: " The wicked shall be turned into hell, and all the nations that forget God." And again it says: " The smoke of their torment ascendeth for ever and ever."

You can not say that you did not hear about heaven, the other alternative, for you hear of it now: " The Lamb which is in the midst of the throne shall lead them to living fountains of water, and God shall wipe away all tears from their eyes." No sorrow, no suffering, no death. Oh, will you be careless any longer, when I tell you that Christ, the Conqueror of earth and hell, offers you now escape from all peril, and offers to introduce you this very hour into the peace and pardon of the Gospel, preparing you for that good land? The sides of Calvary run blood for you. Jesus, who had not where to lay His head, offers you His heart as a pillow of rest. Christ offers with His own body to bridge over the chasm of death, saying: "Walk over Me; I am the way."

O suffering Jesus! the thief scoffed at Thee, and the malefactor spat on Thee, and the soldiers stabbed Thee; but these who sit before Thee to-day have no heart to do that. O Jesus! tell them of Thy love, tell them of Thy sympathy, tell them of the rewards Thou wilt give them in the better land. Groan again, O blessed Jesus! groan again, and perhaps when the rocks fall, their hard hearts may break.

> "Nothing brought Him from above,
> Nothing but redeeming love."

The promise is all free, the path all clear. Come, Mary, and sit to-night at the feet of Jesus. Come, Bartimeus, and have your eyes opened. Come, O prodigal! and sit at thy father's table. Come, O you suffering, sinning, dying the soul! and find rest on the heart of Jesus. The Spirit and Bride say "Come," and Churches militant and triumphant say "Come," and all the voices of the past, mingling with all the voices of the future, in one great thunder of emphasis, bid you "Come now!" Are not those of you who are in the third class ready to pass over into the second division, and become seekers after Christ? Ay, are you not ready to pass over into the first division, and become the pardoned sons and daughters of the Lord Almighty? I can do no more than offer you, through Jesus Christ, peace on earth and everlasting residence in His presence.

> " When God makes up His last account
> Of natives in His holy mount,
> 'Twill be an honor to appear
> As one new-born and nourished there."

Good-night! The Lord bless you! Go to your homes seeking after Christ. Sleep not until you have made your peace with God. Good-night — a deep, hearty, loving, Christian good-night!

THE INSIGNIFICANT.

"And she went, and came, and gleaned in the field after the reapers: and her hap was to light on a part of the field belonging unto Boaz, who was of the kindred of Elimelech."—RUTH ii: 3.

THE time that Ruth and Naomi arrive at Bethlehem is harvest-time. It was the custom when a sheaf fell from a load in the harvest-field for the reapers to refuse to gather it up: that was to be left for the poor who might happen to come along that way. If there were handfuls of grain scattered across the field after the main harvest had been reaped, instead of raking it, as farmers do now, it was, by the custom of the land, left in its place, so that the poor, coming along that way, might glean it and get their bread. But, you say, "What is the use of all these harvest-fields to Ruth and Naomi? Naomi is too old and feeble to go out and toil in the sun; and can you expect that Ruth, the young and the beautiful, should tan her cheeks and blister her hands in the harvest-field?"

Boaz owns a large farm, and he goes out to see the reapers gather in the grain. Coming there, right behind the swarthy, sun-browned reapers, he beholds a beautiful woman gleaning—a woman more fit to bend to a harp or sit upon a throne than to stoop among the sheaves. Ah, that was an eventful day!

It was love at first sight. Boaz forms an attachment for the womanly gleaner—an attachment full of undying interest to the Church of God in all ages; while Ruth, with an ephah, or nearly a bushel of barley, goes home to Naomi to tell her the successes and adventures of the day. That Ruth, who left her native land of Moab in darkness, and traveled through an undying affection for her mother-in-law, is in the harvest-field of Boaz, is affianced to one of the best families in Judah, and becomes in after-time the ancestress of Jesus Christ, the Lord of glory! Out of so dark a night did there ever dawn so bright a morning?

I. I learn, in the first place, from this subject how trouble develops character. It was bereavement, poverty, and exile that developed, illustrated, and announced to all ages the sublimity of Ruth's character. That is a very unfortunate man who has no trouble. It was sorrow that made John Bunyan the better dreamer, and Doctor Young the better poet, and O'Connell the better orator, and Bishop Hall the better preacher, and Havelock the better soldier, and Kitto the better encyclopædist, and Ruth the better daughter-in-law.

I once asked an aged man in regard to his pastor, who was a very brilliant man, " Why is it that your pastor, so very brilliant, seems to have so little heart and tenderness in his sermons?" " Well," he replied, " the reason is, our pastor has never had any trouble. When misfortune comes upon him, his style will be different." After awhile the Lord took a child out of that pastor's house; and though the preacher was just as brilliant as he was before, oh, the warmth, the tenderness of his discourses! The fact is, that trouble is a great educator. You see sometimes a musician sit down at an instrument, and his execution is cold and formal and unfeeling. The reason is that all his life he has been prospered. But let misfortune or bereavement come to that man, and he sits down at the instrument, and you discover the pathos in the first sweep of the keys.

Misfortune and trials are great educators. A young doctor comes into a sick-room where there is a dying child. Perhaps he is very rough in his prescription, and very rough in his manner, and rough in the feeling of the pulse, and rough in his answer to the mother's anxious question; but years roll on, and there has been one dead in his own house; and now he comes into the sick-room, and with tearful eye he looks at the dying child, and he says, "Oh, how this reminds me of my Charlie!" Trouble, the great educator. Sorrow——I see its touch in the grandest painting; I hear its tremor in the sweetest song; I feel its power in the mightiest argument.

Grecian mythology said that the fountain of Hippocrene was struck out by the foot of the winged horse Pegasus. I have often noticed in life that the brightest and most beautiful fountains of Christian comfort and spiritual life have been struck out by the iron-shod hoof of disaster and calamity. I see Daniel's courage best by the flash of Nebuchadnezzar's furnace. I see Paul's prowess best when I find him on the foundering ship under the glare of the lightning in the breakers of Melita. God crowns His children amid the howling of wild beasts and the chopping of blood-splashed guillotine and the crackling fires of martyrdom. It took the persecutions of Marcus Aurelius to develop Polycarp and Justin Martyr. It took the pope's bull and the cardinal's curse and the world's anathema to develop Martin Luther. It took all the hostilities against the Scotch Covenanters and the fury of Lord Claverhouse to develop James Renwick, and Andrew Melville, and Hugh McKail, the glorious martyrs of Scotch history. It took the stormy sea, and the December blast, and the desolate New England coast, and the war-whoop of savages, to show forth the prowess of the Pilgrim Fathers—

> " When amid the storms they sung,
> And the stars heard, and the sea;
> And the sounding aisles of the dim wood
> Rang to the anthems of the free."

It took all our past national distresses, and it takes all our present national sorrows, to lift up our nation on that high career where it will march along after the foreign aristocracies that have mocked and the tyrannies that have jeered, shall be swept down under the omnipotent wrath of God, who hates despotism, and who, by the strength of His own red right arm, will make all men free. And so it is individually, and in the family, and in the Church, and in the world, that through darkness and storm and trouble men, women, churches, nations, are developed.

II. Again, I see in my text the beauty of unfaltering friendship. I suppose there were plenty of friends for Naomi while she was in prosperity; but of all her acquaintances, how many were willing to trudge off with her toward Judah, when she had to make that lonely journey?

One—the heroine of my text.   One—absolutely one.   I suppose when Naomi's husband was living, and they had plenty of money, and all things went well, they had a great many callers; but I suppose that after her husband died, and her property went, and she got old and poor, she was not troubled very much with callers.   All the birds that sung in the bower while the sun shone have gone to their nests, now the night has fallen.

Oh, these beautiful sun-flowers that spread out their color in the morning hour! but they are always asleep when the sun is going down!   Job had plenty of friends when he was the richest man in Uz; but when his property went and the trials came, then there were none so much that pestered as Eliphaz the Temanite, and Bildad the Shuhite, and Zophar the Naamathite.

Life often seems to be a mere game, where the successful player pulls down all the other men into his own lap. Let suspicions arise about a man's character, and he becomes like a bank in a panic, and all the imputations rush on him and break down in a day that character which in due time would have had strength to defend itself.   There are reputations that have been half a century in building, which go down under some moral exposure, as a vast temple is consumed by the touch of a sulphurous match.   A hog can uproot a century plant.

In this world, so full of heartlessness and hypocrisy, how thrilling it is to find some friend as faithful in days of adversity as in days of prosperity!   David had such a friend in Hushai; the Jews had such a friend in Mordecai, who never forgot their cause; Paul had such a friend in

Onesiphorus, who visited him in jail; Christ had such in the Marys, who adhered to Him on the cross; Naomi had such a one in Ruth, who cried out: "Entreat me not to leave thee, or to return from following after thee; for whither thou goest, I will go; and where thou lodgest, I will lodge; thy people shall be my people, and thy God my God; where thou diest will I die, and there will I be buried: the Lord do so to me, and more also, if aught but death part thee and me."

III. Again, I learn from this subject that paths which open in hardship and darkness often come out in places of joy. When Ruth started from Moab toward Jerusalem, to go along with her mother-in-law, I suppose the people said: "Oh, what a foolish creature to go away from her father's house, to go off with a poor old woman toward the land of Judah! They won't live to get across the desert. They will be drowned in the sea, or the jackals of the wilderness will destroy them." It was a very dark morning when Ruth started off with Naomi; but behold her in my text in the harvest-field of Boaz, to be affianced to one of the lords of the land, and become one of the grandmothers of Jesus Christ, the Lord of glory. And so it often is that a path which often starts very darkly ends very brightly.

When you started out for heaven, oh, how dark was the hour of conviction—how Sinai thundered, and devils tormented, and the darkness thickened! All the sins of your life pounced upon you, and it was the darkest hour you ever saw when you first found out your sins. After awhile you went into the harvest-field of God's mercy; you began to glean in the fields of divine promise, and you had more sheaves than you could carry, as the voice of God addressed you, saying: " Blessed is the man whose transgressions are forgiven, and whose sins are covered." A very dark starting in conviction, a very bright ending in the pardon and the hope and the triumph of the Gospel!

So, very often in our worldly business or in our spiritual career, we start off on a very dark path. We must go. The flesh may shrink back, but there is a voice within, or a voice from above, saying, " You must go;" and we have to drink the gall, and we have to carry the cross, and we have to traverse the desert and we are pounded and flailed of misrepresentation and abuse, and we have to urge our way through ten thousand obstacles that have been slain by our own right arm. We have to ford the river, we have to climb the mountain, we have to storm the castle; but, blessed be God, the day of rest and reward will come. On the tip-top of the captured battlements we will shout the victory; if not in this world, then in that world where there is no gall to drink, no burdens to carry, no battles to fight. How do I know it? Know it! I know it because God says so: " They shall hunger no more, neither thirst any more, neither shall the sun light on them, nor any heat, for the Lamb which is in the midst of the throne shall lead them to living fountains of water, and God shall wipe all tears from their eyes."

It was very hard for Noah to endure the scoffing of the people in his day, while he was trying to build the ark, and was every morning quizzed about his old boat that would never be of any practical use; but when the deluge came, and the tops of the mountains disappeared like the backs of sea-monsters, and the elements, lashed up in fury, clapped their hands over a drowned world, then Noah in the ark rejoiced in his own safety and in the safety of his family, and looked out on the wreck of a ruined earth.

Christ, hounded of persecutors, denied a pillow, worse maltreated than the thieves on either side of the cross, human hate smacking its lips in satisfaction after it had been draining His last drop of blood, the sheeted dead bursting from the sepulchers at His crucifixion. Tell me, O Gethsemane and Golgotha! were there ever darker times than those? Like the booming of the midnight sea against the rock, the surges of Christ's anguish beat against the gates of eternity, to be echoed back by all the thrones of heaven and all the dungeons of hell. But the day of reward comes for Christ; all the pomp and dominion of this world are to be hung on His throne, uncrowned heads are to bow before Him on whose head are many crowns, and all the celestial worship is to come up at His feet, like the humming of the forest, like the rushing of the waters, like the thundering of the seas, while all heaven, rising on their thrones, beat time with their scepters: "Hallelujah, for the Lord God omnipotent reigneth! Hallelujah, the kingdoms of this world have become the kingdoms of our Lord Jesus Christ!"

> "That song of love, now low and far,
>   Ere long shall swell from star to star;
>   That light, the breaking day which tips
>   The golden-spired Apocalypse."

IV. Again, I learn from my subject that events which seem to be most insignificant may be momentous. Can you imagine anything more unimportant than the coming of a poor woman from Moab to Judah? Can you imagine anything more trivial than the fact that this Ruth just happened to alight—as they say—just happened to alight on that field of Boaz? Yet all ages, all generations, have an interest in the fact that she was to become an ancestor of the Lord Jesus Christ, and all nations and kingdoms must look at that one little incident with a thrill of unspeakable and eternal satisfaction. So it is in your history and in mine: events that you thought of no importance at all have been of very great moment. That casual conversation, that accidental meeting—you did not think of it again for a long while; but how it changed all the phase of your life!

It seemed to be of no importance that Jubal invented rude instruments of music, calling them harp and organ; but they were the introduction of all the world's minstrelsy; and as you hear the vibration of a stringed instrument, even after the fingers have been taken away from it, so all music now of lute and drum and cornet is only the long-continued strains of Jubal's harp and Jubal's organ. It seemed to be a matter of very little importance that Tubal Cain learned the uses of copper and iron; but that rude foundry of ancient days has its echo in the rattle of Birmingham machinery, and the roar and bang of factories on the Merrimac.

It seemed to be a matter of no importance that Luther found a Bible in a monastery; but as he opened that Bible, and the brass-bound lids fell back, they jarred everything, from the Vatican to the furthest convent in Germany, and the rustling of the wormed leaves was the sound of the wings of the angel of the Reformation. It seemed to be a matter of no importance that a woman, whose name has been forgotten, dropped a tract in the way of a very bad man by the name of Richard Baxter. He picked up the tract and read it, and it was the means of his salvation.

In after-days that man wrote a book called "The Call to the Unconverted," that was the means of bringing a multitude to God, among others Philip Doddridge. Philip Doddridge wrote a book called "The Rise and Progress of Religion," which has brought thousands and tens of thousands into the kingdom of God, and among others the great Wilberforce. Wilberforce wrote a book called "A Practical View of Christianity," which was the means of bringing a great multitude to Christ, among others Legh Richmond. Legh Richmond wrote a tract called "The Dairyman's Daughter," which has been the means of the salvation of unconverted multitudes. And that tide of influence started from the fact that one Christian woman dropped a Christian tract in the way of Richard Baxter— the tide of influence rolling on through Richard Baxter, through Philip Doddridge, through the great Wilberforce, through Legh Richmond, on, on, on, forever, forever. So the insignificant events of this world seem, after all, to be most momentous. The fact that you came up that street or this street seemed to be of no importance to you, and the fact that you went inside of some church may seem to

7

be a matter of very great insignificance to you, but you will find it the turning-point in your history.

V. Again, I see in my subject an illustration of the beauty of female industry.

Behold Ruth toiling in the harvest-field under the hot sun, or at noon taking plain bread with the reapers, or eating the parched corn which Boaz handed to her. The customs of society, of course, have changed, and without the hardships and exposure to which Ruth was subjected, every intelligent woman will find something to do.

I know there is a sickly sentimentality on this subject. In some families there are persons of no practical service to the household or community; and though there are so many woes all around about them in the world, they spend their time languishing over a new pattern, or bursting into tears at midnight over the story of some lover who shot himself! They would not deign to look at Ruth carrying back the barley on her way home to her mother-in-law, Naomi. All this fastidiousness may seem to do very well while they are under the shelter of their father's house; but when the sharp winter of misfortune comes, what of these butterflies? Persons under indulgent parentage may get upon themselves habits of indolence; but when they come out into practical life their soul will recoil with disgust and chagrin. They will feel in their hearts what the poet so severely satirized when he said:

> " Folks are so awkward, things so impolite,
>   They're elegantly pained from morning until night."

Through that gate of indolence how many men and women have marched, useless on earth, to a destroyed eternity! Spinola said to Sir Horace Vere: " Of what did your brother die?" " Of having nothing to do," was the answer. " Ah!" said Spinola, " that's enough to kill any general of us." Oh! can it be possible in this world, where there is so much suffering to be alleviated, so much darkness to be enlightened, and so many burdens to be carried, that there is any person who cannot find anything to do?

Madame de Staël did a world of work in her time; and one day, while she was seated amid instruments of music, all of which she had mastered, and amid manuscript books which she had written, some one said to her: " How do you find time to attend to all these things?" " Oh," she replied, " these are not the things I am proud of. My chief boast is in the fact that I have seventeen trades, by any one of which I could make a livelihood if necessary." And if in secular spheres there is so much to be done, in spiritual work how vast the field! How many dying all around about us without one word of comfort! We want more Abigails, more Hannahs, more Rebeccas, more Marys, more Deborahs consecrated—body, mind, soul—to the Lord who bought them.

VI. Once more I learn from my subject the value of gleaning.

Ruth going into that harvest-field might have said: " There is a straw. and there is a straw, but what is a straw? I can't get any barley for myself or my mother-in-law out of these separate straws." Not so said beautiful Ruth. She gathered two straws, and she put them together, and more straws, until she got enough to make a sheaf. Putting that down, she went and gathered more straws, until she had another sheaf, and another, and another, and another, and then she brought them all together, and she threshed them out, and she had an ephah of barley, nigh a bushel. Oh, that we might all be gleaners!

Elihu Burritt learned many things while toiling in a blacksmith's shop. Abercrombie, the world-renowned philosopher, was a philosopher in Scotland, and he got his philosophy, or the chief part of it, while, as a physician, he was waiting for the door of the sick-room to open. Yet how many there are in this day who say they are so busy they have no time for mental or spiritual improvement; the great duties of life cross the field like strong reapers, and carry off all the hours, and there is only here and there a fragment left, that is not worth gleaning. Ah, my friends, you could go into the busiest day and busiest week of your life and find golden opportunities, which, gathered, might at last make a whole sheaf for the Lord's garner. It is the stray opportunities and the stray privileges which, taken up and bound together and beaten out, will at last fill you with much joy.

There are a few moments left worth the gleaning. Now, Ruth, to the field! May each one have a measure full and running over! Oh, you gleaners, to the field! And if there be in your household an aged one or a sick relative that is not strong enough to come forth and toil in this field, then let Ruth take home to feeble Naomi this sheaf of gleaning: "He that goeth forth and weepeth, bearing precious seed, shall doubtless come again with rejoicing, bringing his sheaves with him." May the Lord God of Ruth and Naomi be our portion forever!

THE THREE RINGS.

"Put a ring on his hand."—LUKE xv: 22.

I WILL not rehearse the familiar story of the fast young man of the parable. You know what a splendid home he left. You know what a hard time he had. And you remember how after that season of vagabondage and prodigality he resolved to go and weep out his sorrows on the bosom of parental forgiveness. Well, there is great excitement one day in front of the door of the old farmhouse. The servants come rushing up and say: " What's the matter? What *is* the matter?" But before they quite arrive, the old man cries out: " Put a ring on his hand." What a seeming absurdity! What can such a wretched mendicant as this fellow that is tramping on toward the house want with a ring? Oh, he is the prodigal son. No more tending of the swine-trough. No more longing for the pods of the carob-tree. No more blistered feet. Off with the rags! On with the robe! Out with the ring! Even so does God receive every one of us when we come back. There are gold rings, and pearl rings, and carnelian rings, and diamond rings; but the richest ring that ever flashed on the vision is that which our Father puts upon a forgiven soul.

I know that the impression is abroad among some peo-

ple that religion bemeans and belittles a man; that it takes
all the sparkle out of his soul; that he has to exchange a
roistering independence for an ecclesiastical strait-jacket.
Not so.   When a man becomes a Christian, he does not go
down, he starts upward.   Religion multiplies one by ten
thousand.   Nay, the multiplier is in infinity.   It is not a
blotting out—it is a polishing, it is an arborescence, it is
an efflorescence, it is an irradiation.   When a man comes
into the kingdom of God he is not sent into a menial service, but the Lord God Almighty from the palaces of
heaven calls upon the messenger angels that wait upon the
throne to fly and "put a ring on his hand."   In Christ are
the largest liberty, and brightest joy, and highest honor,
and richest adornment.   "Put a ring on his hand."

I remark, in the first place, that when Christ receives a
soul into His love, He puts upon him the ring of adoption.   Eight or ten years ago, in my church in Philadelphia, there came the representative of the Howard
Mission of New York.   He brought with him eight or ten
children of the street that he had picked up, and he
was trying to find for them Christian homes; and as the
little ones stood on the pulpit and sung, our hearts melted
within us.   At the close of the services a great-hearted
wealthy man came up and said: "I'll take this little
bright-eyed girl, and I'll adopt her as one of my own
children;" and he took her by the hand, lifted her into his
carriage, and went away.

The next day, while we were in the church gathering up
garments for the poor of New York, this little child came
back with a bundle under her arm, and she said: "There's

my old dress; perhaps some of the poor children would like to have it," while she herself was in bright and beautiful array, and those who more immediately examined her said that she had a ring on her hand. It was a ring of adoption.

There are a great many persons who pride themselves on their ancestry, and they glory over the royal blood that pours through their arteries. In their line there was a lord, or a duke, or a prime minister, or a king. But when the Lord, our Father, puts upon us the ring of His adoption, we become the children of the Ruler of all nations. "Behold what manner of love the Father hath bestowed upon us, that we should be called the sons of God." It matters not how poor our garments may be in this world, or how scant our bread, or how mean the hut we live in, if we have that ring of Christ's adoption upon our hand we are assured of eternal defenses.

Adopted! Why, then, we are brothers and sisters to all the good of earth and heaven. We have the family name, the family dress, the family keys, the family wardrobe. The Father looks after us, robes us, defends us, blesses us. We have royal blood in our veins, and there are crowns in our line. If we are His children, then princes and princesses. It is only a question of time when we get our coronet. Adopted! Then we have the family secrets. "The secret of the Lord is with them that fear Him." Adopted! Then we have the family inheritance, and in the day when our Father shall divide the riches of heaven we shall take our share of the mansions and palaces and temples. Henceforth let us boast no more of an earthly ancestry. The insignia of eternal glory is our coat of arms. This ring of adoption puts upon us all honor and all privilege. Now we can take the words of Charles Wesley, that prince of hymn-makers, and sing:

> "Come, let us join our friends above,
> Who have obtained the prize,
> And on the eagle wings of love
> To joy celestial rise.

> "Let all the saints terrestrial sing
> With those to glory gone;
> For all the servants of our King,
> In heaven and earth, are one."

I have been told that when any of the members of any of the great secret societies of this country are in a distant city and are in any kind of trouble, and are set upon by enemies, they have only to give a certain signal and the members of that organization will flock around for defense. And when any man belongs to this great Christian brotherhood, if he gets in trouble, in trial, in persecution, in temptation, he has only to show this ring of Christ's adoption, and all the armed cohorts of heaven will come to his rescue.

Still further, when Christ takes a soul into His love He puts upon it a marriage-ring. Now, that is not a whim of mine: "And I will betroth thee unto Me forever; yea, I will betroth thee unto Me in righteousness, and in judgment, and in loving-kindness, and in mercies." (Hosea ii: 19.) At the wedding altar the bridegroom puts a ring upon the hand of the bride, signifying love and faithfulness. Trouble may come upon the household, and the carpets may go, the pictures may go, the piano may go, everything else may go—the last thing that goes is that marriage-ring, for it is considered sacred. In the burial hour it is withdrawn from the hand and kept in a casket, and sometimes the box is opened on an anniversary day, and as you look at that ring you see under its arch a long procession of precious memories. Within the golden circle of that ring there is room for a thousand sweet recollections to revolve, and you think of the great contrast between the hour when, at the close of the "Wedding March," under the flashing lights and amid the aroma of orange-blossoms, you set that ring on the round finger of the plump hand, and that other hour when, at the close of the exhaustive watching, when you knew that the soul had fled, you took from the hand, which gave back no responsive clasp, from that emaciated finger, the ring that she had worn so long and worn so well.

On some anniversary day you take up that ring, and you repolish it until all the old luster comes back, and you can see in it the flash of eyes that long ago ceased to weep. Oh, it is not an unmeaning thing when I tell you that when Christ receives a soul into His keeping He puts on it a marriage-ring. He endows you from that moment with all His wealth. You are one—Christ and the soul—one in sympathy, one in affection, one in hope.

There is no power in earth or hell to effect a divorcement after Christ and the soul are united. Other kings have turned out their companions when they got weary of them, and sent them adrift from the palace gate.

Ahasuerus banished Vashti; Napoleon forsook Josephine; but Christ is the husband that is true forever. Having loved you once, He loves you to the end. Did they not try to divorce Margaret, the Scotch girl, from Jesus? They said: "You must give up your religion." She said: "I can't give up my religion." And so they took her down to the beach of the sea, and they drove in a stake at low-water mark, and they fastened her to it, expecting that as the tide came up her faith would fail. The tide began to rise, and came up higher and higher, and to the girdle, and to the lip, and in the last moment, just as the wave was washing her soul into glory, she shouted the praises of Jesus.

Oh, no, you can not separate a soul from Christ! It is an everlasting marriage. Battle and storm and darkness can not do it. Is it too much exultation for a man, who is but dust and ashes like myself, to cry out this morning: "I am persuaded that neither height, nor depth, nor principalities, nor powers, nor things present, nor things to come, nor any other creature shall separate me from the love of God which is in Christ Jesus my Lord"? Glory be to God that when Christ and the soul are married they are bound by a chain, a golden chain—if I might say so—a chain with one link, and that one link the golden ring of God's everlasting love.

I go a step further, and tell you that when Christ receives a soul into His love He puts on him the ring of festivity. You know that it has been the custom in all ages to bestow rings on very happy occasions. There is nothing more appropriate for a birthday gift than a ring.

You delight to bestow such a gift upon your children at such a time. It means joy, hilarity, festivity. Well, when this old man of the text wanted to tell how glad he was that his boy had got back, he expressed it in this way. Actually, before he ordered sandals to be put on his bare feet; before he ordered the fatted calf to be killed to appease the boy's hunger, he commanded: "Put a ring on his hand."

Oh, it is a merry time when Christ and the soul are united! Joy of forgiveness! What a splendid thing it is to feel that all is right between me and God. What a glorious thing it is to have God just take up all the sins of my life and put them in one bundle, and then fling them into the depths of the sea, never to rise again, never to be talked of again. Pollution all gone. Darkness all illumined. God reconciled. The prodigal home. "Put a ring on his hand."

Every day I find happy Christian people. I find some of them with no second coat, some of them in huts and tenement houses, not one earthly comfort afforded them; and yet they are as happy as happy can be. They sing "Rock of Ages" as no other people in the world sing it. They never wore any jewelry in their life but one gold ring, and that was the ring of God's undying affection. Oh, how happy religion makes us! Did it make you gloomy and sad? Did you go with your head cast down? I do not think you got religion, my brother. That is not the effect of religion. True religion is a joy. "Her ways are ways of pleasantness, and all her paths are peace."

Why, religion lightens all our burdens. It smooths all our way. It interprets all our sorrows. It changes the jar of earthly discord for the peal of festal bells. In front of the flaming furnace of trial it sets the forge on which scepters are hammered out. Would you not like to-day to come up from the swine-feeding and try this religion? All the joys of heaven would come out and meet you, and God would cry from the throne: "Put a ring on his hand."

You are not happy. I see it. There is no peace, and sometimes you laugh when you feel a great deal more like crying. The world is a cheat. It first wears you down with its follies, then it kicks you out into darkness. It comes back from the massacre of a million souls to attempt the destruction of your soul to-day. No peace out of God, but here is the fountain that can slake the thirst. Here is the harbor where you can drop safe anchorage.

Would you not like, I ask you—not perfunctorily, but as one brother might talk to another—would you not like to have a pillow of rest to put your head on? And would you not like, when you retire at night, to feel that all is well, whether you wake up to-morrow morning at six o'clock, or sleep the sleep that knows no waking? Would you not like to exchange this awful uncertainty about the future for a glorious assurance of heaven? Accept of the Lord Jesus to-day, and all is well. If on your way home some peril should cross the street and dash your life out, it would not hurt you. You would rise up immediately. You would stand in the celestial streets. You would be amid the great throng that forever worship and are forever happy. If this day some sudden disease should come upon you, it would not frighten you. If you knew you were going you could give a calm farewell to your beautiful home on earth, and know that you are going right into the companionship of those who have already got beyond the toiling and the weeping.

You feel on Saturday night different from the way you feel any other night of the week. You come home from the bank, or the store, or the shop, and you say: "Well, now my week's work is done, and to-morrow is Sunday." It is a pleasant thought. There is refreshment and reconstruction in the very idea. Oh, how pleasant it will be, if, when we get through the day of our life, and we go and lie down in our bed of dust, we can realize: "Well, now the work is all done, and to-morrow is Sunday—an everlasting Sunday."

> " Oh, when, thou city of my God,
>   Shall I thy courts ascend?
>   Where congregations ne'er break up,
>   And Sabbaths have no end."

There are people in this house to-day who are very near the eternal world. If you are Christians, I bid you be of good cheer. Bear with you our congratulations to the bright city. Aged men, who will soon be gone, take with you our love for our kindred in the better land, and when you see them, tell them that we are soon coming. Only a few more sermons to preach and hear. Only a few more heart-aches. Only a few more toils. Only a few more tears. And then—what an entrancing spectacle will open before us!

" Beautiful heaven, where all is light,
Beautiful angels clothed in white,
Beautiful strains that never tire,
Beautiful harps through all the choir;
There shall I join the chorus sweet,
Worshiping at the Saviour's feet."

I stand before you on this Sabbath, the last Sabbath preceding the great feast-day in this Church. On the next Lord's-day the door of communion will be open, and you will all be invited to come in. And so I approach you now with a general invitation, not picking out here and there a man, or here and there a woman, or here and there a child; but giving you an unlimited invitation, saying: " Come, for all things are now ready." We invite you to the warm heart of Christ, and the inclosure of the Christian Church. I know a great many think that the Church does not amount to much—that it is obsolete; that it did its work and is gone now, so far as all usefulness is concerned. It is the happiest place I have ever been in except my own home.

I know there are some people who say they are Christians who seem to get along without any help from others, and who culture solitary piety. They do not want any ordinances. I do not belong to that class. I can not get along without them. There are so many things in this world that take my attention from God, and Christ, and heaven, that I want all the helps of all the symbols and of all the Christian associations; and I want around about me a solid phalanx of men who love God and keep His commandments. Are there any here who would like to enter into that association? Then by a simple, child-like faith, apply for admission into the visible Church, and you will be received. No questions asked about your past history or present surroundings. Only one test—do you love Jesus?

Baptism does not amount to anything, say a great many people; but the Lord Jesus declared, "He that believeth and is baptized shall be saved," putting baptism and faith side by side. And an apostle declares, "Repent and be baptized, every one of you." I do not stickle for any particular mode of baptism, but I put great emphasis on the fact that you ought to be baptized. Yet no more emphasis than the Lord Jesus Christ, the Great Head of the Church, puts upon it.

The world is going to lose a great many of its votaries next Sabbath. We give you warning. There is a great host coming in to stand under the banner of the Lord Jesus Christ. Will you be among them? It is going to be a great harvest-day. Will you be among the gathered sheaves?

Some of you have been thinking on this subject year after year. You have found out that this world is a poor portion. You want to be Christians. You have come almost into the kingdom of God; but there you stop, forgetful of the fact that to be almost saved is not to be saved at all. Oh, my brother, after having come so near to the door of mercy, if you turn back, you will never come at all. After all you have heard of the goodness of God, if you turn away and die, it will not be because you did not have a good offer.

"God's spirit will not always strive
    With hardened, self-destroying man;
Ye who persist His love to grieve
    May never hear his voice again."

May God Almighty this hour move upon your soul and bring you back from the husks of the wilderness to the Father's house, and set you at the banquet, and "put a ring on your hand."

HOW HE CAME TO SAY IT.

"If any man love not the Lord Jesus Christ, let him be Anathema Maranatha."—I Cor. xvi: 22.

THE smallest lad in the house knows the meaning of all those words except the last two, Anathema Maranatha. Anathema, to cut off. Maranatha, at His coming. So the whole passage might be read: "If any man love not the Lord Jesus Christ, let him be cut off at His coming." Well, how could the tender-hearted Paul say that? We have seen him with tears discoursing about human want, and flushed with excitement about human sorrow; and now he throws those red-hot iron words into this letter to the Corinthians. Had he lost his patience? Oh, no. Had he resigned his confidence in the Christian religion? Oh, no. Had the world treated him so badly that he had become its sworn enemy? Oh, no. It needs some explanation, I confess, and I shall proceed to show by what process Paul came to the vehement utterance of my text. Before I close, if God shall give His Spirit, you shall cease to be surprised at the exclamation of the Apostle, and you yourselves will employ the same emphasis, declaring, "If any man love not the Lord Jesus Christ, let him be Anathema Maranatha."

If the photographic art had been discovered early

enough, we should have had the facial proportions of Christ—the front face, the side face, Jesus sitting, Jesus standing—provided He had submitted to that art; but since the sun did not become a portrait painter until eighteen centuries after Christ, our idea about the Saviour's personal appearance is all guess work. Still, tradition tells us that He was the most infinitely beautiful being that ever walked our small earth. If His features had been rugged, and His gait had been ungainly, that would not have hindered Him from being attractive. Many men you have known and loved have had few charms of physiognomy. Wilberforce was not attractive in face. Socrates was repulsive. Suwarrow, the great Russian hero, looked almost an imbecile. And some whom you have known, and honored, and loved, have not had very great attractiveness of personal appearance. The shape of the mouth, and the nose, and the eyebrow, did not hinder the soul from shining through the cuticle of the face in all-powerful irradiation.

But to a lovely exterior Christ joined all loveliness of disposition. Run through the galleries of heaven, and find out that He is *a non-such*. The sunshine of His love mingling with the shadows of His sorrows, crossed by the crystalline stream of His tears and the crimson flowing forth of His blood, make a picture worthy of being called the masterpiece of the eternities. Hung on the wall of heaven, the celestial population would be enchanted but for the fact that they have the grand and magnificent original, and they want no picture. But Christ having gone away from earth, we are dependent upon four indistinct pictures. Matthew took one, Mark another, Luke another, and John another. I care not which picture you take, it is lovely. Lovely? He was altogether lovely.

He had a way of taking up a dropsical limb without hurting it, and of removing the cataract from the eye without the knife, and of starting the circulation through the shrunken arteries without the shock of the electric battery, and of putting intelligence into the dull stare of lunacy, and of restringing the auditory nerve of the deaf ear, and of striking articulation into the stiff tongue, and of making the stark-naked madman dress himself and exchange tombstone for ottoman, and of unlocking from the skeleton grip of death the daughter of Jairus to embosom her in her glad father's arms. Oh, He was lovely—sitting, standing, kneeling, lying down—always lovely.

Lovely in His sacrifice. Why, He gave up everything for us. Home, celestial companionship, music of seraphic harps, balmy breath of eternal summer, all joy, all light, all music, and heard the gates slam shut behind Him as He came out to fight for our freedom, and with bare feet plunged on the sharp javelins of human and satanic hate, until His blood spurted into the faces of those who slew Him. You want the soft, low, minor key of sweetest music to describe the pathos; but it needs an orchestra, under swinging of an archangel's baton, reaching from throne to manger, to drum and trumpet the doxologies of His praise. He took everybody's trouble—the leper's sickness, the widow's dead boy, the harlot's shame, the Galilean fisherman's poor luck, the invalidism of Simon's mother-in-law, the sting of Malchus' amputated ear.

Some people cry very easily, and for some it is very difficult to cry. A great many tears on some cheeks do not mean so much as one tear on another cheek. What is it that I see glittering in the mild eye of Jesus? It was all the sorrows of earth, and the woes of hell, from which He had plucked our souls, accreted into one transparent drop, lingering on the lower eyelash until it fell on a cheek red with the slap of human hands—just one salt, bitter, burning tear of Jesus. No wonder the rock, the sky, and the cemetery were in consternation when He died! No wonder the universe was convulsed! It was the Lord God Almighty bursting into tears. Now, suppose that, notwithstanding all this, a man can not have any affection for Him. What ought to be done with such hard behavior?

It seems to me that there ought to be some chastisement for a man who will not love such a Christ. Does it not make your blood tingle to think of Jesus coming over the tens of thousands of miles that seem to separate God from us, and then to see a man jostle Him out, and push Him back, and shut the door in His face, and trample upon His entreaties? While you may not be able to rise up to the towering excitement of the Apostle in my text, you can at any rate somewhat understand his feelings when he cried out: "After all this, 'if a man love not the Lord Jesus Christ, let him be Anathema Maranatha.'"

Just look at the injustice of not loving Him. Now, there is nothing that excites a man like injustice. You go along the street, and you see your little child buffeted, or a ruffian comes and takes a boy's hat and throws it into the ditch. You say: "What great meanness, what injustice

that is!" You can not stand injustice. I remember, in
my boyhood days, attending a large meeting in Tripler
Hall, New York. Thousands of people were huzzaing,
and the same kind of audiences were assembled at the
same time in Boston, Edinburgh, and London. Why?
Because the Madaii family, in Italy, had been robbed of
their Bible. "A little thing," you say. Ah, that injustice was enough to arouse the indignation of a world. But
while we are so sensitive about injustice as between man
and man, how little sensitive we are about injustice between man and God. If there ever was a fair and square
purchase of anything, then Christ purchased us. He paid
for us, not in shekels, not in ancient coins inscribed with
effigies of Hercules, or Ægina's tortoise, or lyre of Mity-
lene, but in two kinds of coin—one red, the other glittering—blood and tears! If anything is purchased and paid
for, ought not the goods to be delivered? If you have
bought property and given the money, do you not want to
come into possession of it? "Yes," you say, "I will have
it. I bought and paid for it." And you will go to law
for it, and you will denounce the man as a defrauder.
Ay, if need be, you will hurl him into jail. You will say:
"I am bound to get that property. I bought it. I paid
for it!"

Now, transpose the case. Suppose Jesus Christ to be
the wronged purchaser on the one side, and the impenitent
soul on the other, trying to defraud Him of that which
He bought at such an exorbitant price, how do you feel
about that injustice? How do you feel toward that
spiritual fraud, turpitude and perfidy? A man with an

ardent temperament rises and he says that such injustice as between man and man is bad enough, but between man and God it is reprehensible and intolerable, and he brings his fist down on the pew, and he says: "I can stand this injustice no longer. After all this purchase, 'if any man love not the Lord Jesus Christ, let him be Anathema Maranatha'!"

I go still further, and show you how suicidal it is for a man not to love Christ. If a man gets in trouble, and he can not get out, we have only one feeling toward him—sympathy and a desire to help him. If he has failed for a vast amount of money, and can not pay more than ten cents on a dollar—ay, if he can not pay anything—though his creditors may come after him like a pack of hounds, we sympathize with him. We go to his store, or house, and we express our condolence. But suppose the day before that man failed, William E. Dodge had come into his store and said: "My friend, I hear you are in trouble. I have come to help you. If ten thousand dollars will see you through your perplexity, I have a loan of that amount for you. Here is a check for the amount of that loan." Suppose the man said: "With that ten thousand dollars I could get through until next spring, and then everything will be all right; but, Mr. Dodge, I don't want it; I won't take it; I would rather fail than take it; I don't even thank you for offering it." Your sympathy for that man would cease immediately. You would say: "He had a fair offer; he might have got out; he wants to fail; he refuses all help; now let him fail." There is no one in all this house who would have any sympathy for that man.

But do not let us be too hasty. Christ hears of our spiritual embarrassments. He finds that we are on the very verge of eternal defalcation. He finds the law knocking at our door with this dun: "Pay me what thou owest."

We do not know which way to turn. Pay? We can not pay a farthing of all the millions of obligation. Well, Christ comes in and says: "Here is My name; you can use My name. Your name would be worthless, but My red handwriting on the back of this obligation will get you through anywhere." Now suppose the soul says: "I know I am in debt; I can't meet these obligations either in time or eternity; but, oh, Christ, I want not Thy help; I ask not Thy rescue. Go away from me." You would say: "That man, why, he deserves to die. He had the offer of help; he would not take it. He is a free agent; he ought to have what he wants; he chooses death rather than life. Ought you not give him freedom of choice?" Though awhile ago there was only one ardent man who understood the Apostle, now there are hundreds in the house who can say, and do say within themselves: "After all this ingratitude, and rejection, and obstinacy, 'if any man love not the Lord Jesus Christ, let him be Anathema Maranatha.'"

I go a step further, and say it is most cruel for a man not to love Jesus. The meanest thing I could do for you would be needlessly to hurt your feelings. Sharp words sometimes cut like a dagger. An unkind look will sometimes rive like the lightning. An unkind deed may overmaster a sensitive spirit, and if you have made up your

mind that you have done wrong to any one, it does not
take you two minutes to make up your mind to go and
apologize. Now, Christ is a bundle of delicacy and sensitiveness. How you have shocked His nerves! How you
have broken His heart!

Did you, my brother, ever measure the meaning of that
one passage: " Behold, I stand at the door and knock "?
It never came to me as it did this morning while I was
thinking on this subject. " Behold, I stand at the door
and knock." Some January day, the thermometer five
degrees below zero, the wind and sleet beating mercilessly
against you, you go up the steps of a house where you have
a very important errand. You knock with one knuckle.
No answer. You are very earnest, and you are freezing.
The next time you knock harder. After awhile with your
fist you beat against the door. You must get in, but the
inmate is careless or stubborn, and he does not want you
in. Your errand is a failure. You go away.

The Lord Jesus Christ comes up on the steps of your
heart, and with very sore hand he knocks hard at the door
of your soul. He is standing in the cold blasts of human
suffering. He knocks. He says: " Let me in. I have
come a great way. I have come all the way from Nazareth, from Bethlehem, from Golgotha. Let Me in. I am
shivering and blue with the cold. Let Me in. My feet
are bare but for their covering of blood. My head is uncovered but for a turban of brambles. By all these
wounds of foot, and head, and heart, I beg you to let Me
in. Oh, I have been here a great while, and the night is
getting darker. I am faint with hunger. I am dying to

get in. Oh, lift the latch—shove back the bolt! Won't you let Me in? Won't you? ' Behold, I stand at the door and knock!' "

But after awhile, my brother, the scene will change. It will be another door, but Christ will be on the other side of it. He will be on the inside, and the rejected sinner will be on the outside, and the sinner will come up and knock at the door, and say: " Let me in, let me in. I have come a great way. I came all the way from earth. I am sick and dying. Let me in. The merciless storm beats my unsheltered head. The wolves of a great night are on my track. Let me in. With both fists I beat against this door. Oh, let me in. Oh, Christ, let me in. Oh, Holy Ghost, let me in. Oh, God, let me in. Oh, my glorified kindred, let me in." No answer save the voice of Christ, who shall say: " Sinner, when I stood at your door you would not let Me in, and now you are standing at My door, and I can not let you in. The day of your grace is past. Officer of the law, seize him." And while the arrest is going on, all the myriads of heaven rise on gallery and throne, and cry with loud voice, that makes the eternal city quake from capstone to foundation, saying: " If any man love not the Lord Jesus Christ, let him be Anathema Maranatha."

Sabbath audience in the Brooklyn Tabernacle, and all to whom these words shall come on both sides the sea, notice here the tremendous alternative: it is not whether you live in Pierrepont Street or Carlton Avenue, walk Trafalgar Square or the " Canongate;" nor whether your dress shall be black or brown; nor whether you shall be robust or an invalid; nor whether you shall live on the banks of the Hudson, the Shannon, the Seine, the Thames, the Tiber; but it is a question whether you will love Christ or suffer banishment; whether you will give yourselves to Him who owns you or fall under the mill-stone; whether you will rise to glories that have no terminus or plunge to a depth which has no bottom. I do not see how you can take the ten-thousandth part of a second to decide it, when there are two worlds fastened at opposite ends of a swivel, and the swivel turns on one point, and that point is now, now. Is it not fair that you love Him? Is it not right that you love Him? Is it not imperative that you love Him? What is it that keeps you from rushing up and throwing the arms of your affection about His neck?

My text pronounces Anathema Maranatha upon all those who refuse to love Christ. Anathema—cut off. Cut off from light, from hope, from peace, from heaven. Oh, sharp, keen, sword-like words! Cut off! Everlastingly cut off! Behold, therefore, the goodness and severity of God: on them which fell, severity; but toward thee, goodness, if thou continue in His goodness; otherwise thou also shalt be cut off. Maranatha—that is the other word. "When he comes" is the meaning of it.

Will He come? I see no signs of it. I looked into the sky as I rode down to church. I saw no signs of the coming. No signal of God's appearance. The earth stands solid on its foundation. No cry of welcome or of woe. Will He come! He will. Maranatha! Hear it ye mountains, and prepare to fall. Ye cities, and prepare to burn. Ye righteous, and prepare to reign. Ye wicked, and prepare to die. Maranatha! Maranatha!

But, oh, my brother, I am not so aroused by that coming as I am by a previous coming, and that is the coming of our death hour, which will fix everything for us. I can not help now, while preaching, asking myself the question —Am I ready for that? If I am ready for the first I will be ready for the next. Are you ready for the emergency? Shall I tell you when your death hour will come? "Oh, no," says some one, "I don't want to know. I would rather not know." Some one says: "I would rather know, if you can tell me." I will tell you. It will be at the most unexpected moment, when you are most busy, and when you think you can be least spared. I can not exactly say whether it will be in the noon, or at the sun-down when people are coming home, or in the morning when the world is waking up, or while the clock is striking twelve at night. But I tell you what I think, that with some of you it will be before next Saturday night.

A minister of the Gospel said to an audience: "Before next Sabbath some of you will be gone." And a man said during the week: "I shall watch now, and if no one dies in our congregation during this week I shall go and tell the minister his falsehood." A man standing next to him said: "Why, it may be yourself." "Oh, no," he replied; "I shall live on to be an old man." That night he breathed his last.

Standing before some who shall be launched into the great eternity, what are your equipments? About to jump, where will you land? Oh, the subject is overwhelming to me; and when I say these things to you, I say them to myself. "Lord, is it I? Is it I?" Some of us part to-night never to meet again. If never before, I now here commit my soul into the keeping of the Lord Jesus Christ. I throw my sinful heart upon His infinite mercy. But some of you will not do that. You will go over to the store to-morrow, and your comrades will say: "Where were you yesterday?" You will say: "I heard Talmage preach, and I don't believe what he preaches." And you will go on and die in your sins.

Feeling that you are bound unto death eternal I solemnly take leave of you. Be careful of your health, for when your respiration gives out all your good times will have ended. Be careful in walking near a scaffold, for one falling brick or stone might usher you into the great eternity for which you have no preparation. A few months, or weeks, or days, or hours will pass on, and then you will see the last light, and hear the last music, and have the last pleasant emotion, and a destroyed eternity will rush upon you. Farewell, oh, doomed spirit! As you shove off from hope, I wave you this last salutation. Oh, it is hard to part forever and forever! I bid you one long, last, bitter, eternal adieu!

CASTLE JESUS.

" Who have fled for refuge."—HEB. vi: 18.

PAUL is here speaking of the consolations of Christians. He styles them these " who have fled for refuge."

Moses established six cities of refuge—three on the east side of the river Jordan, and three on the west. When a man had killed any one accidentally he fled to one of these cities. The roads leading to them were kept perfectly good, so that when a man started for the refuge nothing might impede him. Along the cross-roads, and wherever there might be any mistake about the way, there were signs put up pointing in the right way, with the word " Refuge." Having gained the limits of one of these cities the man was safe, and the mothers of the priests provided for him.

Some of us have seen our peril, and have fled to Christ, and feel that we shall never be captured. We are among those " who have fled for refuge." Christ is represented in the Bible as a Tower, a High Rock, a Fortress, and a Shelter. If you have seen any of the ancient castles of Europe, you know that they are surrounded by trenches, across which there is a draw-bridge. If an enemy approach, the people, for defense, would get into the castle, have the trenches filled with water, and lift up the draw

(221)

bridge. Whether to a city of safety, or a tower, Paul refers, I know not, and care not, for in any case he means Christ, the safety of the soul.

But why talk of refuge? Who needs it, if the refuge spoken of be a city or a castle, into which men fly for safety? It is all sunlight here. No sound of war in our streets. We do not hear the rush of armed men against the doors of our dwellings. We do not come with weapons to church. Our lives are not at the mercy of an assassin. Why, then, talk of refuge?

Alas! I stand before a company of imperiled men. No flock of sheep was ever so threatened or endangered of a pack of wolves; no ship was ever so beaten of a storm; no company of men were ever so environed of a band of savages. A refuge you must have, or fall before an all-devouring destruction. There are not so many serpents in Africa; there are not so many hyenas in Asia; there are not so many panthers in the forest, as there are transgressions attacking my soul. I will take the best unregenerated man anywhere, and say to him, You are utterly corrupt. If all the sins of your past life were marshaled in single file, they would reach from here to hell. If you have escaped all other sins, the fact that you have rejected the mission of the Son of God is enough to condemn you forever, pushing you off into bottomless darkness, struck by ten thousand hissing thunder-bolts of Omnipotent wrath.

You are a sinner. The Bible says it, and your conscience affirms it. Not a small sinner, or a moderate sinner, or a tolerable sinner, but a great sinner, a protracted sinner, a vile sinner, an outrageous sinner, a condemned

sinner.   As God, with His all-scrutinizing gaze, looks
upon you to-day, He can not find one sound spot in your
soul. Sin has put scales on your eyes, and deadened your
ear with an awful deafness, and palsied your right arm,
and stunned your sensibilities, and blasted you with an infinite blasting. The Bible, which you admit to be true,
affirms that you are diseased from the crown of your head
to the sole of your foot. You are unclean; you are a leper.
Believe not me, but believe God's Word, that over and
over again announces, in language that a fool might understand, the total and complete depravity of the un-
changed heart: " The heart is deceitful above all things,
and desperately wicked."

In addition to the sins of your life there are uncounted
troubles in pursuit of you. Bereavements, losses, disap-
pointments are a flock of vultures ever on the wing. Did
you get your house built, and furnished, and made comfortable any sooner than misfortune came in without
knocking, and sat beside you — a skeleton apparition?
Have not pains shot their poisoned arrows, and fevers
kindled their fire in your brain? Many of you, for years,
have walked on burning marl. You stepped out of one
disaster into another. You may, like Job, have cursed the
day in which you were born. This world boils over with
trouble for you, and you are wondering where the next
grave will gape, and where the next storm will burst. Oh,
ye pursued, sinning, dying, troubled, exhausted souls, are
you not ready now to hear me while I tell you of Christ,
the Refuge?

A soldier, during the war, heard of the sickness of his

wife and asked for a furlough.   It was denied him, and he
ran away.   He was caught, brought back, and sentenced
to be shot as a deserter.   The officer took from his pocket
a document that announced his death on the following
morning.   As the document was read, the man flinched
not and showed no sorrow or anxiety.   But the officer then
took from his pocket another document that contained the
prisoner's pardon.   Then he broke down with deep emotion at the thought of the leniency that had been extended.
Though you may not appear moved while I tell you of
the law that thundered its condemnation, while I tell you
of the pardon and the peace of the Gospel I wonder if they
will not overcome you.

Jesus is a safe refuge.   Fort Hudson, Fort Pulaski, Fort
Moultrie, Fort Sumter, Gibraltar, Sebastopol were taken.
But Jesus is a castle into which the righteous runneth and
is safe.   No battering-ram can demolish its wall.   No
sappers or miners can explode its ramparts, no storm-bolt
of perdition leap upon its towers.   The weapons that guard
this fort are omnipotent.   Hell shall unlimber its great
guns as death only to have them dismantled.   In Christ
our sins are pardoned, discomforted, blotted out, forgiven.
An ocean can not so easily drown a fly as the ocean of
God's forgiveness swallow up, utterly and forever, our
transgressions.   He is able to save unto the uttermost.

You who have been so often overcome in a hand-to-hand
fight with the world, the flesh, and devil, try this fortress.
Once here, you are safe forever.   Satan may charge up the
steep, and shout amid the uproar of the fight, Forward, to
his battalions of darkness; but you will stand in the might

of the great God, your Redeemer, safe in the refuge. The troubles of life, that once overwhelmed you, may come on with their long wagon-trains laden with care and worryment; and you may hear in their tramp the bereavements that once broke your heart; but Christ is your friend, Christ your sympathizer, Christ your reward. Safe in the refuge!

Death at last may lay the siege to your spirit, and the shadows of the sepulcher may shake their horrors in the breeze, and the hoarse howl of the night wind may be mingled with the cry of despair, yet you will shout in triumph from the ramparts, and the pale horse shall be hurled back on his haunches. Safe in the refuge! To this castle I fly. This last fire shall but illumine its towers; and the rolling thunders of the judgment will be the salvo of its victory.

Just after Queen Victoria had been crowned—she being only nineteen or twenty years of age—Wellington handed her a death-warrant for her signature. It was to take the life of a soldier in the army. She said to Wellington: "Can there nothing good be said of this man?" He said: "No; he is a bad soldier, and deserves to die." She took up the death-warrant, and it trembled in her hand as she again asked: "Does no one know anything good of this man?" Wellington said: "I have heard that at his trial a man said that he had been a good son to his old mother." "Then let his life be spared," said the queen, and she ordered his sentence commuted.

Christ is on a throne of grace. Our case is brought before him. The question is asked: "Is there any good

8

about this man?" The law says: "None." Justice says: "None." Our own conscience says: "None." Nevertheless, Christ hands over our pardon, and asks us to take it. Oh, the height and depth, the length and breadth of his mercy!

Again, Christ is a near refuge. When we are attacked, what advantage is there in having a fortress on the other side of the mountain? Many an army has had an intrenchment, but could not get to it before the battle opened. Blessed be God, it is no long march to our castle. We may get off, with all our troops, from the worst earthly defeat in this stronghold. In a moment we may step from the battle into the tower. I sing of a Saviour near.

During the late war the forts of the North were named after the Northern generals, and the forts of the South were named after the Southern generals. This fortress of our soul I shall call Castle Jesus. I have seen men pursued of sins that chased them with feet of lightning, and yet with one glad leap they bounded into the tower. I have seen troubles, with more than the speed and terror of a cavalry troop, dash after a retreating soul, yet were hurled back in defeat from the bulwarks. Jesus near! A child's cry, a prisoner's prayer, a sailor's death-shriek, a pauper's moan reaches him. No pilgrimages on spikes. No journeying with a huge pack on your back. No kneeling in penance in cold vestibule of mercy. But an open door! A compassionate Saviour! A present salvation! A near refuge! Castle Jesus!

Oh, why do you not put out your arm and reach it? Why do you not fly to it? Why be riddled, and shelled, and consumed under the rattling bombardment of perdition, when one moment's faith would plant you in the glorious refuge? I preach a Jesus here; a Jesus now; a fountain close to your feet; a fiery pillar right over your head; bread already broken for your hunger; a crown already gleaming for your brow. Hark to the castle gates rattling back for your entrance! Hear you not the welcome of those who have fled for refuge to lay hold upon the hope set before us?

Again, it is a universal refuge. A fortress is seldom large enough to hold a whole army. I look out upon fourteen hundred millions of the race; and then I look at this fortress, and I say that there is room enough for all. If it had been possible, this salvation would have been monopolized. Men would have said: " Let us have all this to ourselves —no publicans, no plebeians, no lazzaroni, no converted pickpockets. We will ride toward heaven on fierce chargers, our feet in golden stirrups. Grace for lords, and dukes, and duchesses, and counts. Let Napoleon and his marshals come in, but not the common soldier that fought under him. Let the Girards and the Barings come in, but not the stevedores that unloaded their cargoes, or the men who kept their books." Heaven would have been a glorified Windsor Castle, or Tuileries, or Vatican; and exclusive aristocrats would have strutted through the golden streets to all eternity.

Thank God, there is mercy for the poor! The great Doctor John Mason preached over a hundred times the same sermon; and the text was: " To the poor the Gospel is preached." Lazarus went up, while Dives went down; and there are candidates for Imperial splendors in the back alley, and by the peat-fire of the Irish shanty. King Jesus set up His throne in a manger, and made a resurrection day for the poor widow of Nain, and sprung the gate of heaven wide open, so that all the beggars, and thieves, and scoundrels of the universe may come in if they will only repent. I can snatch the knife from the murderer's hand while it is yet dripping with the blood of his victim, and tell him of the grace that is sufficient to pardon his soul. Do you say that I swing open the gate of heaven too far? I swing it open no wider than Christ, when He says: "Whosoever will, let him come." Don't you want to go in with such a rabble? Then you can stay out.

The whole world will yet come into this refuge. The windows of heaven will be opened; God's trumpet of salvation will sound, and China will come from its tea-fields and rice-harvests, and lift itself up into the light. India will come forth, the chariots of salvation jostling to pieces her Juggernauts. Freezing Greenland, and sweltering Abyssinia, will, side by side, press into the kingdom; and transformed Bornesian cannibal preach of the resurrection of the missionary he has slain. The glory of Calvary will tinge the tip of the Pyrenees; and Lebanon cedars shall clap their hands; and by one swing of the sickle Christ shall harvest nations for the skies.

I sing a world redeemed. In the rush of the winds that set the forest in motion, like giants wrestling on the hills, I see the tossing up of the triumphal branches that shall wave all along the line of our King as He comes to take empire. In the stormy diapason of the ocean's organ, and the more gentle strains that in the calm come sounding up from the crystal and jasper keys at the beach, I hear the prophecy: "The earth shall be filled with the knowledge of God as the waters fill the sea."

The gospel morning will come like the natural morning. At first it seems only like another hue of the night. Then a pallor strikes through the sky, as though a company of ministering spirits, pale with tedious watching through the night, had turned in their flight upward to look back upon the earth. Then a faint glow of fire, as though on a barren beach a wrecked mariner was kindling a flickering flame. Then chariots and horses of fire racing up and down the heavens; then perfect day: "Who is she that cometh forth as the morning?"

Come in, black Hottentot and snow-white Caucasian, come in, mitered official and diseased beggar; let all the world come in. Room in Castle Jesus! Sound it through all lands; sound it by all tongues. Let sermons preach it, and bells chime it, and pencils sketch it, and processions celebrate it, and bells ring it: Room in Castle Jesus!

Again, Christ is the only refuge. If you were very sick, and there was only one medicine that would cure you, how anxious you would be to get that medicine. If you were in a storm at sea, and you found that the ship could not weather it, and there was only one harbor, how anxious you would be to get into that harbor. Oh, sin-sick soul, Christ is the only medicine; oh, storm-tossed soul, Christ is the only harbor. Need I tell a cultured audience like this that there is no other name given among men by which ye can be saved? That if you want the handcuffs knocked from your wrists, and the hopples from your feet, and the icy bands from your heart, there is just one Almighty arm in all the universe to do everything? There are other fortresses to which you might fly, and other ramparts behind which you might hide, but God will cut to pieces, with the hail of His vengeance, all these refuges of lies.

Some of you are foundering in terrible Euroclydon. Hark to the howling of the gale, and the splintering of the spars, and the starting of the timbers, and the breaking of the billow, clear across the hurricane deck. Down she goes! Into the life-boat! Quick! One boat! One shore! One oarsman! One salvation! You are polluted; there is but one well at which you can wash clean. You are enslaved; there is but one proclamation that can emancipate. You are blind; there is but one salve that can kindle your vision. You are dead; there is but one trumpet that can burst the grave.

I have seen men come near the refuge but not make entrance. They came up, and fronted the gate, and looked in, but passed on, and passed down; and they will curse their folly through all eternity, that they despised the only refuge. Oh! forget everything else I have said, if you will but remember that there is but one atonement, one sacrifice, one justification, one faith, one hope, one Jesus, one refuge. There is that old Christian. Many a scar on his face tells where trouble lacerated him. He has fought with wild beasts at Ephesus. He has had enough misfortune to shadow his countenance with perpetual despair.

Yet he is full of hope. Has he found any new elixir? "No," he says; "I have found Jesus the refuge."

Christ is our only defense at the last. John Holland, in his concluding moment, swept his hand over the Bible, and said: "Come, let us gather a few flowers from this garden." As it was even-time he said to his wife: "Have you lighted the candles?" "No," she said; "we have not lighted the candles." "Then," said he, "it must be the brightness of the face of Jesus that I see."

Ask that dying Christian woman the source of her comfort. Why that supernatural glow on the curtains of the death-chamber; and the tossing out of one hand, as if to wave the triumph, and the reaching up of the other, as if to take a crown? Hosanna on the tongue. Glory beaming from the forehead. Heaven in the eyes. Spirit departing. Wings to bear it. Anthems to charm it. Open the gates to receive it. Hallelujah! Speak, dying Christian—what light do you see? What sounds do you hear? The thin lips part. The pale hand is lifted. She says: "Jesus the refuge!" Let all in the death-chamber stop weeping now. Celebrate the triumph. Take up a song. Clap your hands. Shout it. Hallelujah! Hallelujah!

But this refuge will be of no worth to you unless you lay hold of it. The time will come when you will wish that you had done so. It will come soon. At an unexpected moment it will come. The castle bridge will be drawn up and the fortress closed. When you see this discomfiture, and look back, and look up at the storm gathering, and the billowy darkness of death has rolled upon the sheeted flash of the storm, you will discover the utter desolation of those who are outside of the refuge.

What you propose to do in this matter you had better do right away. A mistake this morning may never be corrected. Jesus, the Great Captain of salvation, puts forth his wounded hand to-day to cheer you on the race to heaven. If you despise it, the ghastliest vision that will haunt the eternal darkness of your soul will be the gaping, bleeding wounds of the dying Redeemer.

Jesus is to be crucified to-day. Think not of it as a day that is past. He comes before you to-day weary and worn. Here is the cross, and here is the victim. But there are no nails, and there are no thorns, and there are no hammers. Who will furnish these? A man out yonder says: "I will furnish with my sins the nails!" Now we have the cross, and the victim, and the nails. But we have no thorns. Who will furnish the thorns? A man in the audience says: "With my sins I will furnish the thorns!" Now we have the cross, the victim, the nails, and the thorns. But we have no hammers. Who will furnish the hammers? A voice in the audience says: "My hard heart shall be the hammer!" Everything is ready now. The crucifixion goes out! See Jesus dying! "Behold the Lamb of God, that taketh away the sins of the world."

STRIPPING THE SLAIN.

"And it came to pass on the morrow, when the Philistines came to strip the slain, that they found Saul and his three sons fallen in Mount Gilboa."—I. SAM. xxxi: 8.

SOME of you were at South Mountain, or Shiloh, or Ball's Bluff, or Gettysburg, and I ask you if there is any sadder sight than a battle-field after the guns have stopped firing? I walked across the field of Antietam just after the conflict. The scene was so sickening I shall not describe it. Every valuable thing had been taken from the bodies of the dead, for there are always vultures hovering over and around about an army, and they pick up the watches, and the memorandum books, and the letters, and the daguerreotypes, and the hats, and the coats, applying them to their own uses. The dead make no resistance. So there are always camp followers going on and after an army, as when Scott went down into Mexico, as when Napoleon marched up toward Moscow, as when Von Moltke went to Sedan. There is a similar scene in my text.

Saul and his army had been horribly cut to pieces. Mount Gilboa was ghastly with the dead. On the morrow the stragglers came on to the field, and they lifted the latchet of the helmet from under the chin of the dead, and they picked up the swords and bent them on their knee to test the temper of the metal, and they opened the wallets and counted the coin. Saul lay dead along the ground, eight or nine feet in length, and I suppose the cowardly Philistines, to show their bravery, leaped upon the trunk of his carcass, and jeered at the fallen slain, and whistled through the mouth of the helmet. Before night those cormorants had taken everything valuable from the field: "And it came to pass on the morrow, when the Philistines came to strip the slain, that they found Saul and his three sons fallen in Mount Gilboa."

Before I get through to-day I will show you that the same process is going on all the world over, and every day, and that when men have fallen, Satan and the world, so far from pitying them or helping them, go to work remorselessly to take what little is left, thus stripping the slain.

There are tens of thousands of young men every year coming from the country to our great cities. They come with brave hearts and grand expectations. They think they will be Rufus Choates in the law, or Drapers in chemistry, or A. T. Stewarts in merchandise. The country lads sit down in the village grocery, with their feet on the iron rod around the red-hot stove, in the evening, talking over the prospects of the young man who has gone off to the city. Two or three of them think that perhaps he may get along very well and succeed, but the most of them prophesy failure; for it is very hard to think that those whom we knew in boyhood will ever make any stir in the world.

But our young man has a fine position in a dry-goods store. The month is over. He gets his wages. He is not accustomed to have so much money belonging to himself. He is a little excited, and does not know exactly what to do with it, and he spends it in some places where he ought not. Soon there come up new companions and acquaintances from the bar-rooms and the saloons of the city. Soon that young man begins to waver in the battle of temptation, and soon his soul goes down. In a few months, or few years, he has fallen. He is morally dead. He is a mere corpse of what he once was. The harpies of sin snuff up the taint and come on the field. His garments gradually give out. He has pawned his watch. His health is failing him. His credit perishes. He is too poor to stay in the city, and he is too poor to pay his way home to the country. Down! down! Why do the low fellows of the city now stick to him so closely? Is it to help him back to a moral and spiritual life? Oh, no! I will tell you why they stay; they are the Philistines stripping the slain.

Do not look where I point, but yonder stands a man who once had a beautiful home in this city. His house had elegant furniture, his children were beautifully clad, his name was synonymous with honor and usefulness; but evil habit knocked at his front door, knocked at his back door, knocked at his parlor door, knocked at his bedroom door. Where is the piano? Sold to pay the rent. Where is the hat-rack? Sold to meet the butcher's bill. Where are the carpets? Sold to get bread. Where is the wardrobe? Sold to get rum. Where are the daughters? Working their fingers off in trying to keep the family together. Worse and worse, until everything is gone. Who is that going up the front steps of that house? That is a creditor, hoping to find some chair or bed that has not been levied upon. Who are those two gentlemen now going up the front steps? The one is a constable, the other is the sheriff. Why do they go there? The unfortunate is morally dead, socially dead, financially dead. Why do they go there? I will tell you why the creditors, and the constables, and the sheriffs go there. They are, some on their own account, and some on account of the law, stripping the slain.

An ex-member of Congress, one of the most eloquent men that ever stood in the House of Representatives, said in his last moments: "This is the end. I am dying—dying on a borrowed bed, covered by a borrowed sheet, in a house built by public charity. Bury me under that tree in the middle of the field, where I shall not be crowded, for I have been crowded all my life." Where were the jolly politicians and the dissipating comrades who had been with him, laughing at his jokes, applauding his eloquence, and plunging him into sin? They have left. Why? His money is gone, his reputation is gone, his wit is gone, his clothes are gone, everything is gone. Why should they stay any longer? They have completed their work. They have stripped the slain.

There is another way, however, of doing that same work. Here is a man who, through his sin, is prostrate. He acknowledges that he has done wrong. Now is the time for you to go to that man and say: "Thousands of

people have been as far astray as you are, and got back."
Now is the time for you to go to that man and tell him of
the omnipotent grace of God, that is sufficient for any
poor soul. Now is the time to go to tell him how swearing John Bunyan, through the grace of God, afterward
came to the celestial city. Now is the time to go to that
man and tell him how profligate Newton came, through
conversion, to be a world-renowned preacher of righteousness. Now is the time to tell that man that multitudes
who have been pounded with all the flails of sin and
dragged through all the sewers of pollution at last have
risen to positive dominion of moral power.

You do not tell him that, do you? No. You say to
him: " Loan you money? No. You are down. You
will have to go to the dogs. Lend you a shilling? I
would not lend you five cents to keep you from the gallows. You are debauched! Get out of my sight, now!
Down; you will have to stay down!" And thus those
bruised and battered men are sometimes accosted by those
who ought to lift them up. Thus the last vestige of hope
is taken from them. Thus those who ought to go and lift
and save them are guilty of stripping the slain.

The point I want to make is this: sin is hard, cruel, and
merciless. Instead of helping a man up it helps him
down; and when, like Saul and his comrades, you lie on
the field, it will come and steal your sword and helmet and
shield, leaving you to the jackal and the crow.

But the world and Satan do not do all their work with
the outcast and abandoned. A respectable, impenitent
man comes to die. He is flat on his back. He could not

get up if the house were on fire. Adroitest medical skill and gentlest nursing have been a failure. He has come to his last hour. What does Satan do for such a man? Why, he fetches up all the inapt, disagreeable, and harrowing things in his life. He says: "Do you remember those chances you had for heaven, and missed them? Do you remember all those lapses in conduct? Do you remember all those opprobrious words and thoughts and actions? Don't remember them, eh? I'll make you remember them." And then he takes all the past and empties it on that death-bed, as the mail-bags are emptied on the post-office floor. The man is sick. He can not get away from them.

Then the man says to Satan: "You have deceived me. You told me that all would be well. You said there would be no trouble at the last. You told me if I did so and so, you would do so and so. Now you corner me, and hedge me up, and submerge me in everything evil." "Ha! ha!" says Satan, "I was only fooling you. It is mirth for me to see you suffer. I have been for thirty years plotting to get you just where you are. It is hard for you now—it will be worse for you after awhile. It pleases me. Lie still, sir. Don't flinch or shudder. Come now, I will tear off from you the last rag of expectation. I will rend away from your soul the last hope. I will leave you bare for the beating of the storm. It is my business to strip the slain."

While men are in robust health, and their digestion is good, and their nerves are strong, they think their physical strength will get them safely through the last exigency.

They say it is only cowardly women who are afraid at the last, and cry out for God. "Wait till I come to die. I will show you. You won't hear me pray, nor call for a minister, nor want a chapter read me from the Bible." But after the man has been three weeks in a sick-room his nerves are not so steady, and his worldly companions are not anywhere near to cheer him up, and he is persuaded that he must quit life: his physical courage is all gone.

He jumps at the fall of a teaspoon in a saucer. He shivers at the idea of going away. He says: "Wife, I don't think my infidelity is going to take me through. For God's sake don't bring up the children to do as I have done. If you feel like it, I wish you would read a verse or two out of Fannie's Sabbath-school hymn-book or New Testament." But Satan breaks in, and says: "You have always thought religion trash and a lie; don't give up at the last. Besides that, you can not, in the hour you have to live, get off on that track. Die as you lived. With my great black wings I shut out that light. Die in darkness. I rend away from you that last vestige of hope. It is my business to strip the slain."

A man who had rejected Christianity and thought it all trash, came to die. He was in the sweat of a great agony, and his wife said: "We had better have some prayer." "Mary, not a breath of that," he said. "The lightest word of prayer would roll back on me like rocks on a drowning man. I have come to the hour of test. I had a chance, and I forfeited it. I believed in a liar, and he has left me in the lurch. Mary, bring me Tom Paine, that book that I swore by and lived by, and pitch it in the fire,

and let it burn and burn as I myself shall soon burn."
And then, with the foam on his lip and his hands tossing
wildly in the air, he cried out: "Blackness of darkness!
Oh, my God, too late!" And the spirits of darkness
whistled up from the depth, and wheeled around and
around him, stripping the slain.

Sin is a luxury now; it is exhilaration now; it is victory
now. But after awhile it is collision; it is defeat; it is ex-
termination; it is jackalism; it is robbing the dead; it is
stripping the slain. Give it up to-day—give it up! Oh,
how you have been cheated on, my brother, from one
thing to another! All these years you have been under an
evil mastery that you understood not. What have your
companions done for you? What have they done for your
health? Nearly ruined it by carousal. What have they
done for your fortune? Almost scattered it by spendthrift
behavior. What have they done for your reputation?
Almost ruined it with good men. What have they done
for your immortal soul? Almost insured its overthrow.

You are hastening on toward the consummation of all
that is sad. To-day you stop and think, but it is only for
a moment, and then you will tramp on, and at the close of
this service you will go out, and the question will be:
"How did you like the sermon?" And one man will say:
"I liked it very well," and another man will say: "I
didn't like it at all;" but neither of the answers will touch
the tremendous fact that, if impenitent, you are going at
eighteen knots an hour toward shipwreck! Yea, you are
in a battle where you will fall; and while your surviving
relatives will take your remaining estate, and the cemetery

will take your body, the messengers of darkness will take your soul, and come and go about you for the next ten million years, stripping the slain.

Many are crying out: "I admit I am slain, I admit it!" On what battle-field, my brothers? By what weapon? "Polluted imagination," says one man; "Intoxicating liquor," says another man; "My own hard heart," says another man. Do you realize this? Then I come to tell you that the omnipotent Christ is ready to walk across this battle-field, and revive, and resuscitate, and resurrect your dead soul. Let Him take your hand and rub away the numbness; your head, and bathe off the aching; your heart, and stop its wild throb. He brought Lazarus to life; He brought Jairus' daughter to life; He brought the young man of Nain to life, and these are three proofs anyhow that he can bring you to life.

When the Philistines came down on the field, they stepped between the corpses, and they rolled over the dead, and they took away everything that was valuable; and so it was with the people that followed after our army at Chancellorsville, and at Pittsburg Landing, and at Stone River, and at Atlanta, stripping the slain; but the Northern and Southern women—God bless them!—came on the field with basins, and pads, and towels, and lint, and cordials, and Christian encouragement; and the poor fellows that lay there lifted up their arms and said: "Oh, how good that does feel since you dressed it!" and others looked up and said: "Oh, how you make me think of my mother!" and others said: "Tell the folks at home I died thinking about them;" and another looked up and said:

"Miss, won't you sing me a verse of 'Home, Sweet Home,' before I die?" And then the tattoo was sounded, and the hats were off, and the service was read: "I am the resurrection and the life;" and in honor of the departed the muskets were loaded, and the command given: "Take aim—fire!" And there was a shingle set up at the head of the grave, with the epitaph of "Lieutenant —— in the Fourteenth Massachusetts Regulars," or "Captain —— in the Fifteenth Regiment of South Carolina Volunteers." And so to-night, across this great field of moral and spiritual battle, the angels of God come walking among the slain, and there are voices of comfort, and voices of hope, and voices of resurrection, and voices of heaven.

Christ is ready to give life to the dead. He will make the deaf ear to hear, the blind eye to see, the pulseless heart to beat, and the damp walls of your spiritual charnel-house will crash into ruin at His cry: "Come forth!" I verily believe there are souls in this house who are now dead in sin, who in half an hour will be alive forever. There was a thrilling dream, a glorious dream—you may have heard of it. Ezekiel closed his eyes, and he saw two mountains, and a valley between the mountains. That valley looked as though there had been a great battle there, and a whole army had been slain, and they had been unburied; and the heat of the land, and the vultures coming there, soon the bones were exposed to the sun, and they looked like thousands of snow-drifts all through the valley. Frightful spectacle! The bleaching skeletons of a host!

But Ezekiel still kept his eyes shut; and lo! there were

four currents of wind that struck the battle-field, and when those four currents of wind met, the bones began to rattle; and the foot came to the ankle, and the hand came to the wrist, and the jaws clashed together, and the spinal column gathered up the ganglions and the nervous fiber, and all the valley wriggled and writhed, and throbbed, and rocked, and rose up. There, a man coming to life. There, a hundred men. There, a thousand; and all falling into line, waiting for the shout of their commander. Ten thousand bleached skeletons springing up into ten thousand warriors, panting for the fray. I hope that instead of being a dream it may be a prophecy of what we shall see here to-day. Let this north wall be one of the mountains, and the south wall be taken for another of the mountains, and let all the aisles and the pews be the valley between, for there are thousands here to-day without one pulsation of spiritual life.

I look off in one direction, and they are dead. I look off in another direction, and they are dead. Who will bring them to life? Who shall rouse them up? If I should halloo at the top of my voice I could not wake them. Wait a moment! Listen! There is a rustling. There is a gale from heaven. It comes from the north, and from the south, and from the east, and from the west. It shuts us in. It blows upon the slain. There a soul begins to move in spiritual life; there, ten souls; there, a score of souls; there, a hundred souls. The nostrils throbbing in divine respiration, the hands lifted as though to take hold of heaven, the tongue moving as in prayer and adoration. Life! immortal life coming into the slain.

Ten men for God—fifty—a hundred—a regiment—an army for God! Oh, that we might have such a scene here to-day! In Ezekiel's words, and in almost a frenzy of prayer, I cry: "Come from the four winds, O Breath! and breathe upon the slain."

You will have to surrender your heart to-day to God. You can not take the responsibility of fighting against the Spirit in this crisis which will decide whether you are to go to heaven or to hell—to join the hallelujahs of the saved, or the lamentations of the lost. You must pray. You must repent. You must this day fling your sinful soul on the pardoning mercy of God. You must! I see your resolution against God giving way, your determination wavering. I break through the breach in the wall and follow up the advantage gained, hoping to rout your last opposition to Christ, and to make you "ground arms" at the feet of the Divine Conqueror. Oh, you must! You must!

The moon does not ask the tides of the Atlantic Ocean to rise. It only stoops down with two great hands of light, the one at the European beach, and the other at the American beach, and then lifts the great laver of molten silver. And God, it seems to me, is now going to lift this audience to newness of life. Do you not feel the swellings of the great oceanic tides of Divine mercy? My heart is in anguish to have you saved. For this I pray, and preach, and long, glad to be called a fool for Christ's sake, and your salvation.

Some one replies: "Dear me, I do wish I could have these matters arranged with my God. I want to be saved.

God knows I want to be saved; but you stand there talking about this matter, and you don't show me how." My dear brother, the work has all been done. Christ did it with His own torn hand, and lacerated foot, and bleeding side. He took your place, and died your death, if you will only believe it—only accept Him as your substitute.

What an amazing pity that any man should go from this house unblessed, when such a large blessing is offered him at less cost than you would pay for a pin—" without money and without price." I have driven down to-day with the Lord's ambulance to the battle-field where your soul lies exposed to the darkness and the storm, and I want to lift you in, and drive off with you toward heaven. Oh, Christians, by your prayers help to lift these wounded souls into the ambulance! God forbid that any should be left on the field, and that at last eternal sorrow, and remorse, and despair should come up around their soul like the bandit Philistines to the field of Gilboa, stripping the slain.

SOLD OUT.

"Ye have sold yourselves for nought; and ye shall be redeemed without money."—ISA. lii: 3.

THE Jews had gone headlong into sin, and as a punishment they had been carried captive to Babylon. They found that iniquity did not pay. Cyrus seized Babylon, and felt so sorry for these poor captive Jews that, without a dollar of compensation, he let them go home. So that, literally, my text was fulfilled: " Ye have sold yourselves for nought; and ye shall be redeemed without money."

There is enough Gospel in this text for fifty sermons; though I never heard of its being preached on. There are persons in this house who have, like the Jews of the text, sold out. You do not seem to belong either to yourselves or to God. The title-deeds have been passed over to " the world, the flesh, and the devil," but the purchaser has never paid up. " Ye have sold yourselves for nought."

When a man passes himself over to the world he expects to get some adequate compensation. He has heard the great things that the world does for a man, and he believes it. He wants two hundred and fifty thousand dollars. That will be horses, and houses, and a summer-resort, and jolly companionship. To get it he parts with his physical health by overwork. He parts with his conscience. He

parts with much domestic enjoyment. He parts with opportunities for literary culture. He parts with his soul.
And so he makes over his entire nature to the world. He
does it in four installments. He pays down the first installment, and one fourth of his nature is gone. He pays
down the second installment, and one half of his nature is
gone. He pays down the third installment, and three
quarters of his nature are gone; and after many years have
gone by he pays down the fourth installment, and, lo! his
entire nature is gone. Then he comes up to the world and
says: " Good-morning. I have delivered to you the goods.
I have passed over to you my body, my mind, and my
soul, and I have come now to collect the two hundred and
fifty thousand dollars." " Two hundred and fifty thousand dollars?" says the world. " What do you mean?"
" Well," you say, " I come to collect the money you owe
me, and I expect you now to fulfill your part of the contract." " But," says the world, " *I have failed. I am
bankrupt.* I can not possibly pay that debt. I have not
for a long while expected to pay it." " Well," you then
say, " give me back the goods." " Oh, no," says the
world, " they are all gone. I can not give them back to
you." And there you stand on the confines of eternity,
your spiritual character gone, staggering under the consideration that " you have sold yourself for nought."

I tell you the world is a liar; it does not keep its promises. It is a cheat, and it fleeces everything it can put its
hands on. It is a bogus world. It is a six-thousand-year-
old swindle. Even if it pays the two hundred and fifty
thousand dollars for which you contracted, it pays them in

bonds that will not be worth anything in a little while. Just as a man may pay down ten thousand dollars in hard cash and get for it worthless scrip—so the world passes over to you the two hundred and fifty thousand dollars in that shape which will not be worth a farthing to you a thousandth part of a second after you are dead. "Oh," you say, "it will help to bury me, anyhow." Oh, my brother! you need not worry about that. The world will bury you soon enough, from sanitary considerations. After you have been deceased for three or four days you will compel the world to bury you.

Post-mortem emoluments are of no use to you. The treasures of this world will not pass current in the future world; and if all the wealth of the Bank of England were put in the pocket of your shroud, and you in the midst of the Jordan of death were asked to pay three cents for your ferriage, you could not do it. There comes a moment in your existence beyond which all earthly values fail; and many a man has wakened up in such a time to find that he has sold out for eternity, and has nothing to show for it. I should as soon think of going to Chatham Street to buy silk pocket-handkerchiefs with no cotton in them, as to go to this world expecting to find any permanent happiness. It has deceived and deluded every man that has ever put his trust in it.

History tells us of one who resolved that he would have all his senses gratified at one and the same time, and he expended thousands of dollars on each sense. He entered a room, and there were the first musicians of the land pleasing his ear, and there were fine pictures fascinating his eye, and there were costly aromatics regaling his nostril, and there were the richest meats, and wines, and fruits, and confections pleasing the appetite, and there was a soft couch of sinful indulgence on which he reclined; and the man declared afterward that he would give ten times what he had given if he could have one week of such enjoyment, even though he lost his soul by it. Ah! that was the rub. He did lose his soul by it! Cyrus the Conqueror thought for a little while that he was making a fine thing out of this world, and yet before he came to his grave he wrote out this pitiful epitaph for his monument: "I am Cyrus. I occupied the Persian Empire. I was king over Asia. Begrudge me not this monument." But the world in after years plowed up his sepulcher.

The world clapped its hands and stamped its feet in honor of Charles Lamb; but what does he say? "I walk up and down, thinking I am happy, but feeling I am not." Call the roll, and be quick about it. Samuel Johnson, the learned! Happy? "No. I am afraid I shall some day get crazy." William Hazlitt, the great essayist! Happy? "No. I have been for two hours and a half going up and down Paternoster Row with a volcano in my breast." Smollett, the witty author! Happy? "No. I am sick of praise and blame, and I wish to God that I had such circumstances around me that I could throw my pen into oblivion." Buchanan, the world-renowned writer, exiled from his own country, appealing to Henry VIII. for protection! Happy? "No. Over mountains covered with snow, and through valleys flooded with rain, I come a fugitive." Molière, the popular dramatic author! Happy? "No. That wretch of an actor just now recited four of my lines without the proper accent and gesture. To have the children of my brain so hung, drawn, and quartered, tortures me like a condemned spirit."

I went to see a worldling die. As I went into the hall I saw its floor was tessellated, and its wall was a picture-gallery. I found his death-chamber adorned with tapestry until it seemed as if the clouds of the setting sun had settled in the room. The man had given forty years to the world—his wit, his time, his genius, his talent, his soul. Did the world come in to stand by his death-bed, and clearing off the vials of bitter medicine, put down any compensation? Oh, no! The world does not like sick and dying people, and leaves them in the lurch. It ruined this man, and then left him. He had a magnificent funeral. All the ministers wore scarfs, and there were forty-three carriages in a row; but the departed man appreciated not the obsequies.

I want to persuade my audience that this world is a poor investment; that it does not pay ninety per cent. of satisfaction, nor eighty per cent., nor twenty per cent., nor two per cent., nor one; that it gives no solace when a dead babe lies on your lap; that it gives no peace when conscience rings its alarm; that it gives no explanation in the day of dire trouble; and at the time of your decease it takes hold of the pillow-case, and shakes out the feathers, and then jolts down in the place thereof sighs, and groans, and execrations, and then makes you put your head on it. Oh, ye who have tried this world, is

it a satisfactory portion? Would you advise your friends
to make the investment? No. "Ye have sold yourselves
for nought." Your conscience went. Your hope went.
Your Bible went. Your heaven went. Your God went.
When a sheriff under a writ from the courts sells a man
out, the officer generally leaves a few chairs and a bed,
and a few cups and knives; but in this awful vendue in
which you have been engaged the auctioneer's mallet has
come down upon body, mind, and soul: Going! Gone!
"Ye have sold yourselves for nought."

How could you do so? Did you think that your soul
was a mere trinket which for a few pennies you could buy
in a toy shop? Did you think that your soul, if once lost,
might be found again if you went out with torches and
lanterns? Did you think that your soul was short-lived,
and that, panting, it would soon lie down for extinction?
Or had you no idea what your soul was worth? Did you
ever put your forefingers on its eternal pulses? Have you
never felt the quiver of its peerless wing? Have you not
known that, after leaving the body, the first step of your
soul reaches to the stars, and the next step to the furthest
outposts of God's universe, and that it will not die until
the day when the everlasting Jehovah expires? Oh, my
brother, what possessed you that you should part with your
soul so cheap? "Ye have sold yourselves for nought."

But I have some good news to tell you. I want to engage in a litigation for the recovery of that soul of yours.
I want to show that you have been cheated out of it. I
want to prove, as I will, that you were crazy on that subject, and that the world, under such circumstances, has no

right to take the title-deed from you; and if you will join me I shall get a decree from the High Chancery Court of Heaven reinstating you into the possession of your soul. "Oh," you say, "I am afraid of lawsuits; they are so expensive, and I can not pay the cost." Then have you forgotten the last half of my text? "Ye have sold yourselves for nought; and ye shall be redeemed without money."

Money is good for a great many things, but it can not do anything in this matter of the soul. You can not buy your way through. Dollars and pounds sterling mean nothing at the gate of mercy. If you could buy your salvation, heaven would be a great speculation, an extension of Wall Street. Bad men would go up and buy out the place, and leave us to shift for ourselves. But as money is not a lawful tender, what is? I will answer: Blood! Whose? Are we to go through the slaughter? Oh, no; it wants richer blood than ours. It wants a king's blood. It must be poured from royal arteries. It must be a sinless torrent. But where is the king? I see a great many thrones and a great many occupants, yet none seem to be coming down to the rescue. But after awhile the clock of night in Bethlehem strikes twelve, and the silver pendulum of a star swings across the sky, and I see the King of Heaven rising up, and He descends, and steps down from star to star, and from cloud to cloud, lower and lower, until He touches the sheep-covered hills, and then on to another hill, this last skull-covered, and there, at the sharp stroke of persecution, a rill incarnadine trickles down, and we who could not be redeemed by money are redeemed by precious and imperial blood.

We have in this day professed Christians who are so rarefied and etherealized that they do not want a religion of blood. What do you want? You seem to want a religion of brains. The Bible says: "In the blood is the life." No atonement without blood. Ought not the apostle to know? What did he say? "Ye are redeemed not with corruptible things, such as silver and gold, but by the precious blood of Christ." You put your lancet into the arm of our holy religion and withdraw the blood, and you leave it a mere corpse, fit only for the grave. Why did God command the priests of old to strike the knife into the kid, and the goat, and the pigeon, and the bull- ock, and the lamb? It was so that when the blood rushed out from these animals on the floor of the ancient taber- nacle the people should be compelled to think of the com- ing carnage of the Son of God. No blood, no atonement.

I think that God intended to impress us with the vivid- ness of that color. The green of the grass, the blue of the sky, would not have startled and aroused us like this deep crimson. It is as if God had said: "Now, sinner, wake up and see what the Saviour endured for you. This is not water. This is not wine. It is blood. It is the blood of my own Son. It is the blood of the Immaculate. It is the blood of God." Without the shedding of blood is no remission. There has been many a man who in courts of law has pleaded "not guilty," who nevertheless has been condemned because there was blood found on his hands, or blood found in his room; and what shall we do in the last day if it be found that we have recrucified the Lord of Glory and have never repented of it? You must believe in the blood or die. No escape. Unless you let the sacrifice of Jesus go in your stead you yourself must suffer. It is either Christ's blood or your blood.

"Oh," says some one, "the thought of blood sickens me." Good. God intended it to sicken you with your sin. Do not act as though you had nothing to do with that Calvarian massacre. You had. Your sins were the implements of torture. Those implements were not made of steel, and iron, and wood, so much as out of your sins. Guilty of this homicide, and this regicide, and this deicide, confess your guilt to-day. Ten thousand voices of heaven bring in the verdict against you of guilty, guilty. Prepare to die, or believe in that blood. Stretch yourself out for the sacrifice, or accept the Saviour's sacrifice. Do not fling away your one chance.

It seems to me as if all heaven were trying to bid in your soul. The first bid it makes is the tears of Christ at the tomb of Lazarus; but that is not a high enough price. The next bid heaven makes is the sweat of Gethsemane; but it is too cheap a price. The next bid heaven makes seems to be the whipped back of Pilate's hall; but it is not a high enough price. Can it be possible that heaven can not buy you in? Heaven tries once more. It says: "I bid this time for that man's soul the tortures of Christ's martyrdom, the blood on His temple, the blood on His cheek, the blood on His chin, the blood on His hand, the blood on His side, the blood on His knee, the blood on His foot—the blood in drops, the blood in rills, the blood in pools coagulated beneath the cross; the blood that wet the tips of the soldiers' spears, the blood that plashed warm in the faces of His enemies." Glory to God, that bid wins it! The highest price that was ever paid for anything was paid for your soul. Nothing could buy it but blood! The estranged property is bought back. Take it. "You have sold yourselves for nought; and ye shall be redeemed without money." O atoning blood, cleansing blood, life-giving blood, sanctifying blood, glorifying blood of Jesus! Why not burst into tears at the thought that for thee He shed it—for thee the hard-hearted, for thee the lost?

"No," says some one; "I will have nothing to do with it except that, like the Jews, I put both my hands into that carnage and scoop up both palms full, and throw it on my head and cry: 'His blood be on us and on our children!'" Can you do such a shocking thing as that? Just rub your handkerchief across your brow and look at it. It is the blood of the Son of God whom you have despised and driven back all these years. Oh, do not do that any longer! Come out frankly and boldly and honestly, and tell Christ you are sorry. You can not afford to so roughly treat Him upon whom everything depends.

I do not know how you will get away from this subject. You see that you are sold out, and that Christ wants to buy you back. There are three persons who come after you to-night: God the Father, God the Son, and God the Holy Ghost. They unite their three omnipotences in one movement for your salvation. You will not take up arms against the Triune God, will you? Is there enough muscle in your arm for such a combat? By the highest throne in heaven, and by the deepest chasm in hell, I beg you look out. Unless you allow Christ to carry away your sins, they will carry you away. Unless you allow Christ to lift you up, they will drag you down. There is only one hope for you, and that is the blood. Christ, the sin-offering, bearing your transgressions. Christ, the surety, paying your debts. Christ, the divine Cyrus, loosening your Babylonish captivity.

Would you not like to be free? Here is the price of your liberation—not money, but blood. I tremble from head to foot, not because I fear your presence, for I am used to that, but because I fear that you will miss your chance for immortal rescue, and die. This is the alterna-tive divinely put: "He that believeth on the Son shall have everlasting life; and he that believeth not on the Son shall not see life, but the wrath of God abideth on him." In the last day, if you now reject Christ, every drop of that sacrificial blood, instead of pleading for your release as it would have pleaded if you had repented, will plead against you. It will seem to say: "They refused the ransom; they chose to die; let them die; they must die. Down with them to the weeping and the wailing. Depart! go away from me. You would not have me, now I will not have you. Sold out for eternity."

O Lord God of the judgment day! avert that calamity! Let us see the quick flash of the cimeter that slays the sin but saves the sinner. Strike, omnipotent God, for the soul's deliverance! Beat, O eternal sea! with all thy waves against the barren beach of that rocky soul, and make it tremble. Oh! the oppressiveness of the hour, the minute, the second, on which the soul's destiny quivers, and this is that hour, that minute, that second!

I wonder what proportion of this audience will be saved? What proportion will be lost? When the "Schiller" went down, out of three hundred and eighty people only forty were saved. When the "Ville du Havre" went down, out of three hundred and forty about fifty were saved. Out of this audience to-day, how many will get to the shore of heaven? It is no idle question for me to ask, for many of you I shall never see again until the day when the books are open.

Some years ago there came down a fierce storm on the sea-coast, and a vessel got in the breakers and was going to pieces. They threw up some signal of distress, and the people on the shore saw them. They put out in a life-boat. They came on, and they saw the poor sailors, almost exhausted, clinging to a raft; and so afraid were the boatmen that the men would give up before they got to them, they gave them three rounds of cheers, and cried: "Hold on, there! Hold on! We'll save you!" After awhile the boat came up. One man was saved by having the boat-hook put in the collar of his coat; and some in one way, and some in another; but they all got into the boat. "Now," says the captain, "for the shore. Pull away now, pull!" The people on the land were afraid the life-boat had gone down. They said: "How long the boat stays. Why, it must have been swamped, and they have all perished together."

And there were men and women on the pier-heads and on the beach wringing their hands; and while they waited and watched, they saw something looming up through the mist, and it turned out to be the life-boat. As soon as it

9

came within speaking distance the people on the shore cried out: "Did you save any of them? Did you save any of them?" And as the boat swept through the boiling surf and came to the pier-head, the captain waved his hand over the exhausted sailors that lay flat on the bottom of the boat, and cried: "All saved! Thank God! All saved!" So may it be to-day. The waves of your sin run high, the storm is on you, the danger is appalling. Oh! shipwrecked soul, I have come for you. I cheer you with this Gospel hope. God grant that within the next ten minutes we may row with you into the harbor of God's mercy. And when these Christian men gather around to see the result of this service, and the glorified gathering on the pier-heads of heaven to watch and to listen, may we be able to report all saved! Young and old, good and bad! All saved! Saved from sin, and death, and hell. Saved for time. Saved for eternity. "And so it came to pass that they all escaped safe to land."

SUMMER TEMPTATIONS.

"Come ye yourselves apart unto a desert place and rest awhile."
—MARK vi: 31.

HERE Christ advises His apostles to take a vacation. They have been living an excited as well as a useful life, and He advises that they get out into the country. When, six weeks ago, standing in this place, I advocated, with all the energy I could command, the Saturday afternoon holiday, I did not think the people would so soon get that release. By divine fiat it has come, and I rejoice that more people will have opportunity of recreation this summer than in any previous summer. Others will have whole weeks and months of rest. The railway trains are being laden with passengers and baggage on their way to the mountains and the lakes and the sea-shore. Multitudes of our citizens are packing their trunks for a restorative absence.

The city heats are pursuing the people with torch and fear of sunstroke. The long silent halls of sumptuous hotels are all abuzz with excited arrivals. The crystalline surface of Winnipiseogee is shattered with the stroke of steamer, laden with excursionists. The antlers of Adirondack deer rattle under the shot of city sportsmen. The trout make fatal snaps at the hook of adroit sportsmen and toss their spotted brilliance into the game-basket. Already the baton of the orchestral leader taps the music-stand on the hotel green, and American life puts on festal array, and the rumbling of the tenpin alley, and the crack of the ivory balls on the green-baized billiard tables, and the jolting of the bar-room goblets, and the explosive un-corking of champagne bottles, and the whirl and the rustle of the ball-room dance, and the clattering hoofs of the race-courses, attest that the season for the great American watering-places is fairly inaugurated. Music—flute and drum and cornet-à-piston and clapping cymbals — will wake the echoes of the mountains.

Glad I am that fagged-out American life for the most part will have an opportunity to rest, and that nerves racked and destroyed will find a Bethesda. I believe in watering-places. Let not the commercial firm begrudge the clerk, or the employer the journeyman, or the patient the physician, or the church its pastor, a season of inoccupa-tion. Luther used to sport with his children; Edmund Burke used to caress his favorite horse; Thomas Chalmers, in the dark hours of the church's disruption, played kite for recreation—as I was told by his own daughter—and the busy Christ said to the busy apostles: "Come ye apart awhile into the desert and rest yourselves." And I have observed that they who do not know how to rest do not know how to work.

But I have to declare this truth to-day, that some of our fashionable watering-places are the temporal and eternal destruction of "a multitude that no man can number," and amid the congratulations of this season and the prospect of the departure of many of you for the country I must utter a note of warning—plain, earnest, and unmistakable.

I. The first temptation that is apt to hover in this direction is to leave your piety all at home. You will send the dog and cat and canary bird to be well cared for somewhere else; but the temptation will be to leave your religion in the room with the blinds down and the door bolted, and then you will come back in the autumn to find that it is starved and suffocated, lying stretched on the rug stark dead. There is no surplus of piety at the watering-places. I never knew any one to grow very rapidly in grace at the Catskill Mountain House, or Sharon Springs, or the Falls of Montmorency. It is generally the case that the Sabbath is more of a carousal than any other day, and there are Sunday walks and Sunday rides and Sunday excursions.

Elders and deacons and ministers of religion who are entirely consistent at home, sometimes when the Sabbath dawns on them at Niagara Falls or the White Mountains take the day to themselves. If they go to the church, it is apt to be a sacred parade, and the discourse, instead of being a plain talk about the soul, is apt to be what is called *a crack sermon*—that is, some discourse picked out of the effusions of the year as the one most adapted to excite admiration; and in those churches, from the way the ladies hold their fans, you know that they are not so much impressed with the heat as with the picturesqueness of half-disclosed features. Four puny souls stand in the organ-loft and squall a tune that nobody knows, and worshipers, with two thousand dollars' worth of diamonds on the right hand, drop a cent into the poor-box, and then the benediction is pronounced and the farce is ended.

The toughest thing I ever tried to do was to be good at a watering-place. The air is bewitched with " the world, the flesh, and the devil." There are Christians who in three or four weeks in such a place have had such terrible rents made in their Christian robe that they had to keep darning it until Christmas to get it mended! The health of a great many people makes an annual visit to some mineral spring an absolute necessity; but, my dear people, take your Bible along with you, and take an hour for secret prayer every day, though you be surrounded by guffaw and saturnalia. Keep holy the Sabbath, though they denounce you as a bigoted Puritan. Stand off from those institutions which propose to imitate on this side the water the iniquities of Baden-Baden. Let your moral and your immortal health keep pace with your physical recuperation, and remember that all the waters of Hathorne and sulphur and chalybeate springs can not do you so much good as the mineral, healing, perennial flood that breaks forth from the " Rock of Ages." This may be your last summer. If so, make it a fit vestibule of heaven.

II. Another temptation around nearly all our watering-places is the horse-racing business. We all admire the horse. There needs to be a redistribution of coronets among the brute creation. For ages the lion has been called the king of beasts. I knock off its coronet and put the crown upon the horse, in every way nobler, whether in shape or spirit or sagacity or intelligence or affection or usefulness. He is semi-human, and knows how to reason on a small scale. The centaur of olden times, part horse and part man, seems to be a suggestion of the fact that the horse is something more than a beast.

Job sets forth his strength, his beauty, his majesty, the panting of his nostril, the pawing of his hoof, and his enthusiasm for the battle. What Rosa Bonheur did for the cattle, and what Landseer did for the dog, Job, with mightier pencil, does for the horse. Eighty-eight times does the Bible speak of him. He comes into every kingly procession and into every great occasion and into every triumph. It is very evident that Job and David and Isaiah and Ezekiel and Jeremiah and John were fond of the horse. He came into much of their imagery. A red horse—that meant war; a black horse—that meant famine; a pale horse—that meant death; a white horse—that meant victory.

As the Bible makes a favorite of the horse, the patriarch and the prophet and the evangelist and the apostle, stroking his sleek hide, and patting his rounded neck, and tenderly lifting his exquisitely formed hoof, and listening with a thrill to the champ of his bit, so all great natures in all ages have spoken of him in encomiastic terms. Virgil in his Georgics almost seems to plagiarize from the description of Job. The Duke of Wellington would not allow any one irreverently to touch his old war-horse, Copenhagen, on whom he had ridden fifteen hours without dismounting at Waterloo; and when old Copenhagen died, his master ordered a military salute fired over his grave.

John Howard showed that he did not exhaust all his sympathies in pitying the human race, for when sick he writes home: " Has my old chaise-horse become sick or spoiled?"

But we do not think that the speed of the horse should be cultured at the expense of human degradation. Horse-races, in olden times, were under the ban of Christian people, and in our day the same institution has come up under fictitious names, and it is called a " Summer Meeting," almost suggestive of positive religious exercises. And it is called an " Agricultural Fair," suggestive of everything that is improving in the art of farming. But under these deceptive titles are the same cheating and the same betting, the same drunkenness and the same vagabondage and the same abominations that were to be found under the old horse-racing system.

I never knew a man yet who could give himself to the pleasures of the turf for a long reach of time, and not be battered in morals. They hook up their spanking team, and put on their sporting-cap, and light their cigar, and take the reins, and dash down the road to perdition. The great day at Saratoga, and Long Branch, and Cape May, and nearly all the other watering-places, is the day of the races. The hotels are thronged, nearly every kind of equipage is taken up at an almost fabulous price, and there are many respectable people mingling with jockeys, and gamblers, and libertines, and foul-mouthed men and flashy women. The bar-tender stirs up the brandy-smash. The bets run high. The greenhorns, supposing all is fair, put in their money soon enough to lose it. Three weeks before the race takes place the struggle is decided, and the men in the secret know on which steed to bet their money. The two men on the horses riding around long before arranged who shall beat.

Leaning from the stand or from the carriage are men and women so absorbed in the struggle of bone and muscle and mettle that they make a grand harvest for the pick-pockets, who carry off the pocket-books and portemonnaies. Men looking on see only two horses with two riders flying around the ring; but there is many a man on that stand whose honor and domestic happiness and fortune—white mane, white foot, white flank—are in the ring, racing with inebriety, and with fraud, and with profanity, and with ruin—black neck, black foot, black flank. Neck and neck they go in that moral Epsom.

Ah, my friends, have nothing to do with horse-racing dissipations this summer. Long ago the English government got through looking to the turf for the dragoon and light-cavalry horse. They found the turf depreciates the stock, and it is yet worse for men. Thomas Hughes, the member of parliament and the author, known all the world over, hearing that a new turf enterprise was being started in this country, wrote a letter, in which he said: " Heaven help you, then; for of all the cankers of our old civilization there is nothing in this country approaching in unblushing meanness, in rascality holding its head high, to this belauded institution of the British turf." Another famous sportsman writes: " How many fine domains have been shared among these hosts of rapacious sharks during the last two hundred years; and unless the system be altered, how many more are doomed to fall into the same gulf!" The Duke of Hamilton, through his horse-racing proclivities, in three years got through his entire fortune of £70,000, and I will say that some of you are being undermined by it. With the bull-fights of Spain and the bear-baitings of the pit may the Lord God annihilate the infamous and accursed horse-racing of England and America.

III. I go further, and speak of another temptation that hovers over the watering-places; and this is the temptation to sacrifice physical strength. The modern Bethesda was intended to recuperate the physical health; and yet how many come from the watering-places, their health absolutely destroyed! New York and Brooklyn idiots boasting of having imbibed twenty glasses of Congress water before breakfast. Families accustomed to going to bed at ten o'clock at night gossiping until one or two o'clock in the morning. Dyspeptics, usually very cautious about their health, mingling ice-creams, and lemons, and lobster-salads, and cocoa-nuts, until the gastric juices lift up all their voices of lamentation and protest. Delicate women and brainless young men chassezing themselves into vertigo and catalepsy. Thousands of men and women coming back from our watering-places in the autumn with the foundations laid for ailments that will last them all their life long. You know as well as I do that this is the simple truth.

In the summer you say to your good health: "Good-bye, I am going to have a good time for a little while. I will be very glad to see you again in the autumn." Then in the autumn, when you are hard at work in your office, or store, or shop, or counting-room, Good Health will come and say: "Good-bye, I am going." You say: "Where are you going?" "Oh," says Good Health, "I am going to take a vacation!" It is a poor rule that will not work both ways, and your good health will leave you choleric and splenetic and exhausted. You coquetted with your good health in the summer-time, and your good health is coquetting with you in the winter-time. A fragment of Paul's charge to the jailer would be an appropriate inscription for the hotel-register in every watering-place: "Do thyself no harm."

IV. Another temptation hovering around the watering-place is to the formation of hasty and life-long alliances. The watering-places are responsible for more of the domestic infelicities of this country than all the other things combined. Society is so artificial there that no sure judgment of character can be formed. Those who form companionships amid such circumstances go into a lottery where there are twenty blanks to one prize. In the severe tug of life you want more than glitter and splash. Life is not a ball-room where the music decides the step, and bow and prance and graceful swing of long trail can make up for strong common sense. You might as well go among the gayly painted yachts of a summer regatta to find war vessels as to go among the light spray of the summer watering-place to find character that can stand the test of the great struggle of human life. Ah, in the battle of life you want a stronger weapon than a lace fan or a croquet mallet! The load of life is so heavy that in order to draw it, you want a team stronger than one made up of a masculine grasshopper and a feminine butterfly.

If there is any man in the community that excites my
contempt, and that ought to excite the contempt of every
man and woman, it is the soft-handed, soft-headed fop,
who, perfumed until the air is actually sick, spends his
summer in taking killing attitudes, and waving senti-
mental adieus, and talking infinitesimal nothings, and finding his heaven in the set of a lavender kid-glove. Boots
as tight as an Inquisition, two hours of consummate skill
exhibited in the tie of a flaming cravat, his conversation
made up of " Ah's " and " Oh's " and " He-hee's. " It
would take five hundred of them stewed down to make a
teaspoonful of calves-foot jelly. There is only one coun-
terpart to such a man as that, and that is the frothy young
woman at the watering-place, her conversation made up of
French moonshine; what she has on her head only equaled
by what she has on her back; useless ever since she was
born, and to be useless until she is dead: and what they
will do with her in the next world I do not know, except
to set her upon the banks of the River Life for eternity to
look sweet! God intends us to admire music and fair faces
and graceful step, but amid the heartlessness and the infla-
tion and the fantastic influences of our modern watering-
places, beware how you make life-long covenants!

V. Another temptation that will hover over the watering-place is that of baneful literature. Almost every one
starting off for the summer takes some reading matter.
It is a book out of the library or off the bookstand, or
bought of the boy hawking books through the cars. I
really believe there is more pestiferous trash read among
the intelligent classes in July and August than in all the

other ten months of the year. Men and women who at home would not be satisfied with a book that was not really sensible, I found sitting on hotel-piazzas or under the trees reading books the index of which would make them blush if they knew that you knew what the book was.

"Oh," they say, "you must have intellectual recreation!" Yes. There is no need that you take along into a watering-place "Hamilton's Metaphysics" or some thunderous discourse on the eternal decrees, or "Faraday's Philosophy." There are many easy books that are good. You might as well say: "I propose now to give a little rest to my digestive organs; and, instead of eating heavy meat and vegetables, I will for a little while take lighter food—a little strychnine and a few grains of ratsbane." Literary poison in August is as bad as literary poison in December. Mark that. Do not let the frogs and the lice of a corrupt printing-press jump and crawl into your Saratoga trunk or White Mountain valise.

Would it not be an awful thing for you to be struck with lightning some day when you had in your hand one of these paper-covered romances—the hero a Parisian *roué*, the heroine an unprincipled flirt—chapters in the book that you would not read to your children at the rate of $100 a line? Throw out all that stuff from your summer baggage. Are there not good books that are easy to read —books of entertaining travel, books of congenial history, books of pure fun, books of poetry ringing with merry canto, books of fine engravings, books that will rest the mind as well as purify the heart and elevate the whole life? My hearers, there will not be an hour between this and the day of your death when you can afford to read a book lacking in moral principle.

VI. Another temptation hovering all around our watering-places is the intoxicating beverage. I am told that it is becoming more and more fashionable for woman to drink. I care not how well a woman may dress, if she has taken enough of wine to flush her cheek and put glassiness on her eyes, she is intoxicated. She may be handed into a $2500 carriage, and have diamonds enough to confound the Tiffanys—she is intoxicated. She may be a graduate of Packer Institute, and the daughter of some man in danger of being nominated for the Presidency—she is drunk. You may have a larger vocabulary than I have, and you may say in regard to her that she is " convivial," or she is " merry," or she is " festive," or she is " exhilarated," but you can not with all your garlands of verbiage cover up the plain fact that it is an old-fashioned case of drunk.

Now, the watering-places are full of temptations to men and women to tipple. At the close of the tenpin or billiard-game they tipple. At the close of the cotillon they tipple. Seated on the piazza cooling themselves off they tipple. The tinged glasses come around with bright straws, and they tipple. First they take " light wines," as they call them; but " light wines " are heavy enough to debase the appetite. There is not a very long road between champagne at $5 a bottle and whiskey at five cents a glass.

Satan has three or four grades down which he takes men to destruction. One man he takes up, and through one spree pitches him into eternal darkness. That is a rare case. Very seldom, indeed, can you find a man who will be such a fool as that.

When a man goes down to destruction Satan brings him to a plane. It is almost a level. The depression is so slight that you can hardly see it. The man does not actually know that he is on the down grade, and it tips only a little toward darkness—just a little. And the first mile it is claret, and the second mile it is sherry, and the third mile it is punch, and the fourth mile it is ale, and the fifth mile it is porter, and the sixth mile it is brandy, and then it gets steeper and steeper and steeper, and the man gets frightened and says, " Oh, let me get off!" " No," says the conductor, " this is an express train, and it does not stop until it gets to the Grand Central Depot at Smashupton." Ah, " look not thou upon the wine when it is red, when it giveth its color in the cup, when it moveth itself aright. At the last it biteth like a serpent and stingeth like an adder." And if any young man in my congregation should get astray this summer in this direction it will not be because I have not given him fair warning.

My friends, whether you tarry at home—which will be quite as safe and perhaps quite as comfortable—or go into the country, arm yourself against temptation. The grace of God is the only safe shelter, whether in town or country. There are watering-places accessible to all of us. You can not open a book of the Bible without finding out some such watering-place. Fountains open for sin and uncleanliness; wells of salvation; streams from Lebanon; a flood struck out of the rock by Moses; fountains in the wilderness discovered by Hagar; water to drink and water to bathe in; the river of God, which is full of water; water of which if a man drink he shall never thirst; wells of water in the Valley of Baca; living fountains of water; a pure river of water as clear as crystal from under the throne of God.

These are watering-places accessible to all of us. We do not have a laborious packing up before we start—only the throwing away of our transgressions. No expensive hotel bills to pay; it is " without money and without price." No long and dirty travel before we get there; it is only one step away. California in five minutes. I walked around and saw ten fountains, all bubbling up, and they were all different. And in five minutes I can get through this Bible *parterre* and find you fifty bright, sparkling fountains bubbling up into eternal life.

A chemist will go to one of these summer watering-places and take the water and analyze it and tell you that it contains so much of iron, and so much of soda, and so much of lime, and so much of magnesia. I come to this Gospel well, this living fountain and analyze the water, and I find that its ingredients are peace, pardon, forgiveness, hope, comfort, life, heaven. " Ho, every one that thirsteth, come ye " to this watering-place!

Crowd around this Bethesda this morning! Oh, you sick, you lame, you troubled, you dying—crowd around this Bethesda! Step in it! Oh, step in it! The angel of the covenant this morning stirs the water. Why do you not step in it? Some of you are too weak to take a step in that direction. Then we take you up in the arms of our closing prayer and plunge you clean under the wave, hoping that the cure may be as sudden and as radical as with Captain Naaman, who, blotched and carbuncled, stepped into the Jordan, and after the seventh dive came up, his skin roseate-complexioned as the flesh of a little child.

THE BANISHED QUEEN.

" **Also** Vashti the queen made a feast for the women in the royal house which belonged to King Ahasuerus. On the seventh day when the heart of the king was merry with wine, he commanded Mehuman, Biztha, Harbona, Bigtha, and Abagtha, Zethar, and Carcas, the seven chamberlains that served in the presence of Ahasuerus the king, to bring Vashti the queen before the king with the crown royal, to show the people and the princes her beauty: for she was fair to look on. But the Queen Vashti refused to come at the king's commandment by his chamberlains; therefore was the king very wroth, and his anger burned in him."—Esther i: 9–12.

We stand amid the palaces of Shushan. The pinnacles are aflame with the morning light. The columns rise festooned and wreathed, the wealth of empires flashing from the grooves; the ceilings adorned with images of bird and beast, and scenes of prowess and conquest. The walls are hung with shields, and emblazoned until it seems that the whole round of splendors is exhausted. Each arch is a mighty leaf of architectural achievement. Golden stars shining down on glowing arabesque. Hangings of embroidered work in which mingle the blueness of the sky, the greenness of the grass, and the whiteness of the sea-foam. Tapestries hung on silver rings, wedding together the pillars of marble. Pavilions reaching out in every direction. These for repose, filled with luxuriant couches, in which weary limbs sink until all fatigue is submerged. Those for carousal, where kings drink down a kingdom at one swallow.

Amazing spectacle!

Light of silver dripping down over stairs of ivory on shields of gold. Floors of stained marble, sunset red and night black, and inlaid with gleaming pearl.

In connection with this palace there is a garden, where the mighty men of foreign lands are seated at a banquet. Under the spread of oak and linden and acacia the tables are arranged. The breath of honeysuckle and frankincense fills the air. Fountains leap up into the light, the spray struck through with rainbows falling in crystalline baptism upon flowering shrubs—then rolling down through channels of marble, and widening out here and there into pools swirling with the finny tribes of foreign aquariums, bordered with scarlet anemones, hypericums, and many-colored ranunculi.

Meats of rarest bird and beast smoking up amid wreaths of aromatics. The vases filled with apricots and almonds. The baskets piled up with apricots and figs and oranges and pomegranates. Melons tastefully twined with leaves of acacia. The bright waters of Eulæus filling the urns and dropping outside the rim in flashing beads amid the traceries. Wine from the royal vats of Ispahan and Shiraz, in bottles of tinged shell, and lily-shaped cups of silver, and flagons and tankards of solid gold. The music rises higher, and the revelry breaks out into wilder transport, and the wine has flushed the cheek and touched the brain, and louder than all other voices are the hiccough of the inebriates, the gabble of fools, and the song of the drunkards.

In another part of the palace, Queen Vashti is entertaining the princesses of Persia at a banquet. Drunken Ahasuerus says to his servants, "You go out and fetch Vashti from that banquet with the women, and bring her to this banquet with the men, and let me display her beauty." The servants immediately start to obey the king's command; but there was a rule in Oriental society that no woman might appear in public without having her face veiled. Yet here was a mandate that no one dare dispute, demanding that Vashti come in unveiled before the multitude. However, there was in Vashti's soul a principle more regal than Ahasuerus, more brilliant than the gold of Shushan, of more wealth than the realm of Persia, which commanded her to disobey this order of the king; and so all the righteousness and holiness and modesty of her nature rise up into one sublime refusal. She says, "I will not go into the banquet unveiled." Ahasuerus was infuriate; and Vashti, robbed of her position and her estate, is driven forth in poverty and ruin to suffer the scorn of a nation, and yet to receive the applause of after generations, who shall rise up to admire this martyr to kingly insolence. Well, the last vestige of that feast is gone; the last garland has faded; the last arch has fallen; the last tankard has been destroyed; and Shushan is a ruin; but as long as the world stands there will be multitudes of men and women, familiar with the Bible, who will come into this picture-gallery of God and admire the

divine portrait of Vashti the queen, Vashti the veiled,
Vashti the sacrifice, Vashti the silent.

I. In the first place, I want you to look upon Vashti
the queen. A blue ribbon, rayed with white, drawn
around her forehead, indicated her queenly position. It
was no small honor to be queen in such a realm as that.
Hark to the rustle of her robes! See the blaze of her
jewels! And yet, my friends, it is not necessary to have
place and regal robe in order to be queenly. When I see a
woman with stout faith in God, putting her foot upon all
meanness and selfishness and godless display, going right
forward to serve Christ and the race by a grand and a
glorious service, I say: "That woman is a queen," and
the ranks of heaven look over the battlements upon the
coronation; and whether she comes up from the shanty on
the commons or the mansion of the fashionable square, I
greet her with the shout, "All hail, Queen Vashti!"

What glory was there on the brow of Mary of Scotland,
or Elizabeth of England, or Margaret of France, or Cath-
erine of Russia, compared with the worth of some of our
Christian mothers, many of them gone into glory?—or of
that woman mentioned in the Scriptures, who put her all
into the Lord's treasury?—or of Jephtha's daughter, who
made a demonstration of unselfish patriotism?—or of
Abigail, who rescued the herds and flocks of her husband?
—or of Ruth, who toiled under a tropical sun for poor,
old, helpless Naomi?—or of Florence Nightingale, who
went at midnight to stanch the battle wounds of the
Crimea?—or of Mrs. Adoniram Judson, who kindled the
lights of salvation amid the darkness of Burmah?—or of

Mrs. Hemans, who poured out her holy soul in words which will forever be associated with hunter's horn, and captive's chain, and bridal hour, and lute's throb, and curfew's knell at the dying day?—and scores and hundreds of women, unknown on earth, who have given water to the thirsty, and bread to the hungry, and medicine to the sick, and smiles to the discouraged—their footsteps heard along dark lane and in government hospital, and in almshouse corridor, and by prison gate? There may be no royal robe —there may be no palatial surroundings. She does not need them; for all charitable men will unite with the crackling lips of fever-struck hospital and plague-blotched lazaretto in greeting her as she passes: "Hail! Hail! Queen Vashti!"

II. Again, I want you to consider Vashti the veiled. Had she appeared before Ahasuerus and his court on that day with her face uncovered she would have shocked all the delicacies of Oriental society, and the very men who in their intoxication demanded that she come, in their sober moments would have despised her. As some flowers seem to thrive best in the dark lane and in the shadow, and where the sun does not seem to reach them, so God appoints to most womanly natures a retiring and unobtrusive spirit.

God once in awhile does call an Isabella to a throne, or a Miriam to strike the timbrel at the front of a host, or a Marie Antoinette to quell a French mob, or a Deborah to stand at the front of an armed battalion, crying out, "Up! Up! This is the day in which the Lord will deliver Sisera into thy hands." And when the women are called to such out-door work and to such heroic positions, God prepares them for it; and they have iron in their soul, and lightnings in their eye, and whirlwinds in their breath, and the borrowed strength of the Lord Omnipotent in their right arm. They walk through furnaces as though they were hedges of wild-flowers, and cross seas as though they were shimmering sapphire; and all the harpies of hell down to their dungeon at the stamp of womanly indignation.

But these are the exceptions. Generally, Dorcas would rather make a garment for the poor boy; Rebecca would rather fill the trough for the camels; Hannah would rather make a coat for Samuel; the Hebrew maid would rather give a prescription for Naaman's leprosy; the woman of Sarepta would rather gather a few sticks to cook a meal for famished Elijah; Phebe would rather carry a letter for the inspired apostle; Mother Lois would rather educate Timothy in the Scriptures. When I see a woman going about her daily duty, with cheerful dignity presiding at the table, with kind and gentle, but firm discipline presiding in the nursery, going out into the world without any blast of trumpets, following in the footsteps of Him who went about doing good—I say: "This is Vashti with a veil on."

But when I see a woman of unblushing boldness, loud-voiced, with a tongue of infinite clitter-clatter, with arrogant look, passing through the streets with the step of a walking-beam, gayly arrayed in a very hurricane of millinery, I cry out: "Vashti has lost her veil!" When I see a woman struggling for political preferment—trying to force her way on up to the ballot-box, amid the masculine demagogues who stand, with swollen fists and bloodshot eyes and pestiferous breath, to guard the polls—wanting to go through the loaferism and the defilement of popular sovereigns, who crawl up from the saloons greasy and foul and vermin-covered, to decide questions of justice and order and civilization—when I see a woman, I say, who wants to press through all that horrible scum to get to the ballot-box, I say: "Ah, what a pity! Vashti has lost her veil!"

When I see a woman of comely features, and of adroitness of intellect, and endowed with all that the schools can do for one, and of high social position, yet moving in society with superciliousness and *hauteur*, as though she would have people know their place, and with an undefined combination of giggle and strut and rhodomontade, endowed with allopathic quantities of talk, but only homeopathic infinitesimals of sense, the terror of dry-goods clerks and railroad conductors, discoverers of significant meanings in plain conversation, prodigies of badinage and innuendo—I say: "Vashti has lost her veil."

III. Again, I want you this morning to consider Vashti the sacrifice. Who is this that I see coming out of that palace gate of Shushan? It seems to me that I have seen her before. She comes homeless, houseless, friendless, trudging along with a broken heart. Who is she? It is Vashti the sacrifice. Oh! what a change it was from regal position to a wayfarer's crust! A little while ago, approved and sought for; now, none so poor as to acknowledge her acquaintanceship. Vashti the sacrifice!

Ah! you and I have seen it many a time. Here is a

home empalaced with beauty. All that refinement and books and wealth can do for that home has been done; but Ahasuerus, the husband and the father, is taking hold on paths of sin. He is gradually going down. After awhile he will flounder and struggle like a wild beast in the hunter's net—further away from God, further away from the right. Soon the bright apparel of the children will turn to rags; soon the household song will become the sobbing of a broken heart. The old story over again. Brutal Centaurs breaking up the marriage feast of Lapithæ. The house full of outrage and cruelty and abomination, while trudging forth from the palace gate are Vashti and her children. There are homes represented in this house this morning that are in danger of such breaking-up. Oh, Ahasuerus! that you should stand in a home, by a dissipated life destroying the peace and comfort of that home. God forbid that your children should ever have to wring their hands, and have people point their finger at them as they pass down the street, and say, " There goes a drunkard's child." God forbid that the little feet should ever have to trudge the path of poverty and wretchedness! God forbid that any evil spirit born of the wine-cup or the brandy-glass should come forth and uproot that garden, and with a lasting, blistering, all-consuming curse, shut forever the palace gate against Vashti and the children.

One night during the war I went to Hagerstown to look at the army, and I stood on a hill-top and looked down upon them. I saw the camp-fires all through the valleys and all over the hills. It was a weird spectacle, those camp-fires, and I stood and watched them; and the soldiers who were gathered around them were, no doubt, talking of their homes, and of the long march they had taken, and of the battles they were to fight; but after awhile I saw these camp-fires begin to lower; and they continued to lower, until they were all gone out, and the army slept. It was imposing when I saw the camp-fires; it was imposing in the darkness when I thought of that great host asleep. Well, God looks down from heaven, and He sees the fireside of Christendom and the loved ones gathered around these firesides. These are the camp-fires where we warm ourselves at the close of day, and talk over the battles of life we have fought and the battles that are yet to come. God grant that when at last these fires begin to go out, and continue to lower until finally they are extinguished, and the ashes of consumed hopes strew the hearth of the old homestead, it may be because we have

> Gone to sleep that last long sleep,
> From which none ever wake to weep."

Now we are an army on the march of life. Then we shall be an army bivouacked in the tent of the grave.

IV. Once more: I want you to look at Vashti the silent. You do not hear any outcry from this woman as she goes forth from the palace gate. From the very dignity of her nature, you know there will be no vociferation. Sometimes in life it is necessary to make a retort; sometimes in life it is necessary to resist; but there are crises when the most triumphant thing to do is to keep silence. The philosopher, confident in his newly discovered principle, waited for the coming of more intelligent generations, willing that men should laugh at the lightning-rod and cotton-gin and steam-boat—waiting for long years through the scoffing of philosophical schools, in grand and magnificent silence.

Galileo, condemned by mathematicians and monks and cardinals, caricatured everywhere, yet waiting and watching with his telescope to see the coming up of stellar re-enforcements, when the stars in their courses would fight for the Copernican system; then sitting down in complete blindness and deafness to wait for the coming on of the generations who would build his monument and bow at his grave. The reformer, execrated by his contemporaries, fastened in a pillory, the slow fires of public contempt burning under him, ground under the cylinders of the printing-press, yet calmly waiting for the day when purity of soul and heroism of character will get the sanction of earth and the plaudits of heaven.

Affliction enduring without any complaint the sharpness of the pang, and the violence of the storm, and the heft of the chain, and the darkness of the night—waiting until a Divine hand shall be put forth to soothe the pang, and hush the storm, and release the captive. A wife abused, persecuted, and a perpetual exile from every earthly comfort—waiting, waiting, until the Lord shall gather up His dear children in a heavenly home, and no poor Vashti will ever be thrust out from the palace gate.

Jesus, in silence and answering not a word, drinking the gall, bearing the cross, in prospect of the rapturous consummation when

"Angels thronged their chariot wheel,
    And bore Him to His throne;
Then swept their golden harps and sung,
    'The glorious work is done!'"

Oh, woman! does not this story of Vashti the queen, Vashti the veiled, Vashti the sacrifice, Vashti the silent, move your soul? My sermon converges into the one absorbing hope that none of you may be shut out of the palace gate of heaven. You can endure the hardships, and the privations, and the cruelties, and the misfortunes of this life if you can only gain admission there. Through the blood of the everlasting covenant you go through those gates, or never go at all. God forbid that you should at last be banished from the society of angels, and banished from the companionship of your glorified kindred, and banished forever. Through the rich grace of our Lord Jesus Christ, may you be enabled to imitate the example of Rachel, and Hannah, and Abigail, and Deborah, and Mary, and Esther, and Vashti.

THE DAY WE LIVE IN.

" Who knoweth whether thou art come to the kingdom for such a time as this?"—ESTHER iv: 14.

ESTHER the beautiful was the wife of Ahasuerus the abominable. The time had come for her to present a petition to her infamous husband in behalf of the Jewish nation, to which she had once belonged. She was afraid to undertake the work, lest she should lose her own life; but her uncle, Mordecai, who had brought her up, encouraged her with the suggestion that probably she had been raised up of God for that peculiar mission. "Who knoweth whether thou art come to the kingdom for such a time as this?" Esther had her God-appointed work; you and I have ours. It is my business to tell you what style of men and women you ought to be in order that you meet the demand of the age in which God has cast your lot. If you have come expecting to hear abstractions discussed, or dry technicalities of religion glorified, you have come to the wrong church; but if you really would like to know what this age has a right to expect of you as Christian men and women, then I am ready in the Lord's name to look you in the face. When two armies have rushed into battle the officers of either army do not want a philosophical discussion about the chemical properties of human blood or the nature of gunpowder; they want some one to man the batteries and swab out the guns. And now, when all the forces of light and darkness, of heaven and hell, have plunged into the fight, it is no time to give ourselves to the definitions and formulas and technicalities and conventionalities of religion.

What we want is practical, earnest, concentrated, enthusiastic, and triumphant help.

I. In the first place, in order to meet the special demand of this age, you need to be an unmistakably aggressive Christian. Of half-and-half Christians we do not want any more. The Church of Jesus Christ will be better without ten thousand of them. They are the chief obstacle to the Church's advancement. I am speaking of another kind of Christian. All the appliances for your becoming an earnest Christian are at your hand, and there is a straight path for you into the broad daylight of God's forgiveness. You may have come into this Tabernacle the bondsmen of the world, and yet before you go out of these doors you may become princes of the Lord God Almighty. You remember what excitement there was in this country, years ago, when the Prince of Wales came here—how the people rushed out by hundreds of thousands to see him. Why? Because they expected that some day he would sit upon the throne of England. But what was all that honor compared with the honor to which God calls you—to be sons and daughters of the Lord Almighty; yea, to be queens and kings unto God? "They shall reign with Him forever and forever."

But, my friends, you need to be aggressive Christians,

and not like those persons who spend their lives in hugging their Christian graces and wondering why they do not make any progress. How much robustness of health would a man have if he hid himself in a dark closet? A great deal of the piety of the day is too exclusive. It hides itself. It needs more fresh air, more out-door exercise. There are many Christians who are giving their entire life to self-examination. They are feeling their pulses to see what is the condition of their spiritual health. How long would a man have robust physical health if he kept all the days and weeks and months and years of his life feeling his pulse instead of going out into active, earnest, every-day work?

I was once amid the wonderful, bewitching cactus growths of North Carolina. I never was more bewildered with the beauty of flowers, and yet when I would take up one of these cactuses and pull the leaves apart, the beauty was all gone. You could hardly tell that it had ever been a flower. And there are a great many Christian people in this day just pulling apart their Christian experiences to see what there is in them, and there is nothing left in them. This style of self-examination is a damage instead of an advantage to their Christian character. I remember when I was a boy I used to have a small piece in the garden that I called my own, and I planted corn there, and every few days I would pull it up to see how fast it was growing. Now, there are a great many Christian people in this day whose self-examination merely amounts to the pulling up of that which they only yesterday or the day before planted.

O my friends! if you want to have a stalwart Christian character, plant it right out of doors in the great field of Christian usefulness, and though storms may come upon it, and though the hot sun of trial may try to consume it, it will thrive until it becomes a great tree, in which the fowls of heaven may have their habitation. I have no patience with these flower-pot Christians. They keep themselves under shelter, and all their Christian experience in a small, exclusive circle, when they ought to plant it in the great garden of the Lord, so that the whole atmosphere could be aromatic with their Christian usefulness. What we want in the Church of God is more brawn of piety.

The century plant is wonderfully suggestive and wonderfully beautiful, but I never look at it without thinking of its parsimony. It lets whole generations go by before it puts forth one blossom; so I have really more heartfelt admiration when I see the dewy tears in the blue eyes of the violets, for they come every spring. My Christian friends, time is going by so rapidly that we can not afford to be idle.

A recent statistician says that human life now has an average of only thirty-two years. From these thirty-two years you must subtract all the time you take for sleep and the taking of food and recreation; that will leave you about sixteen years. From those sixteen years you must subtract all the time that you are necessarily engaged in the earning of a livelihood; that will leave you about eight years. From those eight years you must take all the days and weeks and months—all the length of time that is passed in childhood and sickness, leaving you about one year in which to work for God. Oh, my soul, wake up! How darest thou sleep in harvest-time and with so few hours in which to reap? So that I state it as a simple fact that all the time that the vast majority of you will have for the exclusive service of God will be less than one year!

"But," says some man, "I liberally support the Gospel, and the church is open and the Gospel is preached: all the spiritual advantages are spread before men, and if they want to be saved, let them come to be saved; I have discharged all my responsibility." Ah! is that the Master's spirit? Is there not an old Book somewhere that commands us to go out into the highways and the hedges and compel the people to come in? What would have become of you and me if Christ had not come down off the hills of heaven, and if He had not come through the door of the Bethlehem caravansary, and if He had not with the crushed hand of the crucifixion knocked at the iron gate of the sepulcher of our spiritual death, crying, "Lazarus, come forth"? Oh, my Christian friends, this is no time for inertia, when all the forces of darkness seem to be in full blast; when steam printing-presses are publishing infidel tracts; when express railroad trains are carrying messengers of sin; when fast clippers are laden with opium and rum; when the night-air of our cities is polluted with the laughter that breaks up from the ten thousand saloons of dissipation and abandonment; when the fires of the second death already are kindled in the cheeks of some who, only a little while ago, were incorrupt. Oh, never since the curse fell upon the earth has there been a time when it was such an unwise, such a cruel, such an awful

10

thing for the Church to sleep! The great audiences are not gathered in the Christian churches; the great audiences are gathered in temples of sin—tears of unutterable woe their baptism, the blood of crushed hearts the awful wine of their sacrament, blasphemies their litany, and the groans of the lost world the organ dirge of their worship.

II. Again, if you want to be qualified to meet the duties which this age demands of you, you must on the one hand avoid reckless iconoclasm, and on the other hand not stick too much to things because they are old. The air is full of new plans, new projects, new theories of government, new theologies, and I am amazed to see how so many Christians want only novelty in order to recommend a thing to their confidence; and so they vacillate and swing to and fro, and they are useless, and they are unhappy. New plans—secular, ethical, philosophical, religious, cis-atlantic, transatlantic—long enough to make a line reaching from the German universities to Great Salt Lake City. Ah, my brother, do not take hold of a thing merely because it is new. Try it by the realities of a Judgment Day.

But, on the other hand, do not adhere to any thing merely because it is old. There is not a single enterprise of the Church or the world but has sometimes been scoffed at. There was a time when men derided even Bible societies; and when a few young men met near a hay-stack in Massachusetts and organized the first missionary society ever organized in this country, there went laughter and ridicule all around the Christian Church. They said the undertaking was preposterous. And so also the work of Jesus Christ was assailed. People cried out, " Who ever heard of such theories of ethics and government? Who ever noticed such a style of preaching as Jesus has?" Ezekiel had talked of mysterious wings and wheels. Here came a man from Capernaum and Gennesaret, and he drew his illustration from the lakes, from the sand, from the ravine, from the lilies, from the corn-stalks. How the Pharisees scoffed! How Herod derided! How Caiaphas hissed! And this Jesus they plucked by the beard, and they spat in his face, and they called him "this fellow!" All the great enterprises in and out of the Church have at times been scoffed at, and there have been a great multitude who have thought that the chariot of God's truth would fall to pieces if it once got out of the old rut.

And so there are those who have no patience with anything like improvement in church architecture, or with anything like good, hearty, earnest church singing, and they deride any form of religious discussion which goes down walking among every-day men rather than that which makes an excursion on rhetorical stilts. Oh, that the Church of God would wake up to an adaptability of work! We must admit the simple fact that the churches of Jesus Christ in this day do not reach the great masses. There are fifty thousand people in Edinburgh who never hear the Gospel. There are one million people in London who never hear the Gospel. There are at least three hundred thousand souls in the city of Brooklyn who come not under the immediate ministrations of Christ's truth; and the Church of God in this day, instead of being a place full of living epistles, read and known of all men, is more like a "dead-letter" post-office.

"But," say the people, "the world is going to be converted; you must be patient; the kingdoms of this world are to become the kingdoms of Christ." Never, unless the Church of Jesus Christ puts on more speed and energy. Instead of the Church converting the world, the world is converting the Church. Here is a great fortress. How shall it be taken? An army comes and sits around about it, cuts off the supplies, and says: "Now we will just wait until from exhaustion and starvation they will have to give up." Weeks and months, and perhaps a year, pass along, and finally the fortress surrenders through that starvation and exhaustion. But, my friends, the fortresses of sin are never to be taken in that way. If they are taken for God it will be by storm; you will have to bring up the great siege guns of the Gospel to the very wall and wheel the flying artillery into line, and when the armed infantry of heaven shall confront the battlements you will have to give the quick command, "Forward! Charge!"

Ah, my friends, there is work for you to do and for me to do in order to this grand accomplishment! Here is my pulpit, and I preach in it. Your pulpit is the bank. Your pulpit is the store. Your pulpit is the editorial chair. Your pulpit is the anvil. Your pulpit is the house scaffolding. Your pulpit is the mechanic's shop. I may stand in this place and, through cowardice or through self-seeking, may keep back the word I ought to utter; while you, with sleeve rolled up and brow besweated with toil, may utter the word that will jar the foundations of heaven with the shout of a great victory. Oh, that this morning this whole audience might feel that the Lord Almighty was putting upon them the hands of ordination. I tell you, every one, go forth and preach this gospel. You have as much right to preach as I have, or as any man has. Only find out the pulpit where God will have you preach, and there preach.

Hedley Vicars was a wicked man in the English army. The grace of God came to him. He became an earnest and eminent Christian. They scoffed at him, and said: "You are a hypocrite; you are as bad as ever you were." Still he kept his faith in Christ, and after awhile, finding that they could not turn him aside by calling him a hypocrite, they said to him: "Oh, you are nothing but a Methodist." That did not disturb him. He went on performing his Christian duty until he had formed all his troop into a Bible-class, and the whole encampment was shaken with the presence of God. So Havelock went into the heathen temple in India while the English army was there, and put a candle into the hand of each of the heathen gods that stood around in the heathen temple, and by the light of those candles, held up by the idols, General Havelock preached righteousness, temperance, and judgment to come. And who will say, on earth or in Heaven, that Havelock had not the right to preach?

In the minister's house where I prepared for college, there was a man who worked, by the name of Peter Croy. He could neither read nor write, but he was a man of God. Often theologians would stop in the house—grave theologians—and at family prayers Peter Croy would be called upon to lead; and all those wise men sat around, wonder-struck at his religious efficiency. When he prayed he reached up and seemed to take hold of the very throne of the Almighty, and he talked with God until the very heavens were bowed down into the sitting-room. Oh, if I were dying I would rather have plain Peter Croy kneel by my bedside and commend my immortal spirit to God than the greatest archbishop, arrayed in costly canonicals. Go preach this Gospel. You say you are not licensed. In the name of the Lord Almighty, this morning, I license you. Go preach this Gospel—preach it in the Sabbath-schools, in the prayer-meetings, in the highways, in the hedges. Woe be unto you if you preach it not.

III. I remark, again, that in order to be qualified to meet your duty in this particular age you want unbounded faith in the triumph of the truth and the overthrow of wickedness. How dare the Christian Church ever get discouraged? Have we not the Lord Almighty on our side? How long did it take God to slay the hosts of Sennacherib or burn Sodom or shake down Jericho? How long will it take God, when He once arises in His strength, to overthrow all the forces of iniquity? Between this time and that there may be long seasons of darkness—the chariot-wheels of God's Gospel may seem to drag heavily; but here is the promise, and yonder is the throne; and when Omniscience has lost its eyesight, and Omnipotence falls back impotent, and Jehovah is driven from His throne, then the Church of Jesus Christ can afford to be despondent, but never until then. Despots may plan and armies may march, and the congresses of the nations may seem to think they are adjusting all the affairs of the world, but the mighty men of the earth are only the dust of the chariot-wheels of God's providence.

I think that before the sun of this century shall set the last tyranny will fall, and with a splendor of demonstration that shall be the astonishment of the universe God will set forth the brightness and pomp and glory and perpetuity of His eternal government. Out of the starry flags and the emblazoned insignia of this world God will make a path for His own triumph, and, returning from universal conquest, He will sit down, the grandest, strongest, highest throne of earth His footstool.

> " Then shall all nations' song ascend
>   To Thee, our Ruler, Father, Friend,
>   Till heaven's high arch resounds again
>   With ' Peace on earth, good will to men.' "

I preach this sermon because I want to encourage all Christian workers in every possible department. Hosts of the living God, march on! march on! His Spirit will bless you. His shield will defend you. His sword will strike for you. March on! march on! The despotism will fall, and paganism will burn its idols, and Mohammedanism will give up its false prophet, and Judaism will confess the true Messiah, and the great walls of superstition will come down in thunder and wreck at the long, loud blast of the Gospel trumpet. March on! march on! The besiegement will soon be ended. Only a few more steps on the long way; only a few more sturdy blows; only a few more battle cries, then God will put the laurel upon your brow, and from the living fountains of heaven will bathe off the sweat and the heat and the dust of the conflict. March on! march on! For you the time for work will soon be passed, and amid the outflashings of the judgment throne, and the trumpeting of resurrection angels, and the upheaving of a world of graves, and the hosanna and the groaning of the saved and the lost, we shall be rewarded for our faithfulness or punished for our stupidity. Blessed be the Lord God of Israel from everlasting to everlasting, and let the whole earth be filled with His glory. Amen and Amen.

CAPITAL AND LABOR.

***

"Whatsoever ye would that men should do to you, do ye even so to them."—MATT. vii: 12.

THE greatest war the world has ever seen is between capital and labor. The strife is not like that which in history is called the Thirty Years' War, for it is a war of centuries, it is a war of the five continents, it is a war hemispheric. The middle classes in this country, upon whom the nation has depended for holding the balance of power and for acting as mediators between the two extremes, are diminishing; and if things go on at the same ratio as they are now going, it will not be very long before there will be no middle class in this country, but all will be very rich or very poor, princes or paupers, and the country will be given up to palaces and hovels.

The antagonistic forces are closing in upon each other. The telegraphic operators' strikes, the railroad employés' strikes, the Pennsylvania miners' strikes, the movements of the Boycotters and the dynamiters are only skirmishes before a general engagement, or, if you prefer it, escapes through the safety-valves of an imprisoned force which promises the explosion of society. You may pooh-pooh it; you may say that this trouble, like an angry child, will cry itself to sleep; you may belittle it by calling it Fourierism, or Socialism, or St. Simonism, or Nihilism, or Communism; but that will not hinder the fact that it is the mightiest, the darkest, the most terrific threat of this century. All attempts at pacification have been dead failures, and monopoly is more arrogant, and the trades unions more bitter. " Give us more wages," cry the employés. " You shall have less," say the capitalists. " Compel us to do fewer hours of toil in a day." " You shall toil more hours," say the others. " Then, under certain conditions, we will not work at all," say these. " Then you shall starve," say those, and the workmen gradually using up that which they accumulated in better times, unless there be some radical change, we shall have soon in this country three million hungry men and women. Now, three million hungry people can not be kept quiet. All the enactments of legislatures and all the constabularies of the cities, and all the army and navy of the United States can not keep three million hungry people quiet. What then? Will this war between capital and labor be settled by human wisdom? Never. The brow of the one becomes more rigid, the fist of the other more clinched.

But that which human wisdom can not achieve will be accomplished by Christianity if it be given full sway. You have heard of medicines so powerful that one drop would stop a disease and restore a patient; and I have to tell you that one drop of my text properly administered will stop all these woes of society and give convalescence and complete health to all classes. " Whatsoever ye would that men should do to you, do ye even so to them."

I shall first show you this morning how this quarrel between monopoly and hard work can not be stopped, and then I will show you how this controversy will be settled.

Futile remedies. In the first place, there will come no pacification to this trouble through an outcry against rich men merely because they are rich. There is no member of a trades-union on earth that would not be rich if he could be. Sometimes through a fortunate invention, or, through some accident of prosperity, a man who had nothing comes to large estate, and we see him arrogant and supercilious, and taking people by the throat just as other people took him by the throat. There is something very mean about human nature when it comes to the top. But it is no more a sin to be rich than it is a sin to be poor. There are those who have gathered a great estate through fraud, and then there are millionaires who have gathered their fortune through foresight in regard to changes in the markets, and through brilliant business faculty, and every dollar of their estate is as honest as the dollar which the plumber gets for mending a pipe, or the mason gets for building a wall. There are those who keep in poverty because of their own fault. They might have been well-off, but they smoked or chewed up their earnings, or they lived beyond their means, while others on the same wages and on the same salaries went on to competency. I know a man who is all the time complaining of his poverty and crying out against rich men, while he himself keeps two dogs, and chews and smokes, and is filled to the chin with whisky and beer!

Micawber said to David Copperfield: " Copperfield, my boy, one pound income, twenty shillings and sixpence expenses: result misery. But, Copperfield, my boy, one pound income, expenses nineteen shillings and sixpence; result, happiness." And there are vast multitudes of people who are kept poor because they are the victims of their own improvidence. It is no sin to be rich, and it is no sin to be poor. I protest against this outcry which I hear against those who, through economy and self-denial and assiduity, have come to large fortune. This bombardment of commercial success will never stop this quarrel between capital and labor.

Neither will the contest be settled by cynical and unsympathetic treatment of the laboring classes. There are those who speak of them as though they were only cattle or draught horses. Their nerves are nothing, their domestic comfort is nothing, their happiness is nothing. They have no more sympathy for them than a hound has for a hare, or a hawk for a hen, or a tiger for a calf. When Jean Valjean, the greatest hero of Victor Hugo's writings, after a life of suffering and brave endurance, goes into incarceration and death, they clap the book shut and say, "Good for him!" They stamp their feet with indignation and say just the opposite of "Save the working-classes." They have all their sympathies with Shylock, and not with Antonio and Portia. They are plutocrats, and their feelings are infernal. They are filled with irritation and irascibility on this subject. To stop this awful imbroglio between capital and labor they will lift not so much as the tip end of the little finger.

Neither will there be any pacification of this angry controversy through violence. God never blessed murder.

The poorest use you can put a man to is to kill him. Blow up to-morrow all the country-seats on the banks of the Hudson, and all the fine houses on Madison Square, and Brooklyn Heights, and Bunker Hill, and Rittenhouse Square, and Beacon Street, and all the bricks and timber and stone will just fall back on the bare head of American labor. The worst enemies of the working-classes in the United States and Ireland are their demented coadjutors. Assassination—the assassination of Lord Frederick Cavendish and Mr. Burke in Phœnix Park, Dublin, Ireland, in the attempt to avenge the wrongs of Ireland, only turned away from that afflicted people millions of sympathizers. The recent attempt to blow up the House of Commons, in London, had only this effect: to throw out of employment tens of thousands of innocent Irish people in England.

In this country the torch put to the factories that have discharged hands for good or bad reason; obstructions on the rail-track in front of midnight express trains because the offenders do not like the president of the company; strikes on shipboard the hour they were going to sail, or in printing-offices the hour the paper was to go to press, or in mines the day the coal was to be delivered, or on house scaffoldings so the builder fails in keeping his contract— all these are only a hard blow on the head of American labor, and cripple its arms, and lame its feet, and pierce its heart. Take the last great strike in America—the telegraph operators' strike—and you have to find that the operators lost four hundred thousand dollars' worth of wages, and have had poorer wages ever since. Traps sprung suddenly upon employers, and violence, never took one knot out of the knuckle of toil, or put one farthing of wages into a callous palm. Barbarism will never cure the wrongs of civilization. Mark that!

Frederick the Great admired some land near his palace at Potsdam, and he resolved to get it. It was owned by a miller. He offered the miller three times the value of the property. The miller would not take it, because it was the old homestead, and he felt about as Naboth felt about his vineyard when Ahab wanted it. Frederick the Great was a rough and terrible man, and he ordered the miller into his presence; and the king, with a stick in his hand —a stick with which he sometimes struck his officers of state—said to this miller: " Now, I have offered you three times the value of that property, and if you won't sell it I'll take it anyhow." The miller said, " Your majesty, you won't." " Yes," said the king, " I will take it." " Then," said the miller, " if your majesty does take it, I will sue you in the Chancery Court." At that threat Frederick the Great yielded his infamous demand. And the most imperious outrage against the working-classes will yet cower before the law. Violence and contrary to the law will never accomplish anything, but righteousness and according to law will accomplish it.

Well, if this controversy between Capital and Labor can not be settled by human wisdom, if to-day Capital and Labor stand with their thumbs on each other's throat—as they do—it is time for us to look somewhere else for relief, and it points from my text roseate and jubilant, and puts one hand on the broadcloth shoulder of Capital, and puts the other hand on the homespun-covered shoulder of Toil, and says, with a voice that will grandly and gloriously settle this, and settle everything, "Whatsoever ye would that men should do to you, do ye even so to them." That is, the lady of the household will say: "I must treat the maid in the kitchen just as I would like to be treated if I were down-stairs, and it were my work to wash, and cook, and sweep, and it were the duty of the maid in the kitchen to preside in this parlor." The maid in the kitchen must say: "If my employer seems to be more prosperous than I, that is no fault of hers; I shall not treat her as an enemy. I will have the same industry and fidelity downstairs as I would expect from my subordinates, if I happened to be the wife of a silk importer."

The owner of an iron mill, having taken a dose of my text before leaving home in the morning, will go into his foundry, and, passing into what is called the puddling-room, he will see a man there stripped to the waist, and besweated and exhausted with the labor and the toil, and he will say to him: "Why, it seems to be very hot in here. You look very much exhausted. I hear your child is sick with scarlet fever. If you want your wages a little earlier this week, so as to pay the nurse and get the medicines, just come into my office any time."

After awhile, crash goes the money market, and there is no more demand for the articles manufactured in that iron mill, and the owner does not know what to do. He says, "Shall I stop the mill, or shall I run it on half time, or shall I cut down the men's wages?" He walks the floor of his counting-room all day, hardly knowing what to do. Toward evening he calls all the laborers together. They stand all around, some with arms akimbo, some with folded arms, wondering what the boss is going to do now. The manufacturer says: "Men, times are very hard; I don't make twenty dollars where I used to make one hundred. Somehow, there is no demand now for what we manufacture, or but very little demand. You see I am at vast expense, and I have called you together this afternoon to see what you would advise. I don't want to shut up the mill, because that would force you out of work, and you have always been very faithful, and I like you, and you seem to like me, and the bairns must be looked after, and your wife will after awhile want a new dress. I don't know what to do."

There is a dead halt for a minute or two, and then one of the workmen steps out from the ranks of his fellows, and says: "Boss, you have been very good to us, and when you prospered we prospered, and now you are in a tight place and I am sorry, and we have got to sympathize with you. I don't know how the others feel, but I propose that we take off twenty per cent. from our wages, and that when the times get good you will remember us and raise them again." The workman looks around to his comrades, and says: "Boys, what do you say to this? all in favor of my proposition will say ay." "Ay! ay! ay!" shout two hundred voices.

But the mill-owner, getting in some new machinery, exposes himself very much, and takes cold, and it settles into pneumonia, and he dies. In the procession to the tomb are all the workmen, tears rolling down their cheeks, and off upon the ground; but an hour before the procession gets to the cemetery the wives and the children of those workmen are at the grave waiting for the arrival of the funeral pageant. The minister of religion may have delivered an eloquent eulogium before they started from the house, but the most impressive things are said that day by the working-classes standing around the tomb.

That night in all the cabins of the working-people where they have family prayers the widowhood and the orphanage in the mansion are remembered. No glaring populations look over the iron fence of the cemetery; but, hovering over the scene, the benediction of God and man is coming for the fulfillment of the Christlike injunction, " Whatsoever ye would that men should do to you, do ye even so to them."

" Oh," says some man here, " that is all Utopian, that is apocryphal, that is impossible." No. Yesterday, I cut out of a paper this: " One of the pleasantest incidents recorded in a long time is reported from Sheffield, England. The wages of the men in the iron works at Sheffield are regulated by a board of arbitration, by whose decision both masters and men are bound. For some time past the iron and steel trade has been extremely unprofitable, and the employers can not, without much loss, pay the wages fixed by the board, which neither employers nor employed have the power to change. To avoid this difficulty, the workmen in one of the largest steel works in Sheffield hit upon a device as rare as it was generous. They offered to work for their employers one week without any pay whatever. How much better that plan is than a strike would be."

But you go with me and I will show you—not so far off as Sheffield, England—factories, banking-houses, store-houses, and costly enterprises where this Christ-like injunction of my text is fully kept, and you could no more get the employer to practice an injustice upon his men, or the men to conspire against the employer, than you could get your right hand and your left hand, your right eye and your left eye, your right ear and your left ear, into physiological antagonism. Now, where is this to begin? In our homes, in our stores, on our farms—not waiting for other people to do their duty. Is there a divergence now between the parlor and the kitchen? Then there is something wrong, either in the parlor or the kitchen, perhaps in both. Are the clerks in your store irate against the firm? Then there is something wrong, either behind the counter, or in the private office, or perhaps in both.

The great want of the world to-day is the fulfillment of this Christ-like injunction, that which He promulgated in His sermon Olivetic. All the political economists under the arch or vault of the heavens in convention for a thousand years can not settle this controversy between monopoly and hard work, between capital and labor. During the Revolutionary War there was a heavy piece of timber to be lifted, perhaps for some fortress, and a corporal was overseeing the work, and he was giving commands to some soldiers as they lifted: " Heave away, there! yo heave!" Well, the timber was too heavy; they could not get it up. There was a gentleman riding by on a horse, and he stopped and said to this corporal, " Why don't you help them lift? That timber is too heavy for them to lift."

"No," he said, "I won't; I am a corporal." The gentleman got off his horse and came up to the place. "Now," he said to the soldiers, "all together—yo heave!" and the timber went to its place. "Now," said the gentleman to the corporal, "when you have a piece of timber too heavy for the men to lift, and you want help, you send to your commander-in-chief." It was Washington. Now, that is about all the Gospel I know—the Gospel of giving somebody a lift, a lift out of darkness, a lift out of earth into heaven. That is all the Gospel I know —the Gospel of helping somebody else to lift.

"Oh," says some wiseacre, "talk as you will, the law of demand and supply will regulate these things until the end of time." No, they will not, unless God dies and the batteries of the Judgment Day are spiked, and Pluto and Proserpine, king and queen of the infernal regions, take full possession of this world. Do you know who Supply and Demand are? They have gone into partnership, and they propose to swindle this earth and are swindling it. You are drowning. Supply and Demand stand on the shore, one on one side, the other on the other side, of the life-boat, and they cry out to you, "Now, you pay us what we ask you for getting you to shore, or go to the bottom!" If you can borrow $5000 you can keep from failing in business. Supply and Demand say, "Now, you pay us exorbitant usury, or you go into bankruptcy." This robber firm of Supply and Demand say to you: "The crops are short. We bought up all the wheat and it is in our bin. Now, you pay our price or starve." That is your magnificent law of supply and demand.

Supply and Demand own the largest mill on earth, and all the rivers roll over their wheel, and into their hopper they put all the men, women, and children they can shovel out of the centuries, and the blood and the bones redden the valley while the mill grinds. That diabolic law of supply and demand will yet have to stand aside, and instead thereof will come the law of love, the law of co-operation, the law of kindness, the law of sympathy, the law of Christ.

Have you no idea of the coming of such a time? Then you do not believe the Bible. All the Bible is full of promises on this subject, and as the ages roll on the time will come when men or fortune will be giving larger sums to humanitarian and evangelistic purposes, and there will be more James Lenoxes and Peter Coopers and William E. Dodges and George Peabodys. As that time comes there will be more parks, more picture-galleries, more gardens thrown open for the holiday people and the working-classes.

I was reading only this morning in regard to a charge that had been made in England against Lambeth Palace, that it was exclusive; and that charge demonstrated the sublime fact that to the grounds of that wealthy estate eight hundred poor families have free passes, and forty croquet companies, and on the half-day holidays four thousand poor people recline on the grass, walk through the paths, and sit under the trees. That is Gospel—Gospel on the wing, Gospel out-of-doors worth just as much as in-doors. That time is going to come.

That is only a hint of what is going to be. The time is going to come when, if you have anything in your house worth looking at—pictures, pieces of sculpture—you are going to invite me to come and see it, you are going to invite my friends to come and see it, and you will say, " See what I have been blessed with. God has given me this, and so far as enjoying it, it is yours also." That is Gospel.

In crossing the Alleghany Mountains, many years ago, the stage halted, and Henry Clay dismounted from the stage, and went out on a rock at the very verge of the cliff, and he stood there with his cloak wrapped about him, and he seemed to be listening for something. Some one said to him, " What are you listening for?" Standing there, on the top of the mountain, he said: " I am listening to the tramp of the footsteps of the coming millions of this continent." A sublime posture for an American statesman! You and I to-day stand on the mountain-top of privilege, and on the Rock of Ages, and we look off, and we hear coming from the future the happy industries, and smiling populations, and the consecrated fortunes, and the innumerable prosperities of the closing nineteenth and the opening twentieth century.

While I speak this morning, there lies in state the dead author and patriot of France, Victor Hugo. The ten thousand dollars in his will he has given to the poor of the city are only a hint of the work he has done for all nations and for all times. I wonder not that they allow eleven days to pass between his death and his burial, his body meantime kept under triumphal arch, for the world can hardly afford to let go this man who for more than eight decades has by his unparalleled genius blessed it. His name shall be a terror to all despots, and an encouragement to all the struggling. He has made the world's burden lighter, and its darkness less dense, and its chain less galling, and its thrones of iniquity less secure. Farewell, patriot, genius of the century, Victor Hugo! But he was not the overtowering friend of mankind.

The greatest friend of capitalist and toiler, and the one who will yet bring them together in complete accord, was born one Christmas night while the curtains of heaven swung, stirred by the wings angelic. Owner of all things —all the continents, all worlds, and all the islands of light. Capitalist of immensity, crossing over to our condition. Coming into our world, not by gate of palace, but by door of barn. Spending His first night amid the shepherds. Gathering after around Him the fishermen to be His chief attendants. With adze, and saw, and chisel, and ax, and in a carpenter-shop showing himself brother with the tradesmen. Owner of all things, and yet on a hillock back of Jerusalem one day resigning everything for others, keeping not so much as a shekel to pay for His obsequies, by charity buried in the suburbs of a city that had cast Him out. Before the cross of such a capitalist, and such a carpenter, all men can afford to shake hands and worship. Here is the every man's Christ. None so high, but He was higher. None so poor, but He was poorer. At His feet the hostile extremes will yet renounce their animosities, and countenances which have glowered with the prejudices and revenge of centuries shall brighten with the smile of heaven as He commands: "Whatsoever ye would that men should do to you, do ye even so to them."

DESPOTISM OF THE NEEDLE.

"So I returned, and considered all the oppressions that are done under the sun: and behold the tears of such as were oppressed, and they had no comforter; and on the side of their oppressors there was power; but they had no comforter."—ECCLES. iv: 1.

VERY long ago the needle was busy. It was considered honorable for women to toil in olden time. Alexander the Great stood in his palace showing garments made by his own mother. The finest tapestries at Bayeux were made by the queen of William the Conqueror. Augustus, the Emperor, would not wear any garments except those that were fashioned by some member of his royal family. So let the toiler everywhere be respected!

The needle has slain more than the sword. When the sewing-machine was invented some thought that invention would alleviate woman's toil and put an end to the despotism of the needle. But no; while the sewing-machine has been a great blessing to well-to-do families in many cases, it has added to the stab of the needle the crush of the wheel; and multitudes of women, notwithstanding the re-enforcement of these wing-machines, can only make, work hard as they will, between two dollars and three dollars per week.

The greatest blessing that could have happened to our

first parents was being turned out of Eden after they had done wrong. Adam and Eve, in their perfect state, might have got along without work, or only such slight employment as a perfect garden with no weeds in it demanded. But as soon as they had sinned, the best thing for them was to be turned out where they would have to work. We know what a withering thing it is for a man to have nothing to do. Old Ashbel Green, at fourscore years, when asked why he kept on working, said: "I do so to keep out of mischief." We see that a man who has a large amount of money to start with has no chance. Of the thousand prosperous and honorable men that you know, nine hundred and ninety-nine had to work vigorously at the beginning. But I am now to tell you that industry is just as important for a woman's safety and happiness. The most unhappy women in our communities to-day are those who have no engagements to call them up in the morning; who, once having risen and breakfasted, lounge through the dull forenoon in slippers down at the heel and with disheveled hair, reading Ouida's last novel, and who, having dragged through a wretched forenoon and taken their afternoon sleep, and having passed an hour and a half at their toilet, pick up their card-case and go out to make calls, and who pass their evenings waiting for somebody to come in and break up the monotony. Arabella Stuart never was imprisoned in so dark a dungeon as that.

There is no happiness in an idle woman. It may be with hand, it may be with brain, it may be with foot; but work she must, or be wretched forever. The little girls of our families must be started with that idea.

The curse of American society is that our young women are taught that the first, second, third, fourth, fifth, sixth, seventh, tenth, fiftieth, thousandth thing in their life is to get somebody to take care of them. Instead of that, the first lesson should be how under God they may take care of themselves. The simple fact is that a majority of them do have to take care of themselves, and that, too, after having, through the false notions of their parents, wasted the years in which they ought to have learned how successfully to maintain themselves. We now and here declare the inhumanity, cruelty, and outrage of that father and mother who pass their daughters into womanhood, having given them no facility for earning their livelihood. Madame de Staël said: " It is not these writings that I am proud of, but the fact that I have facility in ten occupations, in any one of which I could make a livelihood." You say you have a fortune to leave them. Oh, man and woman, have you not learned that like vultures, like hawks, like eagles, riches have wings and fly away? Though you should be successful in leaving a competency behind you, the trickery of executors may swamp it in a night? or some officials in our churches may get up a mining company and induce your orphans to put their money into a hole in Colorado, and if by the most skillful machinery the sunken money can not be brought up again, prove to them that it was eternally decreed that that was the way they were to lose it, and that it went in the most orthodox and heavenly style. Oh, the damnable schemes that professed Christians will engage in until God puts His fingers into the collar of the hypocrite's robe and strips it clear down to the bottom! You have no right, because you are well off, to conclude that your children are going to be as well off. A man died leaving a large fortune. His son fell dead in a Philadelphia grog-shop. His old comrades came in and said as they bent over his corpse: " What is the matter with you, Boggsey?" The surgeon standing over him said: " Hush ye! He is dead!" " Oh, he is dead," they said. " Come, boys; let us go and take a drink in memory of poor Boggsey!" Have you nothing better than money to leave your children? If you have not, but send your daughters into the world with empty brain and unskilled hand, you are guilty of assassination, homicide, regicide, infanticide.

There are women toiling in our cities for two and three dollars per week who were the daughters of merchant princes. These suffering ones now would be glad to have the crumbs that once fell from their fathers' table. That worn-out, broken shoe that she wears is the lineal descendant of the twelve-dollar gaiters in which her mother walked; and that torn and faded calico had ancestry of magnificent brocade that swept Broadway clean without any expense to the street commissioners. Though you live in an elegant residence and fare sumptuously every day, let your daughters feel it is a disgrace to them not to know how to work. I denounce the idea prevalent in society that, though our young women may embroider slippers and crochet and make mats for lamps to stand on without disgrace, the idea of doing anything for a livelihood is dishonorable. It is a shame for a young woman belonging to a large family to be inefficient when the father toils his life away for her support. It is a shame for a daughter to be idle while her mother toils at the wash-tub. It is as honorable to sweep the house, make beds or trim hats as it is to twist a watch-chain.

As far as I can understand, the line of respectability lies between that which is useful and that which is useless. If women do that which is of no value, their work is honorable. If they do practical work, it is dishonorable. That our young women may escape the censure of doing dishonorable work, I shall particularize. You may knit a tidy for the back of an arm-chair, but by no means make the money wherewith to buy the chair. You may with a delicate brush beautify a mantel ornament, but die rather than earn enough to buy a marble mantel. You may learn artistic music until you can squall Italian, but never sing "Ortonville" or "Old Hundred." Do nothing practical if you would in the eyes of refined society preserve your respectability. I scout these fine notions. I tell you a woman, no more than a man, has a right to occupy a place in this world unless she pays a rent for it.

In the course of a life-time you consume whole harvests and droves of cattle, and every day you live, breathe forty hogsheads of good, pure air. You must by some kind of usefulness pay for all this. Our race was the last thing created—the birds and fishes on the fourth day, the cattle and lizards on the fifth day, and man on the sixth day. If geologists are right, the earth was a million of years in the possession of the insects, beasts, and birds before our race came upon it. In one sense we were innovators. The cattle, the lizards, and the hawks had pre-emption right.

The question is not what we are to do with the lizards and summer insects, but what the lizards and summer insects are to do with us. If we want a place in this world, we must earn it. The partridge makes its own nest before it occupies it. The lark by its morning song earns its breakfast before it eats it, and the Bible gives an intimation that the first duty of an idler is to starve when it says: "If he will not work, neither shall he eat." Idleness ruins the health; and very soon nature says: "This man has refused to pay his rent, out with him!" Society is to be reconstructed on the subject of woman's toil. A vast majority of those who would have woman industrious shut her up to a few kinds of work. My judgment in this matter is that a woman has a right to do anything that she can do well. There should be no department of merchandise, mechanism, art, or science barred against her. If Miss Hosmer has genius for sculpture, give her a chisel. If Rosa Bonheur has a fondness for delineating animals, let her make "The Horse Fair." If Miss Mitchell will study astronomy, let her mount the starry ladder. If Lydia will be a merchant, let her sell purple. If Lucretia Mott will preach the Gospel, let her thrill with her womanly eloquence the Quaker meeting-house.

It is said, If woman is given such opportunities she will occupy places that might be taken by men. I say, If she have more skill and adaptedness for any position than a man has, let her have it! She has as much right to her bread, to her apparel, and to her home, as men have. But it is said that her nature is so delicate that she is unfitted for exhausting toil. I ask in the name of all past history what toil on earth is more severe, exhausting, and tremendous than that toil of the needle to which for ages she has been subjected? The battering-ram, the sword, the carbine, the battle-ax, have made no such havoc as the needle. I would that these living sepulchers in which women have for ages been buried might be opened, and that some resurrection trumpet might bring up these living corpses to the fresh air and sunlight.

Go with me and I will show you a woman who by hardest toil supports her children, her drunken husband, her old father and mother, pays her house rent, always has wholesome food on her table, and when she can get some neighbor on the Sabbath to come in and take care of her family, appears in church with hat and cloak that are far from indicating the toil to which she is subjected. Such a woman as that has body and soul enough to fit her for any position. She could stand beside the majority of your salesmen and dispose of more goods. She could go into your wheelwright shops and beat one half of your workmen at making carriages. We talk about woman as though we had resigned to her all the light work, and ourselves had shouldered the heavier. But the day of judgment, which will reveal the sufferings of the stake and Inquisition, will marshal before the throne of God and the hierarchs of heaven the martyrs of wash-tub and needle. Now, I say if there be any preference in occupation, let women have it. God knows her trials are the severest. By her acuter sensitiveness to misfortune, by her hour of anguish, I demand that no one hedge up her pathway to a livelihood. Oh! the meanness, the despicability of men who begrudge a woman the right to work anywhere in any honorable calling!

I go still further and say that woman should have equal compensation with men. By what principle of justice is it that women in many of our cities get only two thirds as much pay as men, and in many cases only half? Here is the gigantic injustice—that for work equally well, if not better, done, woman receives far less compensation than man. Start with the National Government. Women clerks in Washington get nine hundred dollars for doing that for which men receive eighteen hundred dollars. The wheel of oppression is rolling over the necks of thousands of women who are at this moment in despair about what they are to do. Many of the largest mercantile establishments of our cities are accessory to these abominations, and from their large establishments there are scores of souls being pitched off into death, and their employers know it. Is there a God? Will there be a judgment? I tell you, if God rises up to redress woman's wrongs, many of our large establishments will be swallowed up quicker than a South American earthquake ever took down a city. God will catch these oppressors between the two millstones of his wrath and grind them to powder.

Why is it that a female principal in a school gets only eight hundred and twenty-five dollars for doing work for which a male principal gets sixteen hundred and fifty dollars? I hear from all this land the wail of womanhood. Man has nothing to answer to that wail but flatteries. He says she is an angel. She is not. She knows she is not. She is a human being who gets hungry when she has n food, and cold when she has no fire. Give her no more flatteries; give her justice! There are sixty-five thousand sewing-girls in New York and Brooklyn. Across the sunlight comes their death groan. It is not such a cry as comes from those who are suddenly hurled out of life, but a slow, grinding, horrible wasting-away. Gather them before you and look into their faces, pinched, ghastly, hunger-struck! Look at their fingers, needle-pricked and blood-tipped! See that premature stoop in the shoulders! Hear that dry, hacking, merciless cough! At a large meeting of these women held in a hall in Philadelphia, grand speeches were delivered, but a needle-woman took the stand, threw aside her faded shawl, and with her shriveled arm hurled a very thunder-bolt of eloquence, speaking out the horrors of her own experience.

Stand at the corner of a street in New York at six or seven o'clock in the morning as the women go to work. Many of them had no breakfast except the crumbs that were left over from the night before, or the crumbs they chew on their way through the street. Here they come! The working-girls of New York and Brooklyn. These engaged in head work, these in flower-making, in millinery, in paper-box making; but, most overworked of all and least compensated, the sewing-women. Why do they not take the city cars on their way up? They can not afford the five cents. If, concluding to deny herself something else, she gets into the car, give her a seat. You want to see how Latimer and Ridley appeared in the fire. Look at that woman and behold a more horrible martyrdom, a hotter fire, a more agonizing death. Ask that woman how much she gets for her work, and she will tell you six cents for making coarse shirts and find her own thread.

Years ago, one Sabbath night in the vestibule of this church, after service, a woman fell in convulsions. The doctor said she needed medicine not so much as something to eat. As she began to revive, in her delirium she said, gaspingly: "Eight cents! Eight cents! Eight cents! I wish I could get it done, I am so tired. I wish I could get some sleep, but I must get it done. Eight cents! Eight cents! Eight cents!" We found afterward that she was making garments for eight cents apiece, and that she could make but three of them in a day. Hear it! Three times eight are twenty-four. Hear it, men and women who have comfortable homes! Some of the worst villains of our cities are the employers of these women. They beat them down to the last penny and try to cheat them out of that. The woman must deposit a dollar or two before she gets the garments to work on. When the work is done it is sharply inspected, the most insignificant flaws picked out, and the wages refused and sometimes the dollar deposited not given back. The Women's Protective Union reports a case where one of the poor souls, finding a place where she could get more wages, resolved to change employers, and went to get her pay for work done. The employer says: "I hear you are going to leave me?" "Yes," she said, "and I have come to get what you owe me." He made no answer. She said: "Are you not going to pay me?" "Yes," he said, "I will pay you," and he kicked her down-stairs.

Oh, that Women's Protective Union, 19 Clinton Place, New York! The blessings of Heaven be on it for the merciful and divine work it is doing in the defense of toiling womanhood! What tragedies of suffering are presented to them day by day! A paragraph from their report: " ' Can you make Mr. Jones pay me? He owes me for three weeks at $2.50 a week, and I can't get anything, and my child is very sick!' The speaker, a young woman lately widowed, burst into a flood of tears as she spoke. She was bidden to come again the next afternoon and repeat her story to the attorney at his usual weekly hearing of frauds and impositions. Means were found by which Mr. Jones was induced to pay the $7.50."

Another paragraph from their report: "A fortnight had passed, when she modestly hinted a desire to know how much her services were worth. ' Oh, my dear,' he replied, ' you are getting to be one of the most valuable hands in the trade; you will always get the very best price. Ten dollars a week you will be able to earn very easily.' And the girl's fingers flew on with her work at a marvelous rate. The picture of $10 a week had almost turned her head. A few nights later, while crossing the ferry, she overheard the name of her employer in the conversation of girls who stood near: ' What, John Snipes? Why, he don't pay! Look out for him every time. He'll keep you on trial, as he calls it, for weeks, and then he'll let you go, and get some other fool!' And thus Jane Smith gained her warning against the swindler. But the Union held him in the toils of the law until he paid the worth of each of those days of ' trial.' "

Another paragraph: " Her mortification may be imagined when told that one of the two five-dollar bills which

11

she had just received for her work was counterfeit. But her mortification was swallowed up in indignation when her employer denied having paid her the money, and insultingly asked her to prove it. When the Protective Union had placed this matter in the courts, the judge said: ' You will pay Eleanor the amount of her claim, $5.83, and also the costs of the court.' "

How are these evils to be eradicated? Some say: " Give woman the ballot." What effect such ballot might have on other questions I am not here to discuss; but what would be the effect of female suffrage on women's wages? I do not believe that woman will ever get justice by woman's ballot. Indeed, women oppress women as much as men do. Do not women, as much as men, beat down to the lowest figure the woman who sews for them? Are not women as sharp as men on washer-women and milliners and mantua-makers? If a woman asks a dollar for her work, does not her female employer ask her if she will not take ninety cents? You say, " Only ten cents difference." But that is sometimes the difference between heaven and hell. Women often have less commiseration for women than men. If a woman steps aside from the path of rectitude, man may forgive — woman never! Woman will never get justice done her from woman's ballot. Neither will she get it from man's ballot. How then? God will rise up for her. God has more resources than we know of. The flaming sword that hung at Eden's gate when woman was driven out will cleave with its terrible edge her oppressors.

But there is something for women to do. Let young

people prepare to excel in spheres of work, and they will be able after awhile to get larger wages. Unskilled and incompetent labor must take what is given: skilled and competent labor will eventually make its own standard. Admitting that the law of supply and demand regulates these things, I contend that the demand for skilled labor is very great and the supply very small. Start with the idea that work is honorable, and that you can do some one thing better than anybody else. Resolve that, God helping, you will take care of yourself. If you are after awhile called into another relation you will all the better be qualified for it by your spirit of self-reliance, or if you are called to stay as you are, you can be happy and self-supporting.

Poets are fond of talking about man as an oak and woman the vine that climbs it; but I have seen many a tree fall that not only went down itself, but took all the vines with it. I can tell you of something stronger than an oak for an ivy to climb on, and that is the throne of the great Jehovah. Single or affianced, that woman is strong who leans on God and does her best. Many of you will go single-handed through life, and you will have to choose between two characters. Young woman, I am sure you will turn your back upon the useless, giggling, irresponsible nonentity which society ignominiously acknowledges to be a woman, and ask God to make you an humble, active, earnest Christian. What will become of that womanly disciple of the world? She is more thoughtful of the attitude she strikes upon the carpet than how she will look in the judgment; more worried about her freckles than her sins; more interested in her apparel than in her redemption. The dying actress whose life had been vicious said: "The scene closes—draw the curtain." Generally the tragedy comes first and the farce afterward; but in her life it was first the farce of a useless life and then the tragedy of a wretched eternity.

Compare the life and death of such a one with that of some Christian aunt that was once a blessing to your household. I do not know that she was ever asked to give her hand in marriage. She lived single, that, untrammeled, she might be everybody's blessing. Whenever the sick were to be visited or the poor to be provided with bread she went with a blessing. She could pray or sing "Rock of Ages" for any sick pauper who asked her. As she got older there were many days when she was a little sharp, but for the most part auntie was a sunbeam—just the one for Christmas Eve. She knew better than any one else how to fix things. Her every prayer, as God heard it, was full of everybody who had trouble. The brightest things in all the house dropped from her fingers. She had peculiar notions, but the grandest notion she ever had was to make you happy. She dressed well—auntie always dressed well; but her highest adornment was that of a meek and quiet spirit, which, in the sight of God, is of great price. When she died you all gathered lovingly about her; and as you carried her out to rest, the Sunday-school class almost covered the coffin with japonicas; and the poor people stood at the end of the alley, with their aprons to their eyes, sobbing bitterly, and the man of the world said, with Solomon: "Her price was above rubies;" and Jesus, as unto the maiden in Judea, commanded, "I say unto thee, Arise!"

TOBACCO AND OPIUM.

***

"Let the earth bring forth grass, the herb yielding seed."—GEN.
i: 11.

THE two first born of our earth were the grass-blade
and the herb. They preceded the brute creation and the
human family—the grass for the animal creation, the herb
for human service. The cattle came and took possession of
their inheritance, the grass-blade; man came and took
possession of his inheritance, the herb. We have the herb
for food as in case of hunger, for narcotic as in case of insomnia, for anodyne as in case of paroxysm, for stimulant
as when the pulses flag under the weight of disease. The
caterer comes and takes the herb and presents it in all
styles of delicacy. The physician comes and takes the
herb and compounds it for physical recuperation. Millions of people come and take the herb for ruinous physical and intellectual delectation. The herb, which was
divinely created, and for good purposes, has often been
degraded for bad results. There is a useful and a baneful
employment of the herbaceous kingdom.

There sprung up in Yucatan of this continent an herb
that has bewitched the world. In the fifteenth century it
crossed the Atlantic Ocean and captured Spain. Afterward it captured Portugal. Then the French embassadors

took it to Paris, and it captured the French Empire. Then Walter Raleigh took it to London, and it captured Great Britain. Nicotiana, ascribed to that genus by the botanists, but we all know it is the exhilarating, elevating, emparadising, nerve-shattering, dyspepsia-breeding, health-destroying tobacco. I shall not in my remarks be offensively personal, because you all use it, or nearly all! I know by experience how it soothes and roseates the world, and kindles sociality, and I also know some of its baleful results. I was its slave, and by the grace of God I have become its conqueror. Tens of thousands of people have been asking the question during the past two months, asking it with great pathos and great earnestness: "Does the use of tobacco produce cancerous and other troubles?" I shall not answer the question in regard to any particular case, but shall deal with the subject in a more general way.

You say to me, "Did God not create tobacco?" Yes. You say to me, "Is not God good?" Yes. Well, then, you say, "If God is good and he created tobacco, He must have created it for some good purpose." Yes, your logic is complete. But God created the common sense at the same time, by which we are to know how to use a poison and how not to use it. God created that just as He created henbane and nux vomica and copperas and belladonna and all other poisons, whether directly created by Himself or extracted by man.

That it is a poison no man of common sense will deny. A case was reported where a little child lay upon its mother's lap and one drop fell from a pipe to the child's lip, and it went into convulsions and into death. But you say, "Haven't people lived on in complete use of it to old age?" Oh, yes; just as I have seen inebriates seventy years old. In Boston, years ago, there was a meeting in which there were several centenarians, and they were giving their experience, and one centenarian said that he had lived over a hundred years, and that he ascribed it to the fact that he had refrained from the use of intoxicating liquors. Right after him another centenarian said he had lived over a hundred years, and he ascribed it to the fact that for the last fifty years he had hardly seen a sober moment. It is an amazing thing how many outrages men may commit upon their physical system and yet live on. In the case of the man of the jug he lived on because his body was pickled. In the case of the man of the pipe, he lived on because his body turned into smoked liver!

But are there no truths to be uttered in regard to this great evil? What is the advice to be given to the multitude of young people who hear me this day? What is the advice you are going to give to your children?

First of all, we must advise them to abstain from the use of tobacco because all the medical fraternity of the United States and Great Britain agree in ascribing to this habit terrific unhealth. The men whose life-time work is the study of the science of health say so, and shall I set up my opinion against theirs? Dr. Agnew, Dr. Olcott, Dr. Barnes, Dr. Rush, Dr. Mott, Dr. Harvey, Dr. Hosack— all the doctors, allopathic, homeopathic, hydropathic, eclectic, denounce the habit as a matter of unhealth. A distinguished physician declared he considered the use of tobacco caused seventy different styles of disease, and he says: " Of all the cases of cancer in the mouth that have come under my observation, almost in every case it has been ascribed to tobacco."

The united testimony of all physicians is that it depresses the nervous system, that it takes away twenty-five per cent. of the physical vigor of this generation, and that it goes on as the years multiply and, damaging this generation with accumulated curse, it strikes other centuries. And if it is so deleterious to the body, how much more destructive to the mind. An eminent physician, who was the superintendent of the insane asylum at Northampton, Massachusetts, says: " Fully one half the patients we get in our asylum have lost their intellect through the use of tobacco." If it is such a bad thing to injure the body, what a bad thing, what a worse thing it is to injure the mind, and any man of common sense knows that tobacco attacks the nervous system, and everybody knows that the nervous system attacks the mind.

Besides that, all reformers will tell you that the use of tobacco creates an unnatural thirst, and it is the cause of drunkenness in America to-day more than anything else. In all cases where you find men taking strong drink you find they use tobacco. There are men who use tobacco who do not take strong drink, but all who use strong drink use tobacco, and that shows beyond controversy there is an affinity between the two products. There are reformers here to-day who will testify to you it is impossible for a man to reform from taking strong drink until he quits tobacco. In many of the cases where men have been reformed from strong drink and have gone back to their cups, they have testified that they first touched tobacco and then they surrendered to intoxicants.

I say in the presence of this assemblage to-day, in which there are many physicians—and they know that what I say is true on the subject—that the pathway to the drunkard's grave and the drunkard's hell is strewn thick with tobacco-leaves. What has been the testimony on this subject? Is this a mere statement of a preacher whose business it is to talk morals, or is the testimony of the world just as emphatic? What did Benjamin Franklin say? " I never saw a well man in the exercise of common sense who would say that tobacco did him any good." What did Thomas Jefferson say? Certainly he is good authority. He says in regard to the culture of tobacco, " It is a culture productive of infinite wretchdness." What did Horace Greeley say of it? " It is a profane stench." What did Daniel Webster say of it? " If those men must smoke, let them take the horse-shed!" One reason why the habit goes on from destruction to destruction is that so many ministers of the gospel take it. They smoke themselves into bronchitis, and then the dear people have to send them to Europe to get them restored from exhausting religious services! They smoke until the nervous system is shattered. They smoke themselves to death. I could mention the names of five distinguished clergymen who died of cancer of the mouth, and the doctor said, in every case, it was the result of tobacco. The tombstone of many a minister of religion has been covered all over with handsome eulogy, when, if the true epitaph had been written, it would have said: "Here lies a man killed by too much cavendish!" They smoke until the world is blue, and their theology is blue, and everything is blue. How can a man stand in the pulpit and preach on the subject of temperance when he is indulging such a habit as that? I have seen a cuspadore in a pulpit into which the holy man dropped his cud before he got up to read about "blessed are the pure in heart," and to read about the rolling of sin as a sweet morsel under the tongue, and to read about the unclean animals in Leviticus that chewed the cud.

About sixty-five years ago a student at Andover Theological Seminary graduated into the ministry. He had an eloquence and a magnetism which sent him to the front. Nothing could stand before him. But in a few months he was put in an insane asylum, and the physician said tobacco was the cause of the disaster. It was the custom in those days to give a portion of tobacco to every patient in the asylum. Nearly twenty years passed along, and that man was walking the floor of his cell in the asylum, when his reason returned, and he saw the situation, and he took the tobacco from his mouth and threw it against the iron gate of the place in which he was confined, and he said: "What brought me here? What keeps me here? Tobacco! tobacco! God forgive me, God help me, and I will never use it again." He was fully restored to reason, came forth, preached the Gospel of Christ for some ten years, and then went into everlasting blessedness.

There are ministers of religion now in this country who are dying by inches, and they do not know what is the matter with them. They are being killed by tobacco.

They are despoiling their influence through tobacco. They are malodorous with tobacco. I could give one paragraph of history, and that would be my own experience. It took ten cigars to make one sermon, and I got very nervous, and I awakened one day to see what an outrage I was committing upon my health by the use of tobacco. I was about to change settlement, and a generous tobacconist of Philadelphia told me if I would come to Philadelphia and be his pastor he would give me all the cigars I wanted for nothing all the rest of my life. I halted. I said to myself, " If I smoke more than I ought to now in these war times, and when my salary is small, what would I do if I had gratuitous and unlimited supply?" Then and there, twenty-four years ago, I quit once and forever. It made a new man of me. Much of the time the world looked blue before that, because I was looking through tobacco smoke. Ever since the world has been full of sunshine, and though I have done as much work as any one of my age, God has blessed me, it seems to me, with the best health that a man ever had.

I say that no minister of religion can afford to smoke. Put in my hand all the money expended by Christian men in Brooklyn for tobacco, and I will support three orphan asylums as well and as grandly as the three great orphan asylums already established. Put into my hand the money spent by the Christians of America for tobacco, and I will clothe, shelter, and feed all the suffering poor of the continent. The American Church gives a million dollars a year for the salvation of the heathen, and American Christians smoke five million dollars' worth of tobacco.

I stand here to-day in the presence of a vast multitude of young people who are forming their habits. Between seventeen and twenty-five years of age a great many young men get on them habits in the use of tobacco that they never get over. Let me say to all my young friends, you can not afford to smoke, you can not afford to chew. You either take very good tobacco, or you take very cheap tobacco. If it is cheap, I will tell you why it is cheap. It is made of burdock, and lampblack, and sawdust, and colt's-foot, and plantain leaves, and fuller's earth, and salt, and alum, and lime, and a little tobacco, and you can not afford to put such a mess as that in your mouth. But if you use expensive tobacco, do you not think it would be better for you to take that amount of money which you are now expending for this herb, and which you will expend during the course of your life if you keep the habit up, and with it buy a splendid farm and make the afternoon and the evening of your life comfortable?

There are young men whose life is going out inch by inch from cigarettes. Now, do you not think it would be well for you to listen to the testimony of a merchant of New York, who said this: "In early life I smoked six cigars a day at six and a half cents each. They averaged that. I thought to myself one day, I'll just put aside all I consume in cigars and all I would consume if I keep on in the habit, and I'll see what it will come to by compound interest." And he gives this tremendous statistic: "Last July completed thirty-nine years since, by the grace of God, I was emancipated from the filthy habit, and the saving amounted to the enormous sum of $29,102.03 by compound interest. We lived in the city, but the children, who had learned something of the enjoyment of country life from their annual visits to their grandparents, longed for a home among the green fields. I found a very pleasant place in the country for sale. The cigar money came into requisition, and I found it amounted to a sufficient sum to purchase the place, and it is mine. Now, boys, you take your choice. Smoking without a home, or a home without smoking." This is common sense as well as religion.

I must say a word to my friends who smoke the best tobacco, and who could stop at any time. What is your Christian influence in this respect? What is your influence upon young men? Do you not think it would be better for you to exercise a little self-denial! People wondered why George Briggs, Governor of Massachusetts, wore a cravat but no collar. "Oh," they said, "it is an absurd eccentricity." This was the history of the cravat without any collar: For many years before he had been talking with an inebriate, trying to persuade him to give up the habit of drinking and he said to the inebriate, "Your habit is entirely unnecessary." "Ah!" replied the inebriate, "we do a great many things that are not necessary. It isn't necessary that you should have that collar." "Well," said Mr. Briggs, "I'll never wear a collar again if you will stop drinking." "Agreed," said the other. They joined hands in a pledge that they kept for twenty years—kept until death. That is magnificent. That is Gospel, practical Gospel, worthy of George Briggs, worthy of you. Self-denial for others. Subtraction from our advantage that there may be an addition to somebody else's advantage.

But what I have said has been chiefly appropriate for men. Now my subject widens and shall be appropriate for both sexes. In all ages of the world there has been a search for some herb or flower that would stimulate lethargy and compose grief. Among the ancient Greeks and Egyptians they found something they called nepenthe, and the Theban women knew how to compound it. If a person should chew a few of those leaves his grief would be immediately whelmed with hilarity. Nepenthe passed out from the consideration of the world and then came hasheesh, which is from the Indian hemp. It is manufactured from the flowers at the top. The workman with leathern apparel walks through the field and the exudation of the plants adheres to the leathern garments, and then the man comes out and scrapes off this exudation, and it is mixed with aromatics and becomes an intoxicant that has brutalized whole nations. Its first effect is sight, spectacle glorious and grand beyond all description, but afterward it pulls down body, mind, and soul into anguish.

I knew one of the most brilliant men of our time. His appearance in a newspaper column, or a book, or a magazine was an enchantment. In the course of a half hour he could produce more wit and more valuable information than any man I ever heard talk. But he chewed hasheesh. He first took it out of curiosity to see whether the power said to be attached really existed. He took it. He got under the power of it. He tried to break loose. He put his hand in the cockatrice's den to see whether it would bite, and he found out to his own undoing. His friends gathered around and tried to save him, but he could not be saved. The father, a minister of the Gospel, prayed with him and counseled him, and out of a comparatively small salary employed the first medical advice of New York, Philadelphia, Edinburgh, Paris, London, and Berlin, for he was his only son. No help came. First his body gave way in pangs and convulsions of suffering. Then his mind gave way and he became a raving maniac. Then his soul went out blaspheming God into a starless eternity. He died at thirty years of age. Behold the work of accursed hasheesh.

But I must put my emphasis upon the use of opium. It is made from the white poppy. It is not a new discovery. Three hundred years before Christ we read of it; but it was not until the seventh century that it took up its march of death, and, passing out of the curative and the medicinal, through smoking and mastication it has become the curse of nations. In 1861 there were imported into this country one hundred and seven thousand pounds of opium. In 1880, nineteen years after, there were imported five hundred and thirty thousand pounds of opium. In 1876 there were in this country two hundred and twenty-five thousand opium-consumers. Now, it is estimated there are in the United States to-day six hundred thousand victims of opium. It is appalling.

We do not know why some families do not get on. There is something mysterious about them. The opium habit is so stealthy, it is so deceitful, and it is so deathful, you can cure a hundred men of strong drink where you can cure one opium-eater.

I have knelt down in this very church by those who were elegant in apparel, and elegant in appearance, and from the depths of their souls and from the depths of my soul, we cried out for God's rescue. Somehow it did not come. In many a household only the physician and pastor know it—the physician called in for physical relief, the pastor called in for spiritual relief, and they both fail. The physician confesses his defeat, the minister of religion confesses his defeat, for somehow God does not seem to hear a prayer offered for an opium-eater. His grace is infinite, and I have been told there are cases of reformation. I never saw one. I say this not to wound the feelings of any who may feel this awful grip, but to utter a potent warning that you stand back from that gate of hell. Oh, man, oh, woman, tampering with this great evil, have you fallen back on this as a permanent resource because of some physical distress or mental anguish? Better stop. The ecstasies do not pay for the horrors. The Paradise is followed too soon by the Pandemonium. Morphia, a blessing of God for the relief of sudden pang and of acute dementia, misappropriated and never intended for permanent use.

It is not merely the barbaric fanatics that are taken down by it. Did you ever read De Quincey's " Confessions of an Opium-Eater?" He says that during the first ten years the habit handed to him all the keys of Paradise, but it would take something as mighty as De Quincey's pen to describe the consequent horrors. There is nothing that I have ever read about the tortures of the damned that seemed more horrible than those which De Quincey says he suffered. Samuel Taylor Coleridge first conquered the world with his exquisite pen, and then was conquered by opium. The most brilliant, the most eloquent lawyer of the nineteenth century went down under its power, and there is a vast multitude of men and women—but more women than men—who are going into the dungeon of that awful incarceration.

The worst thing about it is, it takes advantage of one's weakness. De Quincey says: "I got to be an opium-eater on account of my rheumatism." Coleridge says: "I got to be an opium-eater on account of my sleeplessness." For what are you taking it? For God's sake do not take it long. The wealthiest, the grandest families going down under its power. Twenty-five thousand victims of opium in Chicago. Twenty-five thousand victims of opium in St. Louis, and, according to that average, seventy-five thousand victims of opium in New York and Brooklyn.

The clerk of a drug store says: "I can tell them when they come in; there is something about their complexion, something about their manner, something about the look of their eyes that shows they are victims." Some in the struggle to get away from it try chloral. Whole tons of chloral manufactured in Germany every year. Baron Liebig says he knows one chemist in Germany who manufactures a half ton of chloral every week. Beware of hydrate of chloral. It is coming on with mighty tread to curse these cities. But I am chiefly under this head speaking of the morphine. The devil of morphia is going to be in this country, in my opinion, mightier than the devil of alcohol. By the power of the Christian pulpit, by the power of the Christianized printing-press, by the power of the Lord God Almighty, all these evils are going to be extirpated—all, all, and you have a work in regard to that, and I have a work. But what we do we had better do right away. The clock ticks now, and we hear it; after awhile the clock will tick and we will not hear it.

I sat at a country fireside, and I saw the fire kindle and blaze, and go out. I sat long enough at that fireside to get a good many practical reflections, and I said: "That is like human life, that fire on the hearth." We put on the fagots and they blaze up, and out, and on, and the whole room is filled with the light, gay of sparkle, gay of flash, gay of crackle. Emblem of boyhood. Now the fire intensifies. Now the flame reddens into coals. Now the heat is becoming more and more intense, and the more it is stirred the redder is the coal. Now with one sweep of flame it cleaves the way, and all the hearth glows with the intensity. Emblem of full manhood. Now the coals begin to whiten. Now the heat lessens. Now the flickering shadows die along the wall. Now the fagots fall apart. Now the household hover over the expiring embers. Now the last breath of smoke is lost in the chimney. The fire is out. Shovel up the white remains. Ashes! Ashes!

WHY ARE SATAN AND SIN
PERMITTED?

" Wherefore do the wicked live?"—Job xxi: 7,

Poor Job! With tusks and horns and hoofs and stings, all the misfortunes of life seemed to come upon him at once. Bankruptcy, bereavement, scandalization, and eruptive disease so irritating that he had to re-enforce his ten finger-nails with pieces of earthenware to scratch himself withal. His wife took the diagnosis of his complaints and prescribed profanity. She thought he would feel better if between the paroxysms of grief and pain he would swear a little. For each boil a plaster of objurgation.

Probably no man was ever more tempted to take the bad advice than when, at last, Job's three exasperating friends came in, Eliphaz, Zophar, and Bildad, practically saying to him, " You old sinner, serves you right; you are a hypocrite; what a sight you are! God has sent these chastisements for your wickedness."

The disfigured invalid, putting down the pieces of broken saucer with which he had been rubbing his arms, with swollen eyelids looks up and says to his garrulous friends in substance, " The most wicked people sometimes have the best health and are the most prospered," and then in that connection hurls the question which every man and woman has asked in some juncture of affairs, "Wherefore do the wicked live?"

They build up fortunes that overshadow the earth. They confound all the life-insurance tables on the subject of longevity, dying octogenarians, perhaps nonagenarians, possibly centenarians. Ahab in the palace, Naboth in the cabinet. Unclean Herod on the throne, consecrated Paul twisting ropes for tent-making. Manasseh, the worst of all the kings of Juda, living longer than any of them. While the general rule is the wicked do not live out half their days, there are exceptions where they live on to great age and in a Paradise of beauty and luxuriance, and die with a whole college of physicians expending its skill in trying further prolongation of life, and have a funeral with casket under mountain of calla-lilies, the finest equipages of the city jingling and flashing into line, the poor, angle-worm of the dust carried out to its hole in the ground with the pomp that might make a spirit from some other world suppose that the Archangel Michael was dead.

Go up among the finest residences of the city, and on some of the door-plates you will find the names of those mightiest for commercial and social iniquity. They are the vampires of society—they are the gorgons of the century. Some of these men have each wheel of their carriage a juggernaut wet with the blood of those sacrified to their avarice. Some of them are like Caligula, who wished that all the people had only one neck that he might strike it off at one blow. Oh, the slain, the slain! A long procession of usurers and libertines and infamous quacks and legal charlatans and world-grabbing monsters. What apostleship of despoliation! Demons incarnate. Hundreds of men concentering all their energies of body, mind, and soul in one prolonged, ever-intensifying, and unrelenting effort to scald and scarify and blast and consume the world. I do not blame you for asking me the quivering, throbbing, burning, resounding, appalling question of my text, "Wherefore do the wicked live?"

In the first place, they live to demonstrate beyond all controversy the long-suffering patience of God. You sometimes say, under some great affront, " I will not stand it;" but perhaps you are compelled to stand it. God, with all the batteries of omnipotence loaded with thunder-bolts, stands it century after century. I have no doubt sometimes an angel comes to Him and suggests, "Now is the time to strike." "No," says God; "wait a year, wait twenty years, wait a century, wait five centuries." What God does is not so wonderful as what He does not do. He has the reserve corps with which He could strike Mormonism and Mohammedanism and Paganism from the earth in a day. He could take all the fraud in New York on the west side of Broadway and hurl it into the Hudson, and all the fraud on the east side of Broadway and hurl it into the East River in an hour. He under-stands the combination lock of every dishonest money-safe, and could blow it up quicker than by any earthly explo-sive. Written all over the earth, written all over history are the words, " Divine forbearance, divine leniency, divine long-suffering."

I wonder that God did not burn this world up two thou-sand years ago, scattering its ashes into immensity, its aerolites dropping into other worlds to be kept in their museums as specimens of a defunct planet. People sometimes talk of God as though He were hasty in His judgments and as though He snapped men up quick. Oh, no! He waited one hundred and twenty years for the people to get into the ark, and warned them all the time—one hundred and twenty years, then the flood came. The Anchor Line gives only a month's announcement of the sailing of the " Circassia," the White Star Line gives only a month's announcement of the sailing of the "Britannic," the Cunard Line gives only a month's announcement of the sailing of the " Oregon;" but of the sailing of that ship that Noah commanded God gave one hundred and twenty years' announcement and warning. Patience antediluvian, patience postdiluvian, patience in times Adamic, Abrahamic, Mosaic, Davidic, Pauline, Lutheran, Whitefieldian. Patience with men and nations. Patience with barbarisms and civilizations. Six thousand years of patience! Overtopping attribute of God, all of whose attributes are immeasurable. Why do the wicked live? That their overthrow may be the more impressive and climacteric. They must pile up their mischief until all the community shall see it, until the nation shall see it, until all the world shall see it. The higher it goes up the harder it will come down and the grander will be the divine vindication.

God will not allow sin to sneak out of the world. God will not allow it merely to resign and quit. This shall not be a case that goes by default because no one appears against it. God will arraign it, handcuff it, try it, bring against it the verdict of all the good, and then gibbet it so high up that if one half of the gibbet stood on Mount Washington and the other on the Himalaya, it would not be any more conspicuous.

About fifteen years ago we had in this country a most illustrious instance of how God lets a man go on in iniquity, so that at the close of the career his overthrow may be the more impressive, full of warning and climacteric. First, an honest chairmaker, then an alderman, then a member of congress, then a supervisor of a city, then school commissioner, then state senator, then commissioner of public works—on and up, stealing thousands of dollars here and thousands of dollars there, until the malfeasance in office overtopped anything the world had ever seen—making the new Court House in New York a monument of municipal crime, and rushing the debt of the city from thirty-six million dollars to ninety-seven millions. Now, he is at the top of millionairedom.

Country-seat terraced and arbored and parterred clear to the water's brink. Horses enough to stock a king's equerry. Grooms and postilions in full rig. Wine cellars enough to make a whole legislature drunk. New York finances and New York politics in his vest pocket. He winked, and men in high place fell. He lifted his little finger, and ignoramuses took important office. He whispered, and in Albany and Washington they said it thundered. Wider and mightier and more baleful his influence, until it seemed as if Pandemonium was to be adjourned to this world, and in the Satanic realm there was to be a change of administration, and Apollyon, who had held dominion so long, should have a successful competitor.

To bring all to a climax, a wedding came in the house of that man. Diamonds as large as hickory nuts. A pin of sixty diamonds representing sheaves of wheat. Musicians in a semicircle, half-hidden by a great harp of flowers. Ships of flowers. Forty silver sets, one of them with two hundred and forty pieces. One wedding-dress that cost five thousand dollars. A famous libertine, who owned several Long Island Sound steamboats, and not long before he was shot for his crimes, sent as a wedding present to that house a frosted silver iceberg, with representations of arctic bears walking on icicle-handles and ascending the spoons. Was there ever such a convocation of pictures, bronzes, of bric-à-brac, of grandeurs, social grandeurs? The highest wave of New York splendor rolled into that house and recoiled perhaps never again to rise so high. But just at that time, when all earthly and infernal observation was concentered on that man, eternal justice, impersonated by that wonder of the American bar, Charles O'Connor, got on the track of the offender. First arraignment, then sentence to twelve years' imprisonment under twelve indictments, then penitentiary on Blackwell's Island, then a lawsuit against him for six million dollars, then incarceration in Ludlow Street jail, then escape to foreign land, to be brought back under the stout grip of the constabulary, then dying of broken heart in a prison cell. God allowed him to go on in iniquity until all the world saw as never before that "the way of the transgressor is hard," and that dishonesty will not declare permanent dividends, and that you had better be an honest chairmaker with a day's wages at a time than a brilliant commissioner of public works, all your pockets crammed with plunder.

What a brilliant figure in history is William the Conqueror, the intimidator of France, of Anjou, of Brittany, victor at Hastings, snatching the crown of England and setting it on his own brow, destroying homesteads that he might have a larger game forest, making a Doomsday Book by which he could keep the whole land under despotic espionage, proclaiming war in revenge for a joke uttered in regard to his obesity. Harvest fields and vineyards going down under the cavalry hoof. Nations horror-struck. But one day while at the apex of all observation he is riding out and the horse put his hoof on a hot cinder, throwing the king so violently against the pommel of the saddle that he dies, his son hastening to England to get the crown before the breath has left his father's body.

The imperial corpse drawn by a cart, most of the attendants leaving it in the street because of a fire alarm that they might go off and see the conflagration. And just as they are going to put his body down in the church which he had built, a man stepping up and saying, " Bishop, the man you praise is a robber. This church stands on my father's homestead. The property on which this church is built is mine. I reclaim my right. In the name of Almighty God I forbid you to bury the king here, or to cover him with my glebe." " Go up," said the ambition of William the Conqueror. " Go up by conquest, go up by throne, go up in the sight of all nations, go up by cruelties." But one day God said, " Come down, come down by the way of a miserable death, come down by the way of an ignominious obsequies, come down in the sight of all nations, come clear down, come down forever." And you and I see the same thing on a smaller scale many and many a time—illustrations of the fact that God lets the wicked live that He may make their overthrow the more climacteric.

What is true in regard to sin is true in regard to its author, Satan, called Abaddon, called the Prince of the Power of the Air, called the serpent, called the dragon. It seems to me any intelligent man must admit that there is a commander-in-chief of all evil.

The Persians called him Ahriman, the Hindus called him Siva. He was represented on canvas as a mythological combination of Thor and Cerberus and Pan and Vulcan and other horrible addenda. I do not care what you call him, that monster of evil is abroad, and his one work is destruction. John Milton almost glorified him by witchery of description, but he is the concentration of all meanness and of all despicability. My little child, seven years of age, said to her mother one day, "Why don't God kill the devil at once, and have done with it?" In less terse phrase we have all asked the same question. The Bible says he is to be imprisoned and he is to be chained down. Why not heave the old miscreant into his dungeon now? Does it not seem as if his volume of infamy were complete? Does it not seem as if the last fifty years would make an appropriate peroration? No; God will let him go on to the top of all bad endeavor, and then when all the earth and all constellations and galaxies and all the universe are watching, God will hurl him down with a violence and ghastliness enough to persuade five hundred eternities that a rebellion against God must perish. God will not do it by piecemeal, God will not do it by small skirmish. He will wait until all the troops are massed, and then some day when in defiant and confident mood, at the head of his army, this Goliath of hell stalks forth, our champion, the son of David, will strike him down, not with smooth stones from the brook, but with fragments from the Rock of Ages. But it will not be done until this giant of evil and his holy antagonist come out within full sight of the two great armies. The tragedy is only postponed to make the overthrow more impressive and climacteric. Do not fret. If God can afford to wait you can afford to wait. God's clock of destiny strikes only once in a thousand years. Do not try to measure events by the second-hand on your little time-piece. Sin and Satan go on only that their overthrow may at last be the more terrific, the more impressive, the more resounding, the more climacteric.

Why do the wicked live? In order that they may build up fortresses for righteousness to capture. Have you not noticed that God harnesses men, bad men, and accomplishes good through them? Witness Cyrus, witness Nebuchadnezzar, witness the fact that the Bastile of oppression was pried open by the bayonets of a bad man. Recently there came to me the fact that a college had been built at the Far West for infidel purposes. There was to be no nonsense of chapel prayers, no Bible reading there. All the professors there were pronounced infidels. The college was opened, and the work went on, but, of course, failed. Not long ago a Presbyterian minister was in a bank in that village on purposes of business, and he over heard in an adjoining room the board of trustees of that college discussing what they had better do with the institution, as it did not get on successfully, and one of the trustees proposed that it be handed over to the Presbyterians, prefacing the word Presbyterians with a very unhappy expletive. The resolutions were passed, and that fortress of infidelity has become a fortress of old-fashioned, orthodox religion, the only religion that will be worth a snap of your finger when you come to die or appear in the Day of Judgment. The devil built the college. Righteousness captured it.

In some city there goes up a great club-house—the architecture, the furniture, all the equipment a bedazzlement of wealth. That particular club-house is designed to make gambling and dissipation respectable.

Do not fret. That splendid building will after a while be a free library, or it will be a hospital, or it will be a gallery of pure art. Again and again observatories have been built by infidelity, and the first thing you know they go into the hand of Christian science. God said in the Bible that He would put a hook in Sennacherib's nose and pull him down by a way he knew not. And God has a hook to-day in the nose of every Sennacherib of infidelity and sin, and will drag him about as He will. Marble halls deserted to sinful amusements will yet be dedicated for religious assemblage. All these castles of sin are to be captured for God as we go forth with the battle-shout that Oliver Cromwell rang out at the head of his troops as he rode in on the field of Naseby: " Let God arise and let His enemies be scattered!" After a great fire in London, amid the ruins there was nothing left but an arch with the name of the architect upon it; and, my friends, whatever else goes down, God stays up.

Why do the wicked live? That some of them may be monuments of mercy.

So it was with John Newton, so it was with Augustine, perhaps so it was with you. Chieftains of sin to become chieftains of grace. Paul, the apostle, made out of Saul, the persecutor. Baxter, the flaming evangel, made out of Baxter, the blasphemer. Whole squadrons, with streamers of Emmanuel floating from the masthead, though once they were launched from the dry-docks of diabolism. God lets these wicked men live that He may make jewels out of them for coronets, that He may make tongues of fire out of them for Pentecosts, that He may make warriors out of them for Armageddons, that he may make conquerors out of them for the day when they shall ride at the head of the white-horse host in the grand review of the resurrection.

Why do the wicked live? To make it plain beyond all controversy that there is another place of adjustment. So many of the bad up, so many of the good down. It seems to me that no man can look abroad without saying—no man of common sense, religious or irreligious, can look abroad without saying, "There must be some place where brilliant scoundrelism shall be arrested, where innocence shall get out from under the heel of despotism." Common fairness as well as eternal justice demands it.

We adjourn to the great assizes, the stupendous injustices of this life. They are not righted here. There must be some place where they will be righted. God can not afford to omit the judgment day or the reconstruction of conditions. For you can not make me believe that that man stuffed with all abomination, having devoured widows' houses and digested them, looking with basilisk or tigerish eyes upon his fellows, no music so sweet to him as the sound of breaking hearts, is, at death, to get out of the landau at the front door of the sepulcher and pass right on through to the back door of the sepulcher, and find a celestial turnout waiting for him, so that he can drive tandem right up primrosed hills, one glory riding as lackey ahead, and another glory riding as postilion behind, while that poor woman who supported her invalid husband and her helpless children by taking in washing and ironing, often putting her hand to her side where the cancerous trouble had already begun, and dropping dead late on Saturday night while she was preparing the garments for the Sabbath day, coming afoot to the front door of the sepulcher, shall pass through to the back door of the sepulcher and find nothing waiting, no one to welcome, no one to tell her the way to the King's gate. I will not believe it. Solomon was confounded in his day by what he represents as princes afoot and beggars a-horseback, but I tell you there must be a place and a time when the right foot will get into the stirrup. To demonstrate beyond all controversy that there is another place for adjustment, God lets the wicked live.

Why do the wicked live? For the same reason that He lets us live—to have time for repentance.

Where would you and I have been if sin had been followed by immediate catastrophe? While the foot of Christ is fleet as that of a roebuck when He comes to save, it does seem as if he were hoppled with great languors and infinite lethargies when He comes to punish. Oh, I celebrate God's slowness, God's retardation, God's putting off the retribution! Do you not think, my brother, it would be a great deal better for us to exchange our impatient hypercriticism of Providence because this man, by watering of stock, makes a million dollars in one day, and another man rides on in one bloated iniquity year after year—would it not be better for us to exchange that impatient hypercriticism for gratitude everlasting that God let us who were wicked live, though we deserved nothing but capsize and demolition? Oh, I celebrate God's slowness! The slower the rail-train comes the better, if the drawbridge is off.

How long have you, my brother, lived unforgiven? Fifteen, twenty, forty, sixty years? Lived through great awakenings, lived through domestic sorrow, lived through commercial calamity, lived through providential crises that startled nations, and you are living yet, strangers to God, and with no hope for a great future into which you may be precipitated. Oh, would it not be better for us to get our nature through the Grace of Christ revolutionized and transfigured? For I want you to know that God sometimes changes His gait, and instead of the deliberate tread He is the swift witness, and sometimes the enemies of God are suddenly destroyed, and that without remedy.

Make God your ally. What an offer that is! Do not fight against Him. Do not contend against your best interests. Yield this morning to the best impulse of your heart, and that is toward Christ and heaven. Do not fight the Lord that made you and offers to redeem you.

Philip of France went out with his army, with bows and arrows, to fight King Edward III. of England; but just as they got into the critical moment of the battle, a shower of rain came and relaxed the bow-strings so that they were of no effect, and Philip and his army were worsted. And all your weaponry against God will be as nothing when he rains upon you discomfiture from the heavens. Do not fight the Lord any longer. Change allegiance. Take down the old flag of sin, run up the new flag of grace. It does not take the Lord Jesus Christ the thousandth part of a second to convert you if you will only surrender, be willing to be saved. The American Congress was in anxiety during the Revolutionary War while awaiting to hear news from the conflict between Washington and Cornwallis, and the anxiety became intense and almost unbearable as the days went by. When the news came at last that Cornwallis had surrendered and the war was practically over, so great was the excitement that the doorkeeper of the House of Congress dropped dead from joyful excitement. And if this long war between your soul and God should come to an end this morning by your entire surrender, the war forever over, the news would very soon reach the heavens, and nothing but the supernatural health of your loved ones before the throne would keep them from being prostrated with overjoy at the cessation of all spiritual hostilities.

WORSHIP IN SONG.

[Preached in the Brooklyn Tabernacle, May 2, 1886.]

It came even to pass, as the trumpeters and singers were as one, to make one sound to be heard in praising and thanking the Lord.—II Chron. v : 13.

The temple was done. It was the very chorus of all magnificence and pomp. Splendor crowded against splendor. It was *the diamond necklace of the earth*. From the huge pillars crowned with leaves of flowers and rows of pomegranate wrought out in burnished metal, down even to the tongs and snuffers made out of pure gold, everything was as complete as the God-directed architect could make it. It seemed as if a vision from heaven had alighted on the mountains.

The day for dedication came. Tradition says that there were in and around about the temple on that day two hundred thousand silver trumpets, forty thousand harps, forty thousand timbrels, and two hundred thousand singers; so that that all modern demonstrations at Düsseldorf or Boston seem nothing compared with that. As this great sound surged up amid the precious stones of the temple, it must have seemed like the River of Life, dashing against the amethyst of the wall of heaven. The sound arose, and God, as if to show that He was well pleased with the music which His children make in all ages, dropped into the midst of the temple a cloud of glory so overpowering that the officiating priests were obliged to stop in the midst of the services.

There has been much discussion as to where music was born. I think that at the beginning, when the morning stars sang together and all the sons of God shouted for joy, that the earth heard the echo. The cloud on which the angels stood to celebrate the creation was the birthplace of song. The stars that glitter at night are only so many keys of celestial pearl on which God's fingers play the music of the spheres. Inanimate nature is full of God's stringed and wind instruments. Silence itself—perfect silence is only a musical rest in God's great anthem of worship. Wind among the leaves, insect humming in the summer air, the rush of billow upon beach, the ocean far out sounding its everlasting psalm, the bobolink on the edge of the forest, the quail whistling up from the grass, are music.

While visiting Blackwell's Island I heard coming from a window of the lunatic asylum a very sweet song. It was sung by one who had lost her reason, and I have come to believe that even the deranged and disordered elements of nature would make music to our ear, if we only had acuteness enough to listen. I suppose that even the sounds in nature that are discordant and repulsive make harmony in God's ear. You know that you may come so near to an orchestra that the sounds are painful instead of pleasurable, and I think that we stand so near devastating storm and frightful whirlwind we cannot hear that which makes to God's ear and the ear of the spirits above us a music as complete as it is tremendous. The Day of Judgment, which will be a day of uproar and tumult, I suppose will bring no dissonance to the ears of those who can calmly listen; although it will be as when some great performer is executing a boisterous piece of music, he sometimes breaks down the instrument on which he plays; so it may be on that last day that the grand march of God, played by the fingers of thunder, and earthquake, and conflagration may break down the world upon which the music is executed.

Not only is inanimate nature full of music but God has wonderfully organized the human voice, so that in the plainest throat and lungs there are fourteen direct muscles which can make over sixteen thousand different sounds! Now, there are thirty indirect muscles which can make, it has been estimated, more than one hundred and seventy-three millions of sounds. Now, I say, when God has so constructed the human voice, and when He has filled the whole earth with harmony, and when He recognized it in the ancient temple, I have a right to come to the conclusion that God loves music.

I propose this morning to speak about sacred music, first showing you its importance, and then stating some of the obstacles to its advancement. I draw the first argument for the importance of sacred music from the fact that God commanded it. Through Paul He tells us to admonish one another in psalms, and hymns, and spiritual songs; through David He cries out: "Sing ye to God all ye kingdoms of the earth." And there are hundreds of other passages I might name, proving that it is as much a man's duty to sing as it is his duty to pray. Indeed, I think there are more commands in the Bible to sing than there are to pray. God not only asks for the human voice, but for the instruments of music. He asks for the cymbal and the harp and the trumpet. And I suppose that, in the last days of the Church, the harp, the lute, the trumpet, and all the instruments of music that have given their chief aid to the theatre and bacchanal, will be brought by their masters and laid down at the feet of Christ, and then sounded in the Church's triumph on her way from suffering into glory. "Praise ye the Lord!" Praise Him with your voices. Praise Him with stringed instruments and with organs.

I draw another argument for the importance of this exercise from the impressiveness of the exercise. You know something of what secular music has achieved. You know it has made its impression upon governments, upon laws, upon literature, upon whole generations. One inspiriting national air is worth thirty thousand men in a standing army. There comes a time in the battle when one bugle is worth a thousand muskets. In the earlier part of our Civil War, the Government proposed to economize in bands of music, and many of them were sent home: but the generals in the army sent word to Washington: "You are making a very great mistake. We are falling back and falling back. We have not enough music." Then the Government changed its mind; more bands of music were sent to the field, and the day of shameful defeat terminated. I have to tell you that no nation or church can afford to severely economize in music.

Why should we rob the programme of worldly gayety when we have so many appropriate songs and tunes composed in our own day, as well as that magnificent inheri-

tance of Church psalmody, which has come down fragrant
with the devotions of other generations—tunes no more
worn out than when our great-grandfathers climbed up
on them from the church pew to glory? Dear old souls,
how they used to sing! When they were cheerful our
grandfathers and grandmothers used to sing " Colchester."
When they were very meditative then the meeting-house
rang with "South Street" and "St. Edmonds." Were
they struck through with great tenderness, they sang
"Woodstock." Were they wrapped in visions of the
glory of the Church, they sang "Zion." Were they overborne with the love and glory of Christ, they sang
"Ariel." And in those days there were certain tunes
married to certain hymns, and they have lived in peace a
great while, these two old people, and we have no right to
divorce them. "What God hath joined together let no
man put asunder." Born as we have been amid this great
wealth of church music, augmented by the compositions
of artists in our day, we ought not to be tempted out of
the sphere of Christian harmony, and try to seek uncon-
secrated sounds. It is absurd for a millionaire to steal.

Many of you are illustrations of what sacred song can
do. Through it you were brought into the kingdom of
Jesus Christ. You stood out against the warning and the
argument of the pulpit, but when in the sweet words of
Charles Wesley, or John Newton, or Toplady, the love of
Jesus was sung to your soul, then you surrendered, as
an armed castle that could not be taken by a host, lifts its
window to listen to a harp's trill.

There was a Scotch soldier dying in New Orleans, and

a Scotch minister came in to give him the consolations of
the Gospel.   The man turned over on his pillow, and said:
"Don't talk to me about religion."   Then the Scotch
minister began to sing a familiar hymn of Scotland that
was composed by David Dickenson, beginning with the
words:

> "O mother dear, Jerusalem,
>   When shall I come to thee?

He sung it to the tune of "Dundee," and everybody in
Scotland knows that; and as he began to sing the dying
soldier turned over on his pillow, and said to the minister:
"Where did you learn that?"   "Why," replied the minister, "my mother taught me that."   "So did mine,"
said the dying Scotch soldier; and the very foundation of
his heart was upturned, and then and there he yielded
himself to Christ.   Oh, it has an irresistible power !
Luther's sermons have been forgotten, but his "Judgment
Hymn" sings on through the ages, and will keep on singing until the blast of the archangel's trumpet shall bring
about that very day which the hymn celebrates.   I would
to God that those who hear me to-day would take these
songs of salvation as messages from heaven; for, just as
certainly as the birds brought food to Elijah by the brook
of Cherith, so these winged harmonies God sent are flying
to your soul with the bread of life.   Open your mouth and
take it, O hungry Elijah !

I have also noticed the power of sacred song to soothe
perturbation.   You may have come in here with a great
many worriments and anxieties, yet perhaps in the singing
of the first hymn you lost all those worriments and anxie-

ties. You have read in the Bible of Saul, and how he was sad and angry, and how the boy David came in and played the evil spirit out of him. *A Spanish king* was melancholy. The windows were all closed. He sat in the darkness. Nothing could bring him forth until Farinelli came and discoursed music for three or four days to him. On the fourth day he looked up, and wept and rejoiced, and the windows were thrown open, and that which all the splendors of the court could not do, the power of song accomplished. If you have anxieties and worriments try this heavenly charm upon them. Do not sit down on the bank of the hymn, but plunge in that the devil of care may be brought out of you.

It also arouses to action. Do you not know that a singing church is always a triumphant church? If a congregation is silent during the exercise, or partially silent, it is the silence of death. If when the hymn is given out you hear the faint hum of here and there a father and mother in Israel, while the vast majority are silent, that minister of Christ who is presiding needs to have a very strong constitution if he does not get the chills. He needs not only the grace of God, but nerves like whalebone. It is amazing how some people with voice enough to discharge all their duties in the world, when they come into the house of God have no voice to discharge this duty. I really believe that if the Church of Christ could rise up and sing as it ought to sing, that where we have a hundred souls brought into the kingdom of Christ there would be a thousand. How was it in olden time? Cajetan said: "Luther conquered us by his songs."

But I must now speak of some of the obstacles in the way of the advancement of this sacred music; and the first is, that it has been impressed into the service of superstition. I am far from believing that music ought always to be positively religious. Refined art has opened places where music has been secularized and lawfully so. The drawing-room, the musical club, the orchestra, the concert, by the gratification of pure taste, and the productions of harmless amusement, and the improvement of talent have become very forces in the advancement of our civilization. Music has as much right to laugh in Surrey Gardens as it has to pray in St. Paul's. In the kingdom of nature we have the glad fifing of the wind as well as the long metre psalm of the thunder. But, while all this is so, every observer has noticed that this art which God intended for the improvement of the ear and the voice and the head and the heart, has often been impressed into the service of error. Tartini, the musical composer, dreamed one night that Satan snatched from his hand an instrument, and played upon it something very sweet—a dream that has often been fulfilled in our day, the voice and the instruments that ought to have been devoted to Christ, captured from the Church and applied to purposes of sin.

Another obstacle has been an inordinate fear of criticism. The vast majority of people singing in church never want anybody else to hear them sing. Everybody is waiting for somebody else to do his duty. If we all sang, then inaccuracies that are evident when only a few sing would be drowned out. God asks you to do as well as you can, and then, if you get the wrong pitch or keep wrong time, he will forgive any deficiency of the ear and imperfection of the voices. Angels will not laugh if you should lose your place in the musical scale, or come in at the close a bar behind.

There are three schools of singing I am told—the German school, the Italian school, and the French school of singing. Now, I would like to add a fourth school, and that is the school of Christ. The voice of a contrite, broken heart, although it may not be able to stand human criticism, makes better music to God's ear than the most artistic performance, when the heart is wanting. I know it is easier to preach on this than it is to practice; but I sing for two reasons—first, because I like it, and next because I want to encourage those who do not know how. I have but very little faculty in that direction, and no culture at all, yet I am resolved to sing though every note should go off like a Chinese gong. God has commanded it, and I dare not be silent. He calls on the beasts, on the cattle, on the dragons to praise Him, and we ought not to be behind the cattle and the dragons.

Another obstacle that has been in the way of the advancement of this holy art has been so much angry discussion on the subject of music. There are those who would have this exercise conducted by musical instruments. In the same church there are those who do not like musical instruments, and so it is organ and no organ, and there is a fight. In another church it is a question whether the music shall be conducted by a precentor or by a drilled choir. Some want a drilled choir, and some want a precentor, and there is a fight. Then there are those who

would like in the church to have the organ played in a
dull, lifeless, droning way, while there are others who
would have it wreathed into fantastics, branching out in
jets and spangles of sound, rolling and tossing in marvel-
lous convolutions, as when in pyrotechnic display you
think a piece is exhausted it breaks out in wheels, rockets,
blue lights and serpentine demonstrations.

Some would have the organ played in almost inaudible
sweetness, and others would have it full of staccato passages that make the audience jump with great eyes and
hair on end as though by a vision of the witch of Endor;
and he who tries to please all will succeed in nothing.
Nevertheless, you are to admit the fact that this contest
which is going on in hundreds of the churches of the
United States to-day, is a mighty hindrance to the advancement of this art. In this way scores and scores of
churches are entirely crippled as to all influence, and the
music is a damage rather than a praise.

Another obstacle in the advancement of this art has
been the erroneous notion that this part of the service
could be conducted by a delegation. Churches have said:
"Oh, what an easy time we shall have. The minister will
do the preaching, and the choir will do the singing, and
we will have nothing to do." And you know as well as I
that there are a great multitude of churches all through
this land, where the people are not expected to sing. The
whole work is done by delegation of four, or six, or ten
persons, and the audience is silent. In such a church in
Syracuse, an old elder persisted in singing, and so the choir
appointed a committee to go and ask the squire if he would

not stop. You know that in a great multitude of churches the choir are expected, and do all the singing, and the great masses of the people are expected to be silent, and if you utter your voice you are interfering. There they stand, the four, with opera-glass dangling at their side, singing, "Rock of Ages, cleft for me," with the same spirit that the night before on the stage they took their part in the "Grand Duchess" or "Don Giovanni."

Now, in this church, we have resolved upon the plan of conducting the music by a precentor. We do it for two reasons, one is that by throwing the whole responsibility upon the mass of the people, making the great multitude the choir, we might rouse more heartiness. The congregation coming on the Sabbath day feel that they cannot delegate this part of the great service to any one else, and so they themselves assume it. We have glorious congregational singing here. People have come many miles to hear it. They are not sure about the preaching, but they can always depend on the singing. We have heard the sound coming up like "the voice of many waters," but it will be done at a better rate after a while, when we shall realize the height, and the depth, and the immensity of this privilege.

Another reason why we adopted this plan. We do not want any choir quarrels. You know very well that in scores of the churches there has been perpetual contention in that direction. The only church fight that ever occurred under my ministry, was over a melodeon in my first settlement. Have you never been in church on the Sabbath day and heard the choir sing, and you said:

"That is splendid music." The next Sabbath you **were** in the church, and there was no choir at all. Why? The leader was mad, or his assistants were mad, or they were all mad together. Some of the choirs are made up of our best Christian people! Some of the warmest friends I have ever had have stood up in them, Sabbath after Sabbath, conscientiously and successfully leading the praises of God. But the majority of the choirs throughout the land are not made up of Christian people, and three fourths of the church fights originate in the organ-loft. I take that back and say, nine tenths. Many of our churches are dying of choirs. Let us, as a church, give still more attention to the music. If a man, with voice enough to sing, keep silent during this exercise, he commits a crime against God and insults the Almighty.

Music ought to rush from the audience like the water from a rock—clear, bright, sparkling. If all the other part of the church service is dull do not have the music dull. With so many thrilling things to sing about, away with all drawling and stupidity! There is nothing that makes me so nervous as to sit in a pulpit and look off on an audience with their eyes three fourths closed and their lips almost shut, mumbling the praises of God. During my recent absence I preached to a large audience, and all the music they made together did not equal one skylark! People do not sleep at a coronation. Do not let us sleep when we come to a Saviour's crowning. In order to a proper discharge of this duty, let us stand up, save as age, or weakness, or fatigue excuse us. Seated in an easy pew we cannot do this duty half so well as when, upright, we throw our whole body into it. Let our song be like an acclamation of victory. You have a right to sing. Do not surrender your prerogative.

We want to rouse all our families upon this subject. We want each family of our congregation to be a singing-school. Childish petulance, obduracy, and intractability would be soothed if we had more singing in the household, and then our little ones would be prepared for the great congregation on Sabbath-day, their voices uniting with our voices in the praises of the Lord. After a shower there are scores of streams that come down the mountain side with voices rippling and silvery, pouring into one river, and then rolling in united strength to the sea. So I would have all the families in my church send forth the voice of prayer and praise, pouring it into the great tide of public worship that rolls on and on to empty into the great wide heart of God. Never can we have our church sing as it ought, until our families sing as they ought.

There will be a great revolution on this subject in all our churches. God will come down by His Spirit and rouse up the old hymns and tunes that have not been more than half awake since the time of our grandfathers. The silent pews in the church will break forth into music, and when the conductor takes his place on the Sabbath day, there will be a great host of voices rushing into the harmony. My Christian friends, if we have no taste for this service on earth, what will we do in heaven, where they all sing and sing forever? I would that our singing to-day might be like the Saturday night rehearsal for the Sabbath morning in the skies, and might begin now by the strength and by the help of God to discharge a duty which none of us have fully performed.

" Let those refuse to sing
Who never knew our God;
But children of the Heavenly king
Should speak their joys abroad."

Come now, clear your throats, and get ready for this duty or you will never hear the end of this. I never shall forget hearing a Frenchman singing the " Marseillaise Hymn" on the Champs Elysées, Paris, just after the battle of Sedan. I never saw such enthusiasm before or since, as he sang that national air. Oh, how the Frenchmen shouted ! Have you ever, in an English assemblage, heard a band play " God Save the Queen ? " If you have you know something about the enthusiasm of a national air. Now, I tell you that these songs we sing Sabbath by Sabbath are the national airs of Jesus Christ and of the kingdom of heaven. When Cromwell's army went into battle, he stood at the head of them one day, and gave out the long metre doxology to the tune of " Old Hundred," and that great host, company by company, regiment by regiment, battalion by battalion, joined in the doxology:

" Praise God from whom all blessings flow,
Praise him all creatures here below;
Praise him above, ye heavenly host,
Praise Father, Son, and Holy Ghost."

And while they sang they marched, and while they marched they fought, and while they fought they got the victory. Oh, men and women of Jesus Christ, let us go into all our conflicts singing the praises of God, and then, instead of falling back, as we often do, from defeat to defeat, we will be marching on from victory to victory !

THE LAUGHTER OF THE BIBLE.

[PREACHED SUNDAY MORNING, APRIL 18, 1886.]

"Then was our mouth filled with laughter."—PSALM cxxvi : 2.
"He that sitteth in the heavens shall laugh."—PSALM ii : 4.

THIRTY-EIGHT times does the Bible make reference to this configuration of the features and quick expulsion of breath which we call laughter. Sometimes it is born of the sunshine, and sometimes of the midnight. Sometimes it stirs the sympathy of angels, and sometimes the cachinnation of devils. All healthy people laugh; whether it pleases the Lord or displeases Him, that depends upon when we laugh and at what we laugh. My theme this morning is the laughter of the Bible—namely, Sarah's laugh, or *that of scepticism;* David's laugh, or *that of spiritual exultation;* the fool's laugh, or *that of sinful merriment;* God's laugh, or *that of infinite condemnation :* heaven's laugh, or *that of eternal triumph.*

Sarah's laugh or that of scepticism. I. Scene: an Oriental tent; the occupants, old Abraham and Sarah, perhaps wrinkled and decrepit. Their three guests are three angels, the Lord Almighty one of them. In return for the hospitality shown by the old people, God promises Sarah that she shall become the ancestress of the Lord Jesus Christ. Sarah laughs in the face of God; she does not believe it. She is affrighted at what she has done. She denies it. She says : "I didn't laugh." Then God retorted, with an emphasis that silenced all disputation: "But thou didst laugh." My friends, the laugh of scepticism in all the ages is only the echo of Sarah's laughter.

God says He will accomplish a thing, and men say it cannot be done. A great multitude laugh at the miracles. They say they are contrary to the laws of nature. What is a law of nature? It is God's way of doing a thing. You ordinarily cross the river by the Bridge; to-morrow you change for one day, and you go across Wall Street Ferry. You made the rule; have you not a right to change it? I ordinarily come in at that door (pointing to a side entrance) of the church. Suppose next Sabbath I should come in at the other door? It is a habit I have. Have I not *a right to change my habit?* A law of nature. God's habit—his way of doing things. If He makes the law, has He not a right to change it at any time He wants to change it? Alas for the folly of those who laugh at God when He says: "I will do a thing," they responding: "You can't do it." God says that the Bible is true—it is all true. Bishop Colenso laughs. Herbert Spencer laughs. John Stuart Mill laughs. All great German universities laugh. Harvard laughs—softly! A great many of the learned institutions of this country, with long rows of professors *seated on the fence* between Christianity and infidelity, laugh softly. They say: "We didn't laugh." That was Sarah's trick. God thunders from the heavens: "But thou didst laugh!"

The Garden of Eden was only a fable. There never was any ark built, or, if it was built, it was too small to hold two of every kind. The pillar of fire by night is only the northern lights. The ten plagues of Egypt only a brilliant specimen of jugglery. The sea parted because the wind blew violently a great while from one direction. The sun and moon did not put themselves out of the way for Joshua. Jacob's ladder was only horizontal and picturesque clouds. The destroying angel smiting the firstborn in Egypt was only cholera infantum become epidemic. The gullet of the whale, by positive measurement, is too small to swallow a prophet. The lame, the dumb, the blind, the halt cured by mere human surgery. The resurrection of Christ's friend only a beautiful tableau, Christ and Lazarus and Mary and Martha acting their parts well. My friends, there is not a doctrine or statement of God's Holy Word that has not been derided by the scepticism of this day.

I take up this Book of King James's translation. I consider it a perfect Bible, but here are sceptics who want it torn to pieces, and now with this Bible in my hand, let me tear out all those portions which the scepticism of this day demands shall be torn out.

What shall go first? "Well," says some one in the audience, "take out all that about the creation, and about the first settlement of the world." Away goes Genesis. "Now," says some one, "take out all that about the miraculous guidance of the children of Israel in the wilderness." Away goes Exodus. "Now," says some one else in the audience, "there are things in Deuteronomy and Kings that are not fit to be read." Away go Deuteronomy and the Kings. "Now," says some one, "the Book of Job is a drama; that ought to come out." Away goes the Book of Job. "Now," says some one, "those passages in the New Testament which imply the divinity of Jesus Christ ought to come out." Away go the evangelists. "Now," says some one, "the Book of Revelation—how preposterous; it represents a man with the moon under his feet and a sharp sword in his hand." Away goes the Book of Revelation. Now there are *a few pieces left*. What shall we do with them? "Oh," says some man in the audience, "I don't believe a word of the Bible from one end to the other." Well, it is all gone. Now, you have put out the last light for the nations. Now it is the pitch darkness of eternal midnight. *How do you like it ?*

But I think, my friends, we had better keep the Bible a little longer intact. It has done pretty well for a good many years. There are old people who find it a comfort to have it on their laps, and children like the stories in it. Let us keep it for a curiosity anyhow. If the Bible is to be thrown out of the school, and out of the court-room, so men no more swear by it, and it is to be put in a dark corridor of the city library, the Koran on one side, and the writings of Confucius on the other, then let us each one keep a copy for himself; for *we might have trouble*, and we would want to be under the delusions of its consolation; and we might die, and we would want the delusion of the exalted residence at God's right hand which it mentions.

Oh, what an awful thing it is to laugh in God's face, and hurl His revelation back at Him! After a while the day will come when they will say they did not laugh. Then all the hypercriticisms, all the caricatures, and all the learned sneers in the *Quarterly Review* will be brought to judgment, and amid the rocking of everything beneath, and amid the flaming of everything above, God will thunder: "But thou didst laugh!" I think the most fascinating laughter at Christianity I ever remember was Theodore Parker's. He made the Word of God seem ridiculous, and he laughed on at our holy religion until he came to die, and then he said: "My life has been a failure; a failure domestically, I have no children; a failure socially, for I am treated in the streets like a pirate; a failure professionally, because I know but one minister that has adopted my sentiments." For a quarter of a century he laughed at Christianity, and ever since Christianity has been laughing at him. Now, it is a mean thing to go into a man's house and steal his goods; but I tell you *the most gigantic burglary ever enacted* is the proposition to steal these treasures of our holy religion. The meanest laughter ever uttered is the laughter of the sceptic.

II. The next laughter mentioned in this Bible is David's laughter or *the expression of spiritual exultation.* "Then was our mouth filled with laughter." He got very much down sometimes, but there are other chapters where for four or five times he calls up the people to praise and exult. It was not a mere twitch of the lips; it was a demonstration that took hold of his whole physical nature. "Then was our mouth filled with laughter."

My friends, this world will never be converted to God until Christians cry less and laugh and sing more. The horrors are a poor bait. If people are to be persuaded to adopt our holy religion, it will be because they have made up their mind it is a happy religion, and they do not like *an ultra-bilious Christianity.* I know there are morbid people who enjoy a funeral. They come early to see the friends take leave of the corpse, and they steal a ride to the cemetery; but all healthy people enjoy a wedding better than they do a burial. Now, you make the religion of Christ sepulchral and hearse-like, and you make it repulsive.

I say plant the rose of Sharon along the church walks, and columbine to clamber over the church wall; and have a smile on the lip, and have the mouth filled with holy laughter. There is no man in the world except the Christian that has a right to feel an untrammelled glee. He is promised everything is to be for the best here, and he is on the way to a delight which will take all the procession with palm branches, and all the orchestra harped and cymballed and trumpeted to express. "Oh," you say, "I have so much trouble!" Have you more trouble than Paul had? What does he say? "Sorrowful, yet always rejoicing. Poor, yet making many rich. Having nothing, yet possessing all things." The merriest laugh I ever heard has been in the sick-room of God's dear children. When Theodosius was put upon the rack, he suffered very great torture at the first. Somebody asked him how he endured all that pain on the rack. He replied: "When I was first put upon the rack, I suffered a great deal; but very soon *a young man in white* stood by my side, and with a soft and comfortable handkerchief he wiped the sweat from my brow, and my pains were relieved; it was a punishment for me to get from the rack, because when the pain was all gone, the angel was gone." Oh, rejoice evermore!

You know how it is in the army—an army in encampment. If to-day news comes that our side has had a defeat, and to-morrow another portion of the tidings comes, saying: "We have had another defeat!" it demoralizes all the host. But if the news come of victory to-day and victory to-morrow, the whole army is impassioned for the contest. Now, in the kingdom of our Lord Jesus Christ, report fewer defeats; tell us the victories; victory over sin and death and hell. Rejoice evermore, and again I say rejoice.

III. The next laughter mentioned in the Bible that I shall speak of is the fool's laughter or the expression of sinful merriment. Solomon was very quick at simile; when he makes a comparison we all catch it. What is the laughter of a fool like? He says: "It is the crackling of thorns under a pot." The kettle is swung, a bunch of brambles is put under it, and the torch is applied to it, and there is a great noise and a big blaze and a sputter, and a quick extinguishment. Then it is darker than it was before. Fool's laughter! The most miserable thing on earth is *a bad man's fun*. There they are, ten men in a bar-room. They have at home wives, mothers, daughters. The impure jest starts at one corner of the barroom, and crackle, crackle, crackle it goes all around. In five hundred such guffaws there is not one item of happiness. They all feel bemeaned, if they have any conscience left. Have nothing to do with men or women who tell immoral stories. I have no confidence either in their Christian character or their morality.

So all merriment that springs out of the defects of

others—caricature of a lame foot, or a curved spine, or a blind eye, or a deaf ear—will be met with the judgments of God, either upon you or your children. Twenty years ago, in this city of Brooklyn, I knew a man who was particularly skilful in imitating the lameness of a neighbor. Not long ago, a son of the skilful mimic had his leg amputated for the very defect which his father had mimicked years before. I do not say it was a judgment of God. I leave you to make your own inference. So all merriment born of dissipation—that which starts at the counter of the drinking restaurant, or from the wine-glass in the home circle—the maudlin simper, the meaningless joke, the saturnalian gibberish, the paroxysm of mirth about nothing, that you sometimes see in the fashionable club-room or the exquisite parlor at twelve o'clock at night, are the crackling of thorns under a pot. Such laughter and such sin ends in death.

When I was a lad a book came out entitled " *Don Jour's Patent Sermons;* " it made a great stir, a very wide laugh all over the country, that book did. It was a caricature of the Christian ministry, and of the Word of God, and of the day of judgment. Oh, we had a great laugh! The commentary on the whole thing is that, not long ago, the author of that book died in poverty, shame, debauchery, kicked out of society, and cursed of Almighty God. The laughter of such men is the echo of their own damnation.

IV. The next laughter that I shall mention as being in the Bible is *the laughter of God's condemnation.* " He that sitteth in the heavens shall laugh." Again "the Lord will laugh at him." Again: "I will laugh at his calamity." With such demonstration will God greet every kind of great sin and wickedness. Bad men build up villainies higher and higher. Good men almost pity God because He is so schemed against by men. Suddenly a pin drops out of the machinery of wickedness, or a secret is revealed, the foundation begins to rock; finally, the whole thing is demolished. What is the matter? I will tell you what is the matter. The crash of ruin is only the reverberation of God's laughter.

On Wall Street there are a great many good men and a great many fraudulent men. A fraudulent man says: " I mean to have my million." He goes to work reckless of honesty, and he gets his first $100,000. He gets after a while his $200,000. After a while he gets his $500,000. " Now," he says, " I have only one more move to make, and I shall have my million." He gathers up all his resources; he makes that last grand move, he fails and loses all, and he has not enough money of his own left to pay the cost of the car to his home. People cannot understand this spasmodic revulsion. Some said it was a turn in Erie Railroad stock, or in Western Union, or in Illinois Central; some said it was Jay Gould; some said it was one speculator, some another. They all guessed wrong. I will tell you what it was: " He that sitteth in the heavens laughed."

A man in New York said he would be the richest man in the city. He left his honest work of chair-making, and got into the city councils some way, and in ten years stole *fifteen million dollars* from the city government.

He held the Legislature of the State of New York in the

grip of his right hand. Suspicions were aroused. The Grand Jury presented indictments. The whole land stood aghast. The man who expected to put half the city in his vest-pocket goes to Blackwell's Island; goes to Ludlow Street Jail; breaks prison, and goes across the sea; is re-arrested and brought back, and again remanded to jail. Why? "He that sitteth in the heavens laughs."

Rome was a great empire; she had Horace and Virgil among her poets; she had Augustus and Constantine among her emperors. But what mean the defaced Pantheon, and the Forum turned into a cattle-market, and the broken-walled Coliseum, and the architectural skeleton of her great aqueducts? What was that thunder? "Oh," you say, "that was the roar of the battering-rams against her walls." No. What was that quiver? "Oh," you say, "that was the tramp of hostile legions." No. The quiver and the roar were the outburst of omnipotent laughter from the defied and insulted heavens. Rome defied God and He laughed her down. Thebes defied God and He laughed her down. Nineveh defied God and He laughed her down. Babylon defied God and He laughed her down.

There is an immense difference between God's laugh and His smile. His smile is eternal beatitude. He smiled when David sang, and Miriam clapped the cymbals, and Hannah made garments for her son, and Paul preached, and John kindled with apocalyptic vision, and when any man has anything to do and does it well. His smile! Why, it is the apple orchards in full bloom. It is morning breaking on a rippling sea. It is heaven at high noon, all the bells beating the marriage peal.   But His laughter —may it never fall on us ! It is a condemnation for our sin. It is a wasting away. We may let the satirist laugh at us, and all our companions laugh at us, and we be made the target for the merriment of earth and hell; but God forbid that we should ever come to the fulfillment of the prophecy against the rejectors of the truth: " I will laugh at your calamity."   But, my friends, all of us who reject the pardon of the Gospel are to come under that tremendous bombardment.

God wants us all to repent; He counsels, He coaxes, He importunes, He begs us. He comes down out of heaven. He puts all the world's sin on one shoulder, He puts all the world's sorrow on the other shoulder, and then, with that Alps on one side and that Himalaya on the other, He starts up the hill back of Jerusalem to achieve our salvation. He puts the palm of His right hand on one long spike, and He puts the palm of His left hand on another long spike, and then, with his hands spotted with His own blood, He gesticulates, saying: "Look ! look ! and live ! With the crimson veil of My sacrifice I will cover all your sins. With my dying groan I will swallow up all your groans. Look ! live !"

But a thousand of you this morning turn your back to that. And then this voice of invitation turns to a tone divinely ominous, that sobs like a simoom or an equinox through the first chapter of Proverbs: "Because I have called and ye refused; I have stretched out my hand and no man regarded; but ye have set at nought all my counsel and would none of my reproof, *I also will laugh* at your calamity." Oh, what a laugh that is! A deep laugh. A long, reverberating laugh. An overwhelming laugh. God grant we may never hear it. But in this day of merciful visitation yield your heart to Christ, that you may spend all your life on earth under His smile and escape forever the thunder of the laugh of God's indignation.

V. The other laughter mentioned in the Bible, the only one I shall speak of, is heaven's laughter, or *the expression of eternal triumph*. Christ said to His disciples: "Blessed are ye that weep now, for ye shall laugh." That makes me know positively that we are not to spend our days in heaven singing long-metre songs. The formalistic and stiff notions of heaven that some people have would make me miserable. I am glad to know that the heaven of the Bible is not only a place of holy worship, but of magnificent sociality. "What," say you, "will the ringing laugh go around the circles of the saved?" I say, yes; pure laughter, cheering laughter, holy laughter. It will be *a laugh of congratulation*.

When we meet a friend who has suddenly come to a fortune, or who has got over some dire sickness, do we not shake hands, do we not laugh with him? And when we get to heaven and see our friends there, some of them having come up out of great tribulation, why, we will say to one of them: "The last time I saw you, you had been suffering for six weeks under a low intermittent fever;" or to another we will say: "You for ten years were limping with the rheumatism, and you were full of complaints when we saw you last. I congratulate you on your eternal recovery." Ye shall laugh. Yes, we shall congratulate all those who have come up out of great financial embarrassments in ths world, because they have become millionaires in heaven.

Ye shall laugh, it will be a laugh of reassociation. It is as natural for us to laugh when we meet those we haven't seen for ten years, as anything is possible to be natural. And when we meet our friends, over whose departure we lamented ten, twenty, thirty years before, will it not be with infinite congratulation? our perceptions quickened, our knowledge improved? We will know each other at a flash, and have to talk over all that happened since we have been separated, the one that has been ten years in heaven telling us of all that has happened in the ten years of his heavenly residence, and we telling him in return what has happened during the ten years of his absence from earth.

We shall laugh. I think George Whitefield and John Wesley will have a laugh of contempt for their earthly collisions, and that Toplady and Charles Wesley will have a laugh of contempt for their earthly misunderstandings, and the two farmers who were in a lawsuit all their days will have a laugh of contempt over their earthly disturbance about a line fence. Exemption from all annoyance. Immersion in all gladness. Ye shall laugh.

Yes; it will be a laugh of triumph. Oh, what a blessed thing it will be to stand on the wall of heaven, and look down at Satan, and hurl at him defiance, and see him shake his chains, and we free from his clutches! Yes; it will be a laugh of royal greeting; a laugh of royal greeting. You know how the Frenchmen cheered when Napoleon came back from Elba.   You know how the English cheered when Wellington came back from Waterloo.   You know how the Americans cheered when Kossuth arrived from Hungary.   You remember how the Romans cheered when Pompey came back victor over nine hundred cities. Every cheer was a laugh.   But oh, the mightier greeting, the gladder greeting, when the snow-white cavalry troops of heaven shall go through the streets; according to Revelation, Christ, in the red, the crimson coat, seated on a white horse, and all the armies of heaven flying on white horses; but when we see and hear that galloping cavalcade, we shall cheer, we shall laugh.

Does not your heart beat and cry this morning at the thought of that great jubilee upon which we are soon to enter?   I pray God that when we get through with this world and are going out of it, we may have the same vision that a Christian had when he said he saw written all over the clouds of the sky the letter W, and they asked him, standing by his side, what he thought that letter W meant. Oh, he says, that stands for Welcome.   So may it be when we quit this world.   W on the gate, W on the door of the mansion, W on the throne.   Welcome, Welcome, Welcome.

I have preached this sermon with five prayerful wishes: That you might see what a mean thing is the laughter of scepticism, what a bright thing is the laugh of spiritual exultation; what a hollow thing is the laugh of sinful merriment; what an awful thing is the laugh of condemnation; what a radiant, rubicund thing is the laughter of eternal triumph.   Avoid the ill, choose the right; be comforted, be comforted.   Blessed are ye that weep now, for ye shall laugh—ye shall laugh !

THE CONGRATULATIONS OF
HEAVEN.

[PREACHED IN THE BROOKLYN TABERNACLE, MAY 16TH, 1886.]

' Joy shall be in heaven over one sinner that repenteth."—ST.
LUKE, xv : 7.

A LOST sheep ! There is nothing more thoroughly lost
than that. I look through the window of a shepherd's
cabin. It is night, and the candles are lighted. The
shepherd's staff stands in the corner. He has just shaken
his coat from the dirt and dust. His neighbors are in,
and he sits down, panting and exhausted, on a rough
bench, while his wife, and children, and friends say to
him: "Come now, tell us the story of how you found it;
the poor thing !" "Well," he says, "this morning I
went out to the yard to count the flocks, and they didn't
count right, for McDonald, you know, we have a hundred
of them, and I counted ninety-five, ninety-six, ninety-
seven, ninety-eight, ninety-nine. I said: 'There's one
missing.' So I counted again—ninety-five, ninety-six,
ninety-seven, ninety-eight, ninety-nine—sure enough there
is one gone. And I whistled for the dogs and started. I
crossed the bridge, and I leaped the gullies, and I tracked
the woods, and I cried, 'So ho ! So ho !' but not a bleat of
the poor lamb did I hear. I said to myself: 'It must
have dropped into a pit, or a pack of wolves have come
down and sucked its life out.' But I went on, for it was

a favorite lamb—it was that one, you know, with a black spot on the right shoulder—the one that came up and licked my hand when I used to cross the field. It was a favorite lamb, and I kept on and I cried as I went. And after a little while I heard the dogs bark, and I said: 'What's that?' and I hastened over the hill, and no sooner had I come over the hill-top than there I saw the poor lamb. It had fallen into a ditch, and it was covered with slush and slime; and when I leaned over and lifted it out, O, I wish you could have seen how lovingly and gratefully it looked into my face. Poor thing! it was so fagged out and so frightened it could not walk; and I lifted it and I put it upon my shoulder, and I started home. O, it was a long tramp, and that coat hanging there shows in just what a condition the lamb was when I shouldered it. But now it is safe in the yard, thank God!" And the shepherd's wife spread the table and brought out the best fare they could afford, and the company sat up very late that night, and they ate, and they drank, and they sang, and they danced, and they told over and over again the story of the lost sheep.

Well, my friends, it was by such rustic yet tender illustrations that Christ told the story of a man going away from God and then coming back, in the familiar parable of the lost sheep, closing with the words of my text: "Likewise, joy shall be in heaven over one sinner that repenteth."

To repent is to feel that you have been very bad, and to turn over a new leaf and to ask God's help and forgiveness; and when a man does that, they hear of it right away in heaven.   There are no gossips in heaven to go around and chatter and laugh when they hear that a man has fallen; but when they hear that a man is saved then there are a great many to go around and tell the tidings; and it is astonishing how soon the news spreads from the North gate of heaven to the South gate, and from the Eastern gate to the Western gate.   In ten minutes all the inhabitants know it, and "there is joy in heaven over one sinner that repenteth."

I would not be surprised if I had found out that there were heavenly congratulations over the day of Pentecost, when three thousand people were converted, or over the parish of Schotts when five hundred souls were converted, or over one of those years in the time of Harland Page, when forty thousand souls were converted, or over the year 1857, when between three and four hundred thousand souls were converted.   It would not astonish me if there were heavenly congratulations over such masses of people saved; but mark the emphasis of my text: "There is joy in heaven over *one*,"—just *one*—"sinner that repenteth."

You have often noticed churches with two towers.   But I suppose that the temple of God on high may have four towers, and sometimes one of them rings, and sometimes they all ring.   Here is a moral man.   He never said a bad word.   He never did a mean action.   Everybody loves him.   He is not a Christian; but after a while he sees that he is a sinner, and he cries to God, and he is saved, and *one* tower of heaven rings out with beautiful chime.

Here is another man.   He is very bad.   He knows it. Everybody knows it.   Still he is kept in respectable society.

He is far from being an outlaw. That man is converted to God. Now, *two* towers in heaven chime out the glorious tidings.

Here is an outcast of society. Last night he was picked up out of the gutter and taken to the station-house. He has gone through all the crimes against God and man. He is utterly loathsome. Nobody wants to touch him. To-night, in all his wretchedness, he cries out: "O Lord, help me! O Lord, forgive me!" Now, *three* towers in heaven chime out the tidings.

Yonder is a poor waif of the street. She has gone down until no one has any pity for her. As she goes under the gaslight and you see her, your soul shivers with a great horror. Going along, to-night, by the Midnight Mission, she hears Christians singing. They are singing a very beautiful tune:

> "All may come, whoever will,
> This man receives poor sinners still."

And she puts into that harbor. She kneels down at the first bench she comes to, and she cries out: "O Thou who didst have mercy on Mary Magdalen, take my bleeding feet off of the hot pavement of hell!" Now, the *four* towers of heaven chime out the tidings; and they who pass along the streets say: "Hark! some great news has come up. Some great sinner is saved; the four towers are ringing." And "there is joy in heaven over one sinner that repenteth."

We see first, in this subject, that we can augment the joy of heaven.

I hear people talk as though they thought that heaven

was as happy as it could be. No! No! I think that one half of the harps are not yet strung, nor one half of the thrones mounted. When all this world is redeemed, do you not suppose that they will be happier in heaven about it? When that Christian mother who died, leaving her son a vagabond, hears in heaven that he has come to God, do you not suppose her joy is augmented? When I was chaplain in the army, and I saw a sergeant with lathered horse, and blood on his spurs, dash past in full run, I said: "He has got some important message." Now look and see those two angels, wing to wing, flying for the throne of God. I see by their shining faces that they have good news to tell. What is the matter? Do you tell me they cannot bring any joy to the glorified? They will! They will! "For there is joy in heaven over one sinner that repenteth." There is a man yonder, standing in the gallery, who, if he would, might light up a bonfire on the hills of heaven. He might, with the torch of his own repentance, kindle up great gladness there. When your little child was on earth, before the sweet thing flew away from you into heaven, how you used to try to make her happy—did you not? You crowded your pockets many a time with gifts and you came home, and when your night-key rattled in the door she rushed out and cried: "Father, what you brought me?" O, now, that those loved ones are in glory, would you not like to give them new gladness? You may, weeping father. You may, weeping mother. Your repentance, to-night, would be sufficient motive to send those children skipping with eternal gladness, for "there is joy in heaven over one sinner that repenteth."

I believe that if this whole audience should, to-night, come to God, there would be as great joy in heaven as there ever has been there; perhaps greater joy than has ever been since the first pearly gate swung on its hinges; and instead of being a Pentecost of three thousand, it would be a turning to God of five thousand. O, heaven smite with all thy hammers, to-night, and let our chains fall off. O, Holy Spirit, with the gleaming sword of thy truth, strike, and let our souls be free. A general said to his army after they had gained a slight battle: "Hush, now; no shouting, no shouting." But it would be impossible to keep quiet the armies of heaven, to-night, if it were announced that we all had come to God. There would be shouting, shouting, shouting, for "there is joy in heaven among the angels of God over one sinner that repenteth."

In some families they keep a vacant chair at the table, and the plate that was once occupied by the loved one who has gone away. That has been the habit in a great many families. Perhaps it may not have been in yours, because if you had kept vacant chairs for all those who have gone from you, there would have been more chairs for the dead than for the living. In heaven they have vacant chairs, not made so by death, for they never die there, but vacant chairs kept so by your loved ones, because they will not allow any one to sit there till you come up and occupy them. Father, mother, brother, sister, will you go there? Will you start to-night? "Aye!" says some one in this part of the house. "Aye!" says some one in that part of the house. And "there is joy in heaven over one sinner that repenteth."

Again, my subject teaches me that *heaven is not so very far off after all*. I often hear people talk as though heaven were a great distance. The departed must go hundreds of thousands of miles until they get to a star, and then hundreds of thousands of miles until they get to another star, and then millions of miles from that and then they get to heaven. They tell us that heaven is the centre of the universe and that we are on the outer rim of the universe. But we have learned to calculate distance by the time it takes to travel it, and by the speed and the frequency of the intercommunication, and by that estimate, heaven is not far off. It certainly is not twelve hours off, for Jesus said to the dying thief: *"this day— this day, shalt thou be with me in paradise."* And I suppose that the wing of the soul, when it leaves the body, is so swift, that it does not take a day, or an hour, or a minute, or the ten thousandth part of a second for it to flash into glory; and as to the intercommunication, there are hundreds of souls every day going up from the church on earth to the church in heaven, and thousands of ministering spirits every day coming down from heaven to earth, and all the King's highway from earth to heaven is thronged with messengers, coming, going; coming, going!

Some years ago, a foolish undertaking was made, by which it was proposed to gain the attention of another world, and on the highest mountains of Siberia, it was proposed to build some mounds in mathematical figures with which to attract the attention of another world—a most preposterous undertaking. Blessed be God, we need go through no such artifices to attract the attention of heaven! The heart of heaven beats close against the heart of this world, for "there is joy in heaven among the angels of God over one sinner that repenteth."

I had occasion to send a telegram, under the sea, and it being considerable expense, I put it in as small space as possible. You can send a very important telegram with two words. I have thought to-night that if ministering spirits flying up from this place to the throne of God, wanted to announce the redemption of any soul here, it would take only two words: "John repented," "Mary repented," "Father repented," "Mother repented," "child repented;" and "there is joy in heaven over one sinner that repenteth."

Again: This subject teaches me that *the salvation of the soul must be of surpassing importance.* If you had made $100,000 in Wall street, that would not have been reported in heaven. If you had been elected President of the United States, perhaps that might not have been reported in heaven. When the French government passed from Thiers to McMahon, I do not suppose it was reported in heaven. When in the recent English elections, the contest was between Conservatives and Liberals, the result, I do not suppose, was reported in heaven. But there is one item that must go up, there is one thing that must be told. Let the flying hoofs of God's courier clash through the portals, and the news fly from gate to temple, and from temple to mansion, and from mansion to throne, that one soul has been converted.

A few years ago, among the White Mountains, a stage driver was very reckless. He had a large company of

passengers and drove six horses. Coming along a dangerous place, the leaders shied off, and the stage was thrown
over the rocks. A few men leaped out and were saved,
others went down and were bruised and some were slain.
When those who were saved got home, how their friends
must have congratulated them, that they got off from all
that peril. Well! the angels of God look down and see
men driving along the edge of eternal disasters, drawn by
leaping, foaming, uncontrollable perils; and when a man
just before he comes to the fatal capsize, leaps off and
comes away in safety, do you wonder that the angels of
God clap their hands and cry: "Good! Good! saved from
hell! Saved for heaven! Saved forever!"

The redemption of a soul must be a very wonderful
thing or heaven would not make such a time about it.
It must be a great thing or there would not be so much
excitement in that land where coronations are every-day
occurrences, and the stones of the field are amethysts and
chrysoprases. It takes a great thing to make the Supreme
Court or the House of Congress adjourn—the death of a
member or some very important event. It must be a great
thing to make heaven adjourn all its honors and all other
subjects, which thing it does when a soul is converted; for
"there is joy in heaven over one sinner that repenteth."
Oh, yes, the matter of soul saving is so great a work, that
I do not wonder that Bellamy, and Nettleton, and Richard
Cecil, and Fletcher, and George Whitefield, and Bishop
Taylor, and Robert Hall, and Paul, and angels, and Christ,
and God stripped themselves for the work. Around that
one soul sweep to-night, in circle of cloud, and mist, and

fire, and song, and rapture, and woe, all God's universe. At its fall, devils beat the gongs of darkness. At its redemption, heaven puts its lip to trumpet, its finger to harp, its hammer to bell; and "there is joy in heaven over one sinner that repenteth."

Now, it is on such a thing as that, I plead to-night. I bring a message from the throne of God: "Repent, poor soul. Give up thy sin and take Christ." I ask you to make no experiment. I know what I am talking about. Over fifty years ago, my parents carried me to the old church at Somerville, and under the hands of Mr. Van Kleeck, the good minister, the waters of baptism were put upon my face; but that did not save me. Afterward, I learned to kneel at the family altar, and father and mother and a brother and a sister—all four of whom have been sometime in glory—were there. But that did not save me. Afterward, my brother Daniel said to me: "De Witt, if you would like to go to school and to college, and get an education, I will pay your way through." He kept the promise; but that did not save me. I have had a great many good friends, influential friends; but they could not save me. I read Doddridge's "Rise and Progress" and Baxter's "Call to the Unconverted" until I was almost wild; but that did not save me. I heard from Presbyterian pulpits and from Methodist camp-meetings sermons enough mighty to wake the dead; but they did not save me. Then, Christ came. He came with a brow red with carnage, and limping with the wound in the foot, and He said: "Poor soul, it is high time you took your foot off my bleeding heart. I forgive you. Repent! Repent!"

And though there may have been greater joy in heaven over some other souls because of results wider reaching. still I *know* that when I gave my soul to Christ, there were some in heaven made happier by the thought; for "there is joy in heaven over one sinner that repenteth," and that is me!

Can you not come to-day, and give your heart to God? Standing here, I really believe that if you do not come to God to-night, some of you never will. Some of you are putting it off for one thing, and others for another thing. Perhaps it is because you have to make some sacrifices in order to become Christians. Can you not make sacrifices? I wish you could have heard the story of a young man who once stood up in this church. He had to give up a living for Christ. He was in a business that he thought was inconsistent with the Christian service, and he said to his wife: "I can't be a Christian and do this." "Then," she replied, "give up the business." They gave up their living, for Christ. What can you give up? "Oh," says some one here: "my heart is so hard. It is so full of sin, I can't look up." Can't you? Perhaps you can do as the boy did in the hospital. He said to the lad on the couch in the same ward of the hospital: "Jesus comes through these wards every night, and He takes away these children into heaven. I wonder why He don't take me? I am so sick and I am so tired. I think to-night I shall hold up my hand while I sleep, and Jesus going through the wards of the hospital will see my hand up, and then He will know I want to go away with Him, and He will take me." The next morning, the nurse walked through the wards of the hospital, and sure enough Charlie was dead. He laid with one hand extended in the air, and by the other hand he held the elbow. During the night, Christ had walked through the wards of the hospital, and He had seen the wasted hand of the poor little sufferer lifted toward Him, and He answered the prayer, and took him. Oh soul, sick and dying in sin, can you not to-night, lift one hand of solicitation to Jesus of Nazareth as He passes by? This very moment He bends over you. Oh Gospel-hardened man, oh Gospel-hardened woman, can you not this night try to catch the attention of the Master? And are you not willing to say:

"I'm a sinner and nothing at all,
But Jesus Christ is my all in all?"

THE BEAUTIES OF SPRING.

[Delivered in the Brooklyn Tabernacle, Friday
Evening, May 7th, 1886.]

I HAVE been to-day in rhapsody. From the rail-car
window I saw in Pennsylvania and New Jersey one of the
most glorious pageants of vernal splendor that any eye ever
gazed on. The spring is born and the shower of to-night
is its infant baptism from the fount of the clouds, the hills
and mountains standing as sponsors. This is the first week
of the lilacs—Persian flowers, but for many years Americanized. Day before yesterday for the first they appeared
in the gardens and fields. Most generous of flowers, for
when the lilac throws out one bloom it throws out a
thousand blooms, and they toss all at once against the
gardens and the arbors a great purple sea of loveliness.
That means the arrival of the full spring. I never feel
sure that this season has arrived until this particular
flower unfurls its glory.

Often has this pleasant season been driven back.
Marching up the mountain-side, ever and anon it was defeated and hurled down the rocks, yet marching up again,
it has planted its green standards on the topmost cliff, led
on by bands of music in the treetops. The ploughs shar-
pened their coulters and charged on the tufted glebe, and
harrows with iron teeth chewed up the clods and sowers
scattered the seed. The trees put bridal blossoms in their

hair and the waters clapped their hands with gladness, and ponds with multitudinous life made the bogs quake.

Have you thought of the goodness of God in making green the dominant color? If a dull brown had ruled, that would have depressed the nations with melancholy, or too much crimson would have made the eye weary with its intense blaze. Instead of that to touch the eye with unwearying pleasure, God strews the earth with green, the color half way between the blue and the red. As sea-monsters, struck by harpoons, shove quickly away, so black winter clouds, struck through by lances of light, swim off the heavens. Tree branches have pulled on their sleeves of verdure and roots their boots of sod. Buds burst like harmless bombshells, scattering aroma on the fields. Joy of fishes in the water. Joy of insects in the air. Joy of cattle in the fields. Joy of wings in the sky: Gracious and blessed God! All this sunshine got its shape from Thy robes. All this verdure is only the track of Thy foot. All this music Thou didst strike from Thy harp. To-day at sunrise Nature went to morning prayers, reading the 14th psalm: "Praise ye the Lord, mountains and all hills, fruitful trees and all cedars." Fowl in the yard. Flocks on the hill. Insects drinking dew from cups of hyacinth. Jasmine climbing over the stone wall. Rivers tossing gold in their hands. Martins coming back to the rafters of the barn or becoming eaves-droppers of our houses.

Have you thanked God for his goodness in this springtime? The wind thanks him and hums its praise among the tree branches. The birds thank him, and for the drop of water they dip from the brook fill all the sky with roundelay. The honey-suckles thank him and burn incense all the day. The sea thanks him with organ diapason of tempest. Ofttimes the human heart is the only silent and broken instrument in all this orchestra of earth and air and ocean. Do not let our ungrateful soul be the only discord in this grand march of the eighteen hundred and eighty-sixth springtide.

See in all these capitals of the resurrection foliage the divine wisdom. Could all the combined ingenuity of philosophers and artists and inventors make one dandelion? The cup of one China aster holds more of the wine of wisdom than all nations could drink. What architect could plan the pillar of a pond lily? Break off the branch of a tree and know that in its sap is a wonderful chemistry of alum and sugar and tannin and salt and carbonate of lime, and know that God has given to the vegetable lungs and feet and ancestry as old as the ages, and descendants for all time, and that sometimes within a square inch it has 300,000 cells, any one of which it would take an infinite God to build. Explain to me, ye learned universities, one rutabaga! Rise up, O boasting philosophy of the world, and try if you can girdle one grain of corn. Oh, the shining firmament of one drop of dew! Oh, the untrodden continents in one crystal of snow! Oh, the gorgeousness of upholstery in the mountain moss! Oh, the triumphal arch in one tree branch! Oh, the God in an atom! Where is the loom in which he wove the curtains of the morn? From what vats of beauty were dipped the green and the blue and the gold and the crimson? In what moulds were run out the Appenines and the Caucasian range? What harp of God gave the warble to the lark and the sweet call of the robin and the carol to the canary and the chirp to the grasshopper? The very wisdom that guides all your affairs and mine, He who pairs the birds, chose for us our companions. He who helps the chaffinch guard her brood will be the God of our children. He who last month helped a swallow build her nest will give us a habitation. He who this morning fed the squirrel in the woods will feed us. He who gathered the down for the pheasant's breast will give us apparel. He who swings a bridge of gossamer for the insect to walk over will mark out our pathway. Ye who are worried about your health and worried about your property and worried about your children and worried about everything, listen to-morrow morning to one of the English sparrows flying out of the parks, and hear God say: "Ye are of more value than many sparrows."

And I am also impressed by the nest-building at this season going on in our orchards and woods and forests. What architects the birds are! The eagle constructs its nest at some inaccessible height and of very rough materials, gathering the sticks with its claws and hoisting them from great distances. The eider-duck from her own breast takes the feathers to line her nest. The magpie encircles her home with briers to keep back intruders. The black-bird covers its nest with loam. I have examined birds' nests by the hour in amazement, finding them constructed with mathematical accuracy and skill surpassing human ingenuity, sometimes among the rocks, sometimes in the branches of trees, sometimes in the eaves of houses, but always with reference to safety from enemies and the devastation of the elements. Would to God that we were as wise in building our nests! He who builds in the honors and gains of the world builds too high. He who builds in sensualities builds too low. There are weasels, there are foxes, there are hawks of temptation that are hunting for prey, and the only safe tree in which to build a nest is the tree of the cross and the only safe rock the Rock of Ages.

But this springtime, now fully begun, fills me with thoughts of what a superlative place heaven is. For if this earth, sin-blasted and cursed, can appear so beautiful, what must be the attractions of a sinless world. Our world is only the corpse of a dead paradise, the charred hulk of a giant vessel that foundered 6,000 years ago, and has ever since been beating on the rocks. It is only the ruins of a great temple, where lambs of innocence were to have been offered, but on whose altars swine and vultures have been sacrificed. Yet now, if the springtime reveals so much loveliness, although the original curse still reigns, what shall be the glory of that country from which sin shall be excluded, and even suns and moons are too common, for "the Lamb shall be the light thereof?"

I would not dare to say that, in addition to the spiritual excellence of heaven, there will not be a physical beauty— a rose of Sharon, once trodden down by the horsehoofs of the crucifying soldiers, there in heaven, and the humble lily, transplanted from the valley to the heights of Lebanon, and the hawthorn, white and scarlet, reminding the beholder of his innocence and the blood which made him so, and the passion flower, living in this frigid world a day, there blooming in more temperate zones throughout the long years of God's lifetime; a river of life flowing over beds of precious stones and riches, not such as go down with wrecked argosies, but such as He alone could strew who hath sown the mountains with diamonds and the sea with pearl, and birds with wing never torn by sportsman or tempest, ever and anon dipping its surface, as you wander to its source and catch the crystal stream where it drops fresh from the everlasting rock. What a transition when we go into that eternal springtime and walk the hanging gardens of the king, the walls made up of layers, having in them the yellow of jasper, the blue of sapphire, the green of emerald and the fire of jacynth. And then stepping out of the garden into the temple, every hand on a harp, every voice taking the key of rapture, every foot on a throne, and sing, soft as slumbers yet loud as storms, chorus of elders, chorus of saints, chorus of martyrs, chorus of seraphim, chorus of cherubim, chorus of morning stars, "unto Him who hath loved us and washed us from our sins in His own blood and made us kings and priests unto God and the Lamb forever and ever." Amen and amen.

EASTER JOY.

[The Brooklyn Tabernacle was elaborately decorated (April 25, 1886), both in platform and galleries. Within the church a scene of rare beauty was presented, the platform being covered with flowers arranged in various devices and breathing forth a delicate aroma. The building was so crowded that the doors were held open by the pressure, and many persons were turned away, being unable to get farther than the iron gate on the street.]

"Now is Christ risen from the dead, and become the first-fruits of them that slept."—1 Cor. 15: 20.

On this glorious Easter morning, amid the music and the flowers, I give you *Christian salutation*. This morning, Russian meeting Russian on the streets of St. Petersburg hails him with the salutation, "Christ is risen!" and is answered by his friend in salutation, "He is risen indeed!" In some parts of England and Ireland, to this very day, there is the superstition that on Easter morning the sun dances in the heavens; and well may we forgive such a superstition which illustrates the fact that the natural world seems to sympathize with the spiritual.

Hail! Easter morning. Flowers! flowers! All of them a-voice, all of them a-tongue, all of them full of speech to-day. I bend over one of the lilies and I hear it say: "Consider the lilies of the field, how they grow; they toil not, neither do they spin, yet Solomon in all his glory was not arrayed like one of these." I bend over a rose, and it seems to whisper: "I am the Rose of Sharon." And then

I stand and listen. From all sides there comes the chorus of flowers, saying: "If God so clothed the grass of the field, which to-day is, and to-morrow is cast into the oven, shall He not much more clothe you, O ye of little faith?"

Flowers! Flowers! Braid them into the bride's hair. Flowers! Flowers! Strew them over the graves of the dead, sweet prophecy of the resurrection. Flowers! Flowers! Twist them into a garland for my Lord Jesus on Easter morning, and "Glory be to the Father, and to the Son, and to the Holy Ghost; as it was in the beginning, is now, and ever shall be."

Why, if a rainbow this morning had fallen and struck the platform, the scene could not have been more radiant. Oh, how bright and how beautiful the flowers, and how much they make me think of Christ and His religion, that brightens everything it touches, brightens our life, brightens our character, brightens society, brightens the Church, brightens everything! You who go with gloomy countenance pretending you are better than I am because of your lugubriousness, you cannot cheat me. You old hypocrite! I know you. Pretty case you are for a man that professes to be more than conqueror. It is not religion that makes you gloomy, it is the lack of it. There is just as much religion in a wedding as in a burial, just as much religion in a smile as in a tear. Those gloomy Christians we sometimes see are the people to whom I like to lend money, for I never see them again! The women came to the Saviour's tomb and they dropped spices all around the tomb, and those spices were the seed that began to grow, and from them came all the flowers of this

Easter morn. The two angels robed in white took hold of the stone at the Saviour's tomb and they hurled it with such force down the hill that it crushed in the door of the world's sepulchre, and the stark and the dead must come forth.

I care not how labyrinthine the mausoleum or how costly the sarcophagus or however beautifully parterred the family grounds, ye want them all broken up by the Lord of the resurrection. They must come out. Father and mother—they must come out. Husband and wife— they must come out. Brother and sister—they must come out. Our darling children—they must come out. The eyes that we close with such trembling fingers must open again in the radiance of that morn. The arms we folded in dust must join ours in an embrace of reunion. The voice that was hushed in our dwelling must be returned. Oh, how long some of you seem to be waiting—waiting for the resurrection, waiting! And for these broken hearts to-day I make a soft, cool bandage out of Easter flowers.

Six years ago the night before Easter, I received an Easter card on which there was a representation of that exquisite flower, the trumpet creeper, and under it the words: "The trumpet shall sound and the dead shall rise." There was especial reason why at that time I should have that card sent me, and I present the same consolation to-day to all in this house; and who has escaped?

My friends, this morning, I find in the risen Christ a prophecy of our own resurrection, my text setting forth the idea that as Christ has risen so His people will rise.

He the first sheaf of the resurrection harvest. He "the first-fruits of them that slept." Before I get through this morning I will walk through all the cemeteries of the dead, through all the country graveyards, where your loved ones are buried, and I will pluck off these flowers, and I will drop a sweet promise of the Gospel—a rose of hope, a lily of joy on every tomb—the child's tomb, the husband's tomb, the wife's tomb, the father's grave, the mother's grave; and, while we celebrate the resurrection of Christ, we will at the same time celebrate the resurrection of all the good. "Christ the first-fruits of them that slept."

If I should come to you this morning and ask you for the names of the great conquerors of the world, you would say Alexander, Cæsar, Philip, Napoleon I. Ah! my friends, you have forgotten to mention the name of a greater conqueror than all these—a cruel, a ghastly conqueror. He rode on a black horse across Waterloo and Atlanta and Chalons, the bloody hoofs crushing the hearts of nations. It is the conqueror, Death.

He carries a black flag, and he takes no prisoners. He digs a trench across the hemispheres and fills it with the carcasses of nations. Fifty times would the world have been depopulated had not God kept making new generations. Fifty times the world would have swung lifeless through the air—no man on the mountain, no man on the sea, an abandoned ship ploughing through immensity. Again and again has he done his work with all generations. *He is a monarch* as well as a conqueror; his palace a sepulchre; his fountains the falling tears of a world. Blessed be God, in the light of this Easter morning I see the prophecy that his sceptre shall be broken, and his palace shall be demolished. The hour is coming when all who are in their graves shall come forth. Christ risen, we shall rise. Jesus "the first-fruits of them that slept." Now, around this doctrine of the resurrection there are a great many mysteries.

You come to me this morning, and say, If the bodies of the dead are to be raised, how is this, and how is that? and you ask me a thousand questions I am incompetent to answer; but there are a great many things *you believe* that you are not able to *explain*. You would be a very foolish man to say: "I won't believe anything I can't understand."

Why, putting down one kind of flower-seed, comes there up this flower of this color? Why, putting down another flower-seed, comes there up a flower of this color? One flower white, another flower yellow, another flower crimson. Why the difference when the seeds look to be very much alike—are very much alike? Explain these things. Explain that wart on the finger. Explain the difference why the oak-leaf is different from the leaf of the hickory. Tell me how the Lord Almighty can turn the chariot of His omnipotence on a rose-leaf. You ask me questions about the resurrection I cannot answer. I will ask you a thousand questions about every-day life you cannot answer.

I find my strength in this passage: "All who are in their graves shall come forth." I do not pretend to make the explanation. You go on and say: "Suppose a returned missionary dies in Brooklyn; when he was in China his foot was amputated; he lived years after in

England, and there he had an arm amputated; he is
buried to-day in Greenwood; in the resurrection will the
foot come from China, will the arm come from England,
and will the different parts of the body be reconstructed
in the resurrection? How is that possible?"

You say that "the human body changes every seven
years, and by seventy years of age a man has had ten
bodies; in the resurrection which will come up?" You
say, "A man will die and his body crumble into the dust,
and that dust be taken up into the life of the vegetable;
an animal may eat the vegetable, men eat the animal; in
the resurrection, that body, distributed in so many directions, how shall it be gathered up?" Have you any more
questions of this style to ask? Come on, and ask them.
I do not pretend to answer them. I fall back upon the
announcement of God's Word: "All who are in their
graves shall come forth."

You have noticed, I suppose, in reading the story of
the resurrection, that almost every account of the Bible
gives the idea that the characteristic of that day will be a
great sound. I do not know that it will be very loud, but
I know it will be very penetrating. In the mausoleum
where silence has reigned a thousand years that voice must
penetrate. In the coral cave of the deep that voice must
penetrate. Millions of spirits will come through the gates
of eternity and they will come to the tombs of the earth,
and they will cry: "Give us back our bodies; we gave
them to you in corruption, surrender them now in incor-
ruption. Hundreds of spirits hovering about the crags of
Gettysburg, for there the bodies are buried. A hundred

thousand spirits coming to Greenwood, for there the bodies are buried, waiting for the reunion of body and soul.

All along the sea route from New York to Liverpool, at every few miles where a steamer went down, departed spirits coming back, hovering over the wave. There is where the City of Boston perished. Found at last. There is where the President perished. Steamer found at last. There is where the Central America went down. Spirits hovering—hundreds of spirits hovering, *waiting for the reunion of body and soul*. Out on the prairie a spirit alights. There is where a traveller died in the snow. Crash! goes Westminster Abbey, and the poets and orators come forth; wonderful mingling of good and bad. Crash! go the Pyramids of Egypt, and the monarchs come forth.

Who can sketch the scene? I suppose that one moment before that general rising there will be an entire silence, save as you hear the grinding of a wheel, or the clatter of the hoofs of a procession passing into the cemetery. Silence in all the caves of the earth. Silence on the side of the mountain. Silence down in the valleys and far out into the sea. Silence! But in a moment, in the twinkling of an eye, as the archangel's trumpet comes pealing, rolling, crashing across the mountain and sea, the earth will give one terrific shudder, and the graves of the dead will heave like the waves of the sea, and Ostend and Sebastopol and Chalons will stalk forth in the lurid air, and the drowned will come up and lift up their wet locks above the billow; and all the land and all the sea become *one moving mass of life*—all faces, all ages, all conditions gazing in one direction and upon one throne—the throne of resurrection. "All who are in their graves shall come forth."

"But," you say, "if this doctrine of the resurrection is true, as prefigured by this Easter morning, Christ 'the first-fruits of them that slept,' Christ rising a promise and a prophecy of the rising of all His people, can you tell us something about the resurrected body?" I can. There are mysteries about that, but I shall tell you three or four things in regard to the resurrected body that are beyond guessing and beyond mistake

I. In the first place, I remark in regard to your resurrected body: *it will be a glorious body.* The body we have now is a mere skeleton of what it would have been if sin had not marred and defaced it. Take the most exquisite statue that was ever made by an artist, and chip it here and chip it there with a chisel, and batter and bruise it here and there, and then stand it out in the storms of a hundred years, and the beauty would be gone. Well, the human body has been chipped and battered and bruised and damaged with the storms of thousands of years—the physical defects of other generations coming down from generation to generation, we inheriting the infelicities of past generations; but in the morning of the resurrection the body will be adorned and beautified according to the original model. And there is no such difference between a gymnast and an emaciated wretch in a lazaretto, as there will be a difference between our bodies as they are now and our resurrected forms.

There you will see the perfect eye, after the waters of death have washed out the stains of tears and study.

There you will see the perfect hand, after the knots of toil have been untied from the knuckles. There you will see the form erect and elastic, after the burdens have gone off the shoulder—the very life of God in the body.

In this world, the most impressive thing, the most expressive thing, is the human face; but that face is veiled with the griefs of a thousand years; but in the resurrection morn *that veil will be taken away* from the face, and the noonday sun is dull and dim and stupid compared with the outflaming glories of the countenances of the saved. When those faces of the righteous, those resurrected faces, turn toward the gate, or look up toward the throne, it will be like the dawning of a new morning on the bosom of everlasting day! O glorious, resurrected body!

II. But I remark also in regard to that body, which you are to get in the resurrection, it will be an immortal body. These bodies are wasting away. Somebody has said as soon as we begin to live we begin to die. Unless we keep putting the fuel into the furnace the furnace dies out. The blood-vessels are canals taking the breadstuffs to all parts of the system. We must be reconstructed hour by hour, day by day. Sickness and death are all the time trying to get their prey under the tenement, or to push us off the embankment of the grave; but, blessed be God, in the resurrection we will get a body immortal. No malaria in the air, no cough, no neuralgic twinge, no rheumatic pang, no fluttering of the heart, no shortness of breath, no ambulance, no dispensary, no hospital, no invalid's chair, no spectacles to improve the dim vision; but health, immortal health! O ye who have aches and pains indescribable this morning—

O ye who are never well—O ye who are lacerated with physical distresses, let me tell you of the resurrected body, *free from all disease.* Immortal! Immortal!

III. I go further, and say in regard to that body which you are to get in the resurrection, it will be a powerful body. We walk now eight or ten miles, and we are fatigued; we lift a few hundred pounds, and we are exhausted; unarmed, we meet a wild beast, and we must run, or fly, or climb, or dodge because we are incompetent to meet it; we toil eight or ten hours vigorously, and then we are weary; but in the resurrection we are to have a body that *never gets tired.* Is it not a glorious thought?

Plenty of occupation in heaven. I suppose Broadway, New York, in the busiest season of the year, at noonday, is not so busy as heaven is all the time. Grand projects of mercy for other worlds. Victories to be celebrated. The downfall of despotisms on earth to be announced. Great songs to be learned and sung. Great expeditions on which God shall send forth His children. *Plenty to do, but no fatigue.* If you are seated under the trees of life, it will not be to rest, but to talk over with some old comrade old times—the battles where you fought shoulder to shoulder.

Sometimes in this world we feel we would like to have such a body as that. There is so much work to be done for Christ, there are so many tears to be wiped away, there are so many burdens to lift, there is so much to be achieved for Christ, we sometimes wish that from the first of January to the last of December we could toil on without stopping to sleep, or take any recreation, or to rest, or even to take food—that we could toil right on without stopping a moment in our work of commending Christ and heaven to all the people. But we all get tired.

It is a characteristic of the human body in this condition; we must get tired. Is it not a glorious thought that after a while, after the service of God, we are going to have a body that will never get weary? O glorious resurrection day! Gladly will I fling aside this poor body of sin and fling it into the tomb, if at Thy bidding I shall have a body that never wearies. That was a splendid resurrection hymn that was sung at my father's burial:

> "So Jesus slept, God's dying Son
> Passed through the grave and blessed the bed.
> Rest here, blest saint, till from His throne
> The morning breaks to pierce the shade."

O blessed resurrection! Speak out, sweet flowers, beautiful flowers. While you tell of a risen Christ, tell of the righteous who shall rise. May God fill you this morning with anticipation!

I heard of a father and son who, among others, were shipwrecked at sea. The father and the son climbed into the rigging. The father held on, but the son after a while lost his hold in the rigging and was dashed down. The father supposed he had gone hopelessly under the wave. The next day the father was brought ashore from the rigging in an exhausted state, and laid in a bed in a fisherman's hut, and after many hours had passed he came to consciousness, and saw lying beside him on the same bed his boy. Oh, my friends! what a glorious thing it will be if we wake up at last to find our loved ones beside us! coming up from the same plot in the graveyard, coming up in the same morning light—the father and son alive forever, all the loved ones alive forever, nevermore to weep, nevermore to part, nevermore to die.

May the God of peace, that brought again from the dead our Lord Jesus, the great Shepherd of the sheep, through the blood of that everlasting covenant, make you perfect in every good work, to do His will; and let this brilliant scene of the morning transport our thoughts to the grander assemblage before the throne. This august assemblage is nothing compared with it. The one hundred and forty and four thousand, and the "great multitude that no man can number," some of our best friends among them, we, after a while, to join the multitude. Blessed anticipation.

> "Blest are the saints beloved of God,
> Washed are their robes in Jesu's blood,
> Brighter than angels, lo! they shine,
> Their wonders splendid and sublime.
>
> "My soul anticipates the day,
> Would stretch her wings and soar away,
> To aid the song, the palm to bear,
> And bow, the chief of sinners, there."